At Table

LESLEY CHAMBERLAIN

The Food and Cooking of Russia

With a new introduction by the author

UNIVERSITY OF NEBRASKA PRESS
LINCOLN AND LONDON

© 1982 by Lesley Chamberlain
Introduction to the Bison Books Edition © 2006 by Lesley Chamberlain
Manufactured in the United States of America

⊗

First Nebraska paperback printing: 2006

Library of Congress Cataloging-in-Publication Data
Chamberlain, Lesley.
The food and cooking of Russia / Lesley Chamberlain; with a new
introduction by the author.—Bison Books ed.
p.   cm.
Originally published: London: Allen Lane, 1982.
Includes bibliographical references and index.
ISBN-13: 978-0-8032-6461-8 (pbk.: alk. paper)
ISBN-10: 0-8032-6461-5 (pbk.: alk. paper)
1. Cookery, Russian.   I. Title.
TX723.3.C47   2006
641.5947—dc22   2005028451

This Bison Books edition follows the original in beginning the
introduction on arabic page 11; the text remains unaltered.

Introduction to the Bison Books Edition

Russia in 1978, the year I conceived and began working on this book, was a dreary and mysterious place seen through Western eyes. The Cold War, dividing the world into two power blocs, American and Soviet, was at its height, bringing with it in both Russia and the West fear and a distorted picture of "the other side." I had two university degrees in Russian, several visits to the country, and a great deal of reading behind me by the time I was assigned as a trainee Reuter correspondent to Moscow in August that year. I spoke Russian well, and I probably should have been thinking about my lofty mission as a reporter conveying to the free world information from the yet-to-be-named "evil empire." But what most concerned me was how to convey Russian life as it was. I wanted to send home news of everything that was left over when politics was pushed aside.

Of course that could never quite be done. The repressions and injustices of Soviet political life reached into the private life of every family. Moreover, my presence in Moscow was legitimized by the fact that I was both by profession and conviction on the other side. I drove a car with a license plate labeling me a Western journalist. In truth, too, I had never been a Communist supporter, and I rejected a Marxist reading of history. But I was quite sure Russians were "normal" people who had hopes and fears, who grew up in a wide variety of family circumstances, loved or hated their teachers, fell in love, achieved or failed in their ambitions, enjoyed books, films, holidays, walks in the country, and meals together. Against a background of decisions taken by their government that influenced world events, Russians led "ordinary lives," which I wanted to portray. I probably should have written a novel, but what was possible at the time was a cookbook.

Many things made it an exciting project. It was my first book, and it gave me a purpose that, I have to admit, I couldn't find in my designated political work. I wanted to write always about exceptions to the rule, particular people and practices that defied generalization, and also to recapture the sights and sounds and smells of places I had visited in a Russia that, if it wasn't timeless, was a place where people lived and not just a token in a political game. The result was that I traveled as much as I could in my free time. (I still use the wonderful iron pans I bought in Georgia.)

When I was in Moscow I tried to shop in our often poorly stocked local shops and markets rather than in the opulent grocery store reserved for foreigners. Of course I often succumbed to convenience. I piled my cart high with luxury goods behind shuttered windows and, like many of my Western press colleagues, felt ashamed. "Ordinary" Russians, whose lives were blighted by constant consumer shortages and daily lines, knew exactly what was going on. We should have shown solidarity.

My slender excuse was that I needed ingredients to try out my recipes, and I just couldn't find them anywhere else. I had the feeling I was helping to keep alive a culinary tradition that was in danger of disappearing. It was an unusual cause to adopt: not a great one in human terms, but one that gave me a way of writing about and finding readers interested in a real Russia. Lives in which no one had time to cook and so many ingredients were unobtainable were one real outcome of the inefficient command economy. I could at least draw attention to the way Communist ideology tried to conceal this lapse by dismissing the culinary arts as a bourgeois fetish.

My joy was to work with Russian books, past and present, and to research meals I enjoyed in restaurants and occasionally in private apartments, pressing my questions on the few Russians who felt brave enough to answer them. The idea that talking to a Western journalist about food was somehow dangerous or subversive seems absurd today, but it was the case then that every conversation with a foreigner had to be reported to the authorities, and most people understandably preferred to avoid such a situation. I always remember the friendly director of Moscow's then very small and rather bizarre Culinary Museum who gave me such an interesting interview and promised me an Easter cake recipe if I popped back the following week. When I returned he had evidently been forbidden to pass it on.

So I worked with books. The culinary bible of the day, available in the Russian-language bookshop for foreigners but hard to find in ordinary Russian shops, was the *Kniga o vkusnoi i zdorovoi pishche* (The book of tasty and healthy food), which had appeared in seven editions since it first appeared in 1939. It proved an invaluable guide to everyday recipes that could, on a good day, actually be made from what the Soviet food industry produced. The margins contained descriptions of flour types and fish varieties; a guide to the difference between various types of yogurt, buttermilk, fermented milk, and sour cream; a gloss on grains and another on herbs and spices. I still have my 1977 edition of that blue Rexine-covered book, spattered with the juices of experimental meals long ago consumed or discarded and covered with notes of my work in progress. Most of the vocabulary was routine—this was a cookbook, not Tolstoy, after all—but whenever I drew a blank in Russian-English dictionaries, I found the answer in the Great Soviet Encyclopedia or some other reference book. If I could get the Latin for whatever plant or fish puzzled me, then it would be easy to find the common English name.

In fact, Russian food culture wasn't dying in 1978–79. It was preserved in the folk memory and in family practices and waiting for more propitious times to reemerge. One good sign was a weekly column on food history written for the newspaper *Nedelya* (The week) by an extraordinary freelance academic, Vil'yam Pokhlyobkin. His column also alerted me to his excellent book *Natsionalnye kukhni nashikh narodov* (Moscow 1978), which translates as "the national cuisines of our peoples." This included Russian cooking alongside Belorussian, Ukrainian, Uzbek, and Lithuanian cuisines among others. The concept was geoculturally forced. Most of the "Soviet" peoples represented in Pokhlyobkin's volume had no desire to be called "our" at all. But the level of information was high and the separate treatment of overlapping culinary styles already a milestone. Twenty years later I would meet Vil'yam, still flourishing in his nineties, at the other end of a transformed Europe when he won a prize in Italy for his book on the history of vodka.

But I needed more sources than just Pokhlyobkin and particularly enjoyed reaching back into Russian culinary history. Unlike Soviet writers, I was free to draw links between the present-day Russian way with food and the old world of the tsars. A reader's ticket for the national library in Moscow, then named after Lenin, allowed me to spend a couple of evenings a week consulting microfiches of cookbooks from the age of Alexander I and after. Like older books in other food cultures, the huge, vague quantities mentioned in the recipes had to be scaled down for the modern domestic kitchen: from the bucket to the cup, from forty eggs to four. I worked on my recipes in my Moscow apartment and then again when I returned to England. The Lenin Library also introduced me to the standard later-nineteenth-century cookbook of the rising middle class, Elena Molokhovets's *Podarok molodym khozyaikam* ("A gift to young housewives," available in English as *Classic Russian Cooking*, translated by Joyce Toomre [Indiana University Press, 1992]). I was soon able to buy an American reprint of this classic volume, whose author was the Russian equivalent to England's Mrs. Beeton (or America's Catherine Beecher). Last but not least, my library reading showed me just how much Russian history was encoded in food styles through the centuries and added an important dimension to the present book.

I personally tested all of the two hundred or so recipes I included in *The Food and Cooking of Russia*, and many of them, such as black bread and buckwheat blini, the yogurt and barley soup called *spas* or *tanabour*, *solyanka* soup, millet porridge, baked cheesecake with semolina, "Rasputin's red bean salad," and *manty* (Turkmenian fish-stuffed pasta flavored with cardamom), became personal favorites. Add to that list almost any of the beetroot recipes, especially those served hot. For me, the best Russian cooking was and still is everyday fare, close to peasant traditions. It is labor intensive by modern standards but also extremely healthy, with its emphasis on whole grains, fresh vegetables and herbs, seeds and sunflower oil, yogurt and sour cream. Thirty years ago, when most of these ingredients had to be bought in special health or whole-food shops in London, it was a delight to find them in plain packaging on the shelves of every Russian grocer. The Russian food world, imprisoned by the Soviet command economy, was caught in a time warp that was actually beneficial.

Unlike the West, Russia had not "progressed" to fast food in 1978. Now, unfortunately, it has. By an irony of history, Russia has passed from one form of the decline of its food culture under a dying economy to a new one threatened by rampant commercialism. Now *The Food and Cooking of Russia* takes its place in a world where all traditional cuisines need rescuing for the sake of the culinary art, and health, and our sense of history. I hope that, restored to print and unchanged from the original edition, this book will be able to exercise some influence and provide a basis for knowledge.

Contents

List of Illustrations

Acknowledgements

I am most grateful to Weidenfeld & Nicolson Ltd for permission to quote from Vladimir Nabokov's *Speak, Memory*, and to Jane Grigson for permission to reprint, slightly adapted, one of her recipes. I also owe a debt to the many people in Moscow and at home who have helped me with valuable comments and information, among them Princess Natasha Golitsyn and Mrs E. Glassborow, Mrs Olive Stevens, Mrs Sofka Skipwith, the GB-USSR Association and the staff of Rasputin's restaurant in London.

Illustration Acknowledgements

British Library: 31, 53, 213, 224, 247; Illustrated London News Picture Library: 265; Mansell Collection: 305; School of Slavonic and East European Studies Library, University College London: 100, 163; Viollet, Roger: 17.

NOTE: Metric equivalents may differ from one recipe to another. The quantities given have been rounded up or down according to the requirements of each individual recipe. Use either imperial or metric quantities, not a combination of the two.

Alas, fat men know better how to
manage their affairs than thin men...

NIKOLAI GOGOL: *Dead Souls*

Introduction

A BRIEF HISTORY OF RUSSIAN FOOD

That the Russians have a special gift for borrowing foreign ideas and making them their own is as true in the kitchen as it is in any of the finer Russian arts. The French helped create beef Stroganov, the Germans and Scandinavians inspired the *zakuski* table, the Caucasians introduced *shashlyk*, but today all of them count as traditional Russian dishes. What makes the best of Russian cooking, therefore, is a surprising combination of tastes and techniques. Some have been preserved in peasant cooking since the Middle Ages, others are the result of almost four centuries of foreign influence on the palates of the nobility. I have collected what I think are some of the best recipes in this mixed tradition.

The gap between the top and bottom of society has made for great food variety. One has to go back to the Middle Ages to find a period when social class did not determine what a Russian had for dinner. The medieval table was uniformly modest, unvaried and virtually meatless. Except for honey the diet was generally sour and included many pickles and sour yeast doughs. Rye was used to make soursweet bread and that bread used in turn to make *kvas* beer. Cabbage, swede, turnip and beetroot were the staple vegetables. Simple Russian cooking has remained in this tradition, with enormous influence exercised upon it by the Russian Orthodox Church. The Church calendar divided foods into two groups. For over half the days of the year only Lenten fare was allowed: vegetables, fish and mushrooms. Milk, eggs and meat graced the table on the remaining days. The effect of this division is still noticeable today. Even under the influence of foreign chefs, Russian cooking developed keeping these sets of ingredients carefully apart.

Isolating foods that would normally have combined well undoubtedly led to many dull, monotonous dishes comprising only one or two ingredients. Flavour was added with four basic seasonings: onion, garlic, horseradish and dill. To ring the changes, parsley, anise, coriander, bay leaves, black pepper and cloves were also used, along with different flavoured oils – poppy seed, nut, olive and later sunflower. But the results were plain rather than subtle, and salt was added only after food had been cooked.

It was enslavement to the East that relieved this tedium and gave the Russian table its first important introduction to the cooking of other lands. The principalities of Central Russia were invaded by the Mongols in the early thirteenth century, and subjected to 250 years of foreign rule until the state of Muscovy became strong enough to assume power. The East yielded new spices – ginger, cardamom, sweet sedge, cinnamon and saffron – and pasta. Travellers and merchants brought back dried fruits, candied peels, preserves, treacles, lemons, and tea which was to become the great Russian beverage.

But foreign imports meant privilege and division. Only the upper ranks enjoyed the costly package of luxuries from the East. At the same time more meat and game began to appear on their tables, along with caviare and sturgeon. They imported herrings and French wines and were ready to experiment. The lavish banquets given by Ivan the Terrible included cranes seasoned with ginger, guinea fowl with cinnamon, and Romanée (Burgundy) wine.

By the middle of the eighteenth century, while the peasant diet remained unchanged, the upper classes were eating large, rich meals embracing seven or eight courses. A full meal or *obed* began with a soup, and moved through meat and fish courses to savoury pies and the classic Russian grain dish, *kasha*. Honey cakes and other sweet pies followed. Thanks to close ties with Northern Europe, wrought by Tsar Peter the Great, they had their first introduction to meat cutlets (*kotlety*), sausages (*sosiski*), omelettes (*omlety*), mousse (*muss*) and compote (*kompot*). The language of food was quickly Europeanized. The potato came from Germany in the 1770s and took a German name. Tomatoes arrived from Italy at about the same time and kept their Italian name. With an established taste for Eastern sweetmeats, the upper classes took to tea and cakes between meals and the first sugar refineries opened in Russia.

One important modification of the Russian table, encouraged by the Dutch, German and Swedish chefs whom Peter the Great employed, was the *zakuski* table. It gave the classic *obed* a new beginning. A course in its own right and often served on a separate board or in a different room, the *zakuski* table found a place on the menu for the matured foreign cheeses, sandwiches and salads which did not otherwise fit into the Russian dining pattern. More foreign words, such as *buterbrod* (from the German for open sandwich), were borrowed. Happily the traditional delicacies of smoked fish, caviare and pickles fitted alongside the new foods like old friends.

The eighteenth century was also when fresh milk products, butter and cream, were first eaten as delicacies by the aristocracy. The old Russian staples were *tvorog* (curd cheese), *smetana* (sour cream), and other forms of curdled and soured milk. In the nineteenth century French chefs virtually took over. They did not so much introduce new ingredients as revolutionize the existing repertoire. Working for private employers, setting up restaurants in Moscow and St Petersburg and training a new kind of Russian chef, they taught the radical lesson of how to combine and blend many different ingredients to make a perfect dish.

There was an old Russian tradition of not chopping or cutting foods up before they reached the table. The French school introduced for the first time meat off the bone (*eskalop*, *antrekot*, *bifshteks*), which could be served in a sauce of many ingredients. It also developed salads and salad dressings, and popularized white bread, sweet, short, yeastless egg doughs and cake mixtures. Finally, the new cooking called for exact recipes, where Russian chefs had been content before to give vague instructions and measures.

Under the guidance of foreign chefs who were interested in traditional Russian food, Russia came close by the end of the century to achieving a good standard of everyday cuisine practised by all but the peasantry. As early as the 1860s a new wave of home-grown gastronomic expertise became apparent in the person of Elena Molokhovets, Russia's equivalent of Mrs Beeton. Her classic *Gift to Young Housewives* was over 1,000 pages long, and is still considered a kitchen bible by Soviet home cooks. Mrs Molokhovets was full of respect for Russian traditions and the dictates of the Church calendar, but French in the techniques and refinements she brought to the ordinary table.

During Soviet rule Russian cuisine has undoubtedly lapsed from the art it had become by the time of the 1917 Revolution. Shortages of ingredients and lack of variety are a great deal to blame. The standardization and nationalization of restaurants have also been a disincentive to good service, high gastronomic standards and inventive menus. For home cooks only very rarely does a cookery book appear in the shops. Some of the blame can probably be apportioned to ideology too. Before the Revolution, good food was the province of the bourgeoisie and the aristocracy. The ideology of the new state said that neither was to have any influence in forming the manners of Soviet culture. As the poet Vladimir Mayakovsky quipped:

> Eat your pineapples, enjoy your hazel hen,
> Your last day is on its way, bourgeois men.

Under these combined circumstances, peasant traditions have remained strong since 1917. Moscow's markets do the greater part of their trade as always in pickled cabbage, cucumbers and other vegetables in vinegar brine. *Kvas*, still regarded as the national drink, can be bought at any time of the day from huge barrels parked on the street. And although mechanization has meant the demise of many traditional yeast dough cakes, there is not a bakery in Moscow that cannot offer half a dozen different rye breads.

If the influence of the Church has dwindled almost to nothing, the Soviet Russian table is still divided in practice between ordinary and festive eating. On high days and holidays Russians organize themselves veritable banquets, and markets the day before are tellingly well-stocked and teeming with customers. Meat, fish, rich cakes, fruit, cream, champagne and vodka are consumed in large quantities. It is this festive side of things that foreigners eating in restaurants and at official dinners see. For a Russian, going to a restaurant is a special occasion even if the food is not good. But the daily diet is strikingly basic by comparison. Meat is scarce or expensive or both. Caviare is virtually unobtainable through ordinary channels. Pride of place still goes to soups, curd cheese, sour cream, sausage, bread and grain.

Just as the population of the Russian cities has always been extraordinarily varied in ethnic origins, so in the end it is difficult to pin down the limits of Russian food. What are considered characteristic dishes have been drawn from an extensive geographical area from the Baltics to China. With Germany and Poland, Russian cooking shares some of its best-known dishes like *borshch*, black bread, herring *zakuski*, its extensive use of sour cream and curd cheese, its yeast cakes and its pickles. It overlaps largely with Central European Jewish cooking, which migrating Russian Jews have helped spread all over Europe and the United States. Hence *blini* and *blintzes*, compotes of stewed vegetables, boiled fish with horseradish, beetroot and salted cucumbers, an abundance of sugar in savoury cooking, classic dishes like stuffed goose neck, and again pickles and black bread. I discovered quite by accident a London Jewish delicatessen where the white egg bread (challah) is called by its Russian name, *bulka*. Today

Russian cooking is tending more and more to embrace the exotic cookery of the Caucasian and Central Asian Soviet republics. An assimilation which properly began with the absorption of these territories into the Russian Empire at the beginning of the nineteenth century has been greatly boosted by the amount of travelling within the Soviet Union which Russians may now do cheaply and generally freely. Bringing Azerbaijani *plov* (pilaff) to Moscow, of course, is like bringing curry to London. Empires will enrich the native kitchen.

Georgia has been most influential in improving the standards of Soviet Russian cooking, and has taken the place France used to occupy. It has introduced rich stews flavoured with exotic vegetables, such as tomatoes, aubergines and peppers, and a variety of herbs – basil, tarragon, thyme and savory. The Russians have learned to cook with beans and to use walnuts to make dressings and sauces, a habit which is almost unique to Georgia in the cooking of the world. Wine, grapes and grape juice, olive oil, plenty of garlic and firm cheeses have allowed Russia to discover a gastronomic paradise in the same way British cooks discovered the Mediterranean. Russian cooks made similar discoveries in Moldavia, particularly the use of cornmeal. Armenia suggested exciting combinations of meat and fruit, fish and fruit, and not just the Northern staples like apples and pears, but apricots which originated in the region, peaches, cherries, plums and pomegranates. Armenian cooking also backed up the general wider use of fresh herbs in salads and as a garnish to cheese as well as in cooking, and added hot spices, particularly red (cayenne) pepper. It provided ways of cooking bulghur wheat, introduced chick peas, and rang the changes with flat bread. More than any other meat the Russians learned to cook lamb from the Southern republics, from where most of it was imported in the last century and still is today. Azerbaijani cooking extended the Southern repertoire further with its rice dishes, its sour soups, lamb, game and chestnuts.

In this collection of recipes, I have tried to provide dishes representative of the many influences in Russian food today. There are peasant recipes and lavish recipes, French and Georgian style dishes and some thoroughly Central Russian ideas. Russian native cooking is limited, but only that fact and the various reasons for it can explain the enormous influence that French and other cuisines have had upon it. Moreover, because of the controversial importance of this foreign borrowing in Russia's pursuit of a national identity, because of the power of the Church and lately because of the Revolution, Russian eating has been subject to strong ideological pressures throughout its history. The natural tradition is not one of good food for its own sake. For centuries Russians have impressed and even staggered foreigners with the heartiness of their appetites for food and drink. The emphasis on quantity has not encouraged a gourmet tradition. Finally, as the wine trade knows, *le goût russe* is extremely sweet. The habit of bringing out savoury flavours with a little sugar used as a seasoning is excellent, but in sweets, cakes and drinks the proportion of sweetness to taste is often excessive. I have adjusted my recipes accordingly.

RUSSIAN MEALS AND MEALTIMES

The most important Russian meal of the day is *obed*, a movable feast that can take place any time between midday and eight o'clock in the evening. Depending on when *obed* is taken, breakfast (*zavtrak*) and supper (*uzhin*) are adjusted accordingly. But names can be confusing. *Zavtrak* may take place as late as one o'clock in the afternoon, when we would obviously call it lunch. Anything that preceded it would then be a *first zavtrak*. *Obed* would still be to come but there would probably be no supper.

Changes in mealtimes over the last four centuries have been tied to a shortening of the working day and the adoption of foreign habits by the aristocracy. The need for two breakfasts, *obed*, high tea, supper and a snack before bed has lessened. Tea, which the aristocracy cultivated in the last century, is a matter of taste in Central Russia, though afternoon coffee and cake in the German style are unquestionably a part of daily life in the Baltic states.

Since the sixteenth century, what was eaten when at the Russian table has varied enormously according to wealth, fashion and social position. An account of what Peter the Great ordered to his table at the end of the seventeenth century rightly pointed out the similarity between the Tsar's table and the unique state of his country:

His taste was not an imperial one. He loved and most frequently ordered for his own special enjoyment a soup with four cabbages in it; gruel; pig, with sour cream for sauce; cold roast meat, with pickled cucumbers or salad; lemons and lampreys; salt meat, ham and Limburg cheese . . . At his repast he quaffed quass [*kvas*], a sort of beer, which would have disgusted an Egyptian; and he finished with Hungarian or French wine. All this was the repast of a man who seemed, like the nation of which he was head, in a transition state, between barbarism and civilization, beginning dinner with cabbage water, and closing the banquet with goblets of Burgundy.

DORAN, *Table Traits with Something on Them*

A Russian provincial governor entertaining Siberian and Chinese merchants.

By the nineteenth century the aristocracy had a far clearer idea of where it was going: in the direction of France, though still with Russian habits in tow. Lady Londonderry, who kept a journal of her visit to Moscow and St Petersburg in 1836–7, wrote that *obed* was taken at four or five in the afternoon. It was generally rather French: 'cups of soup, beefsteaks, fish etc., the finest fruit and thick cream'. Those who partook of it preferred to give it a French name, either *dîner* or *déjeuner dînatoire*. *Déjeuner dînatoire*, dinner at lunch-time, was exactly what *obed* was, and clearly they were sticking to their Russian habits at heart. A second meal which Lady Londonderry called supper would be served at about eleven in the evening. At a soirée, such as a ball at the Imperial Court, it would be followed by dancing, and after the dancing, tea . . .

. . . the ball began at nine. After the polonaises were quadrilles and at twelve o'clock we passed through a *salle des maréchaux* and a long gallery with between three and four hundred pictures of Dawe's to the supper room, an enormous *salle* with scagliola columns and blue glass lustres and lighted by four thousand candles. This was really fairyland – the endless vista, the quantities of massy plate, the abundance of lovely flowers, and, to crown all, the whole having the appearance of an *orangerie*, the supper tables being so constituted as to let the stems of the immense orange trees through so that we literally sat under their shade and perfume. The scene was perfect enchantment and eight hundred and fifty sat down to supper without the slightest confusion or squeeze. The Empress, according to the strict old etiquette of Russian hospitality, went round all the tables and spoke to every person until she fainted away . . .

Not all suppers even among the aristocracy were so grand. On less formal occasions they were often amalgamated with the last glass of tea of the day. Supper food would be a variety of hot and cold *zakuski*.

Tea in the afternoon was a thoroughly foreign affair. Princess Dolgorouky's granddaughter remembered her thus:

The drawing-room led to Granny's boudoir, the walls and furniture in red brocade and black lacquer. There she sat in a comfortable arm-chair with a great black and gold Chinese screen round the back to keep off any draughts, beside her a table with copies of *La Revue des Deux Mondes* and whatever books she was reading, generally yellow paper-backed French ones, as French was her language with English next and Russian last. Her generation spoke Russian only to servants. At tea-time a table would be laid with a gleaming silver samovar and tea-pot, from which she dispensed very weak tea with lemon and tiny petit-fours.

In this and similar households breakfast was also light, often soft white bread or buns. Vladimir Nabokov remembered spreading his rye bread with imported English golden syrup and drinking hot chocolate with it.

Preparing lunch was often left to a mixed team of chefs employed by aristocratic and diplomatic families. The Dolgoroukys kept four altogether, of whom only one was Russian. A journalist travelling in St Petersburg during the last century compared the *obed* she enjoyed with a Count and his family at home, and an official *obed* given by the same Count in his ministerial role at the Foreign Office. *Zakuski* were too fancy for the family meal, which began with soup and *pirozhki*, followed by duck with pickled cherries and frost-bitten potatoes(!). Afterwards the Countess served a plate of crumbled green cheese[1] into which she put a piece of bread and butter, butter side down, and then passed on the plate to the others round the table who served themselves in the same way. Then came veal cutlets, and finally a compote of stewed fruit. *Kvas* stood on the table in a large decanter. The official meal, on the other hand, was wholly French: oysters, consommé, crab, saddle of lamb, parfait de foie gras with champagne, melon and blackcurrant punch, pheasant, green salad, asparagus with mousseline sauce, duchess potatoes, ice cream, cheese, dessert. It was typical of the 'Russian' menus which Urbain Dubois included in his *Cuisine de tous les pays*. These dinners did not wholly exclude Russian recipes but borrowed from them to transform them. *Pirozhki* were served as 'petits-pâtés du Caucase', filled with béchamel sauce, Parmesan cheese and mushrooms. Sterlet and sturgeon were dressed up in champagne and rich stocks, or served 'nobly' garnished with lemon, parsley and crayfish in a mushroom and truffle sauce. Fruit salads were fresh and extravagant.

From all this it was an enormous jump to the ordinary Russian table. In the poorer households *obed* would probably be soup, *kasha* and a pie; with greater resources it could extend to a meat or fish course. *Uzhin* had the same basic ingredients but was less in quantity.

Mrs Molokhovets recommended to the middle classes she was addressing that they take three courses in the continental manner but eat Russian dishes. Suggested *obedy* included:

> Borshch/baked carp/buckwheat *kasha* with sour cream
> Noodle soup with mushrooms/boiled beef/*syrniki*
> Fish, egg and rice pie/clear soup/roast turkey with
>   marinated cherries/rice pudding
> Bouillon with *pirozhki* or *blini*/beef/cranberry *kisel*

---

1. Green cheese was made by grating hardened curd cheese and mixing it with pounded horseradish leaves which had been soaked in water for several days, sour cream and pounded fenugreek leaves. The cheese was left at room temperature for 6 days, stirred each day, and more cream and horseradish leaves were added. It was then pressed in muslin under a weight, and finally hung up to dry in fresh air. Soviet industry produces a modern version, which looks like green Parmesan ready grated and can be used to give a strong cheese flavour in cooking.

This pattern is the most typical of Russian food as it developed up to the Revolution. It could be richer for special occasions. The number of courses could increase to up to 10, and more French ideas would creep in. Puddings would be more elaborate, and there would be both fish and meat or game served:

1). Green *shchi*
   Kotlety
   Stuffed turnips
   Roast beef
   Apple *plombir*

2). *Blini*
   Asparagus soup
   Chicken with lemon sauce
   Carrots garnished with tripe
   Carp
   Tort (gâteau)

Full menus approached the extravagance of official banquets. Two soups would be offered, one of them cold in summer to arouse the appetite.

Bouillon with *pirozhki*
Botvinya
Fillet of beef
Fish in aspic with salad and mayonnaise
Cauliflower
Strawberry air pie
Raspberry punch (like a water ice/sorbet)
Wild duck or partridge with marinated salads
Ice cream or crème
Fruits and berries
Tea or coffee

Served with the meal in order of courses:

sherry or madeira
red wine
ale
hock
malaga
champagne
liqueurs

Suppers would consist of one or two dishes otherwise served at *obed*. Lunches where *obed* was still to come would often be cold *zakuski*, especially when taken in a restaurant.

PLANNING A RUSSIAN MEAL

Russians today eat a large breakfast which can include meat, porridge, fish, chicken, raw onion and pickles as well as eggs, cheesecake, buttermilk, bread and cakes. *Obed* comes any time from midday to late afternoon. In a restaurant it will consist of *zakuski*, soup, a main course of meat, poultry or fish, ice cream and coffee. To suit Western tastes – most Russian dishes being rather robust – it is easy to fashion a meal around one or two of them, a soup and pancakes for example. A variety of cold *zakuski* is a good starter when entertaining a lot of people. It also makes an excellent lunch with the addition of boiled new potatoes. For a dinner party choose just one *zakuska*, hot or cold and served in suitable proportions, or start with cheese and fresh herbs like the Armenians and Azerbaijanis. A good pie will serve very well as a main course and is probably best followed by a light pudding of fruit. Beware only of the same flavours – dill, sour cream, cabbage, mushrooms and pickles – turning up at every course. Russians use sour cream and dill pickles as abundantly as the Mediterraneans use olive oil and tomatoes.

WHAT TO DRINK

The old Russian drinks, *kvas* and *sbiten'*, complemented the traditional sourness of Russian peasant food, which does not fit well with wine. Lager beer and cider make good substitutes. *Zakuski* should be accompanied by ice-cold vodka (see page 30), which is acceptable with every course of a meal except pudding. That traditionally is the time for champagne, although in my experience vodka and wine or vodka and champagne are not happy marriages. I would stick to one or the other.

A RUSSIAN KITCHEN AND ITS TOOLS

From medieval times until the seventeenth century the Russian kitchen was divided into three areas – one where the oven stood, one where the bread was kneaded and left to rise, and one where other jobs were done such as chopping and mixing. Bread could be cooked by an open fire (*ochag*), but the pride of the old Russian kitchen was the oven (*pech'*), and food was either baked in it from start to finish or first boiled and then baked. Temperature regulations for baking were given, even in the last century, not in degrees but to fit in with bread-baking, that is *before bread* (very hot) and *after bread* (hot but falling). The heat was always indirect and never rising. In the mid eighteenth century a change was made to cooking on top of a stove (*plita*), which allowed for a greater variety of techniques.

The implements I have found invaluable in preparing Russian food have been a mincer, a pestle and mortar, chopping boards and a meat mallet. Small (10 cm or 5 inch diameter) pancake pans of cast iron which I was able to buy in Russia have also been useful. Traditionally they used to be fitted together in sixes and connected by one long handle, and the whole contraption could be placed in the oven to bake the pancakes (see illustration on page 224).

For cakes, and Easter baking in particular, it is useful to have a tall cylindrical baking tin or something close to it, in which you can make *baba* and *kulich*. A wooden or plastic mould is needed for pressed Easter curd cheese or *paskha*, or, in the last resort, you can use a flower pot. For straining generally, making curd cheese, and for lining the *paskha* mould, muslin or cheesecloth is necessary.

A stoneware crock with a lid is ideal for making sauerkraut, pickling or salting herrings and other preserving jobs. A wooden barrel is excellent if you go in for large quantities, otherwise improvise with plastic. Salted and pickled foods, pressed curd cheese and the Georgian way with chicken, chicken *tabaka*, all call for heavy weights to press down evenly over the food beneath them. These can be rigged up rather cumbersomely with a plate first and then a weight of some kind, perhaps a clean brick or a cast-iron lid from a casserole. In Russia special chicken *tabaka* pans consisting of a heavy griddle-bottomed cast iron pan and an even heavier flat lid which fits inside it can be bought from hardware shops and are a good investment.

There you will also find huge brass-covered shallow jam pans with long wooden handles. They resemble old warming pans without lids but are usually bigger. The original copper pans are valued antiques. Look out for something similar if you are considering going in for home preserving in a big way.

For samovars and tea glasses see page 297. Long metal skewers are needed for *shashlyk*.

SPECIAL INGREDIENTS

HERBS

These are vital to almost all savoury dishes and should invariably be used fresh. In particular you will need **parsley**, which is fairly easily bought fresh in greengrocers' and some supermarkets, and **dill**, which you will probably have to grow yourself. Dried dill is tolerable, but avoid dried parsley like the plague. Both these herbs flourish on my indoor window-sills, and I don't claim to have green fingers. Use both the feathery leaves of the dill and the stalks, chopped finely, and the leaves and stem of parsley. If you grow Hamburg parsley, which is the variety the Russians like, the root is full of flavour. It is called for in most recipes which include making a stock with meat or fish and root vegetables. It may be replaced by a small amount of parsnip, which is sweeter, or caraway root. If you buy dried dill, note the difference between dill *weed* which is the dried green feathery part of the plant and the one you need, and dill *seed* which is often easier to find but generally for use only in pickling. It has a very strong flavour. Plant the seeds and you will get dill weed.

Dishes influenced by Caucasian cooking call for a wider variety of fresh herbs. In soups and stews, **basil, tarragon, mint, thyme** and **savory** may be replaced by dried herbs, but for salads grow or buy them fresh or substitute the fresh herbs you do have. A good standby is **chervil**, originally native to Russia. **Lovage**, used in some Southern dishes, is easy to grow from seed, but it is recommended for planting in the garden rather than a window-box because it grows very tall. The taste of the leaves is a cross between celery and fenugreek, one of the main ingredients in curry powder.

Coriander leaves may be grown very easily from the little round seeds available in many shops. The seeds have their own uses in a variety of dishes.

SPICES AND SPICE MIXTURES

Ginger, cinnamon, nutmeg (buy whole nutmeg and grate it fresh), **cloves, black pepper** and **cardamom** are easily found in supermarkets and other shops, but you may have to hunt for **star anise** in delicatessens. It is sometimes sold in whole dry pods by good coffee shops for putting in coffee. The seeds can be crushed. **Allspice** should not be confused with the 'mixed spice' bought ready ground in supermarkets. Allspice is another name for **Jamaican pepper**, which comes whole and looks like black peppercorns except that the pods are paler and larger. It may be crushed or used whole. **Poppy seeds** are available from whole food shops and delicatessens, where you can buy them loose by weight. Avoid little spice jars of poppy seed if possible – Russian cooking demands sizeable quantities of seeds in baking, and buying them this way will cost you a small fortune. The Azerbaijanis use dried **barberries** as a traditional flavouring, but I have never seen the fruit on sale either fresh or dried. I have replaced it with other spices in recipes. **Saffron**, widely used in all the Southern republics and in old Russian baking, presents a problem only in that it is priced almost according to its weight in gold. The Georgians use a substitute which they call *Izmeretinsky shafran*, after a province of Georgia. This apparently is the dried and powdered petal of the plant Holy Thistle, which gives food a yellow colour and a mild flavour. Powdered dried marigold petals are used in the same way and so, further East, is **turmeric**, the yellow powder that goes into curry powder and is used to colour commercial mustards. **Red** or **cayenne pepper** is widely used in Southern recipes and is easy to buy in any supermarket.

Two unusual spice mixtures which I first came across in Russian cooking are made up from these and other spices and herbs. The first is **adzhika**, a mixture of cayenne pepper, chilli powder, salt, black pepper, and crushed bay leaves, and the second **khmeli suneli**. The 'bouquet' which **suneli** means contains crushed fenugreek, bay leaf, coriander, dill, celery seed, parsley, basil, thyme, saffron and mint. There are no specific proportions and it may be made up like curry powder, to taste. The result is hot but not as hot as curry powder. The saffron may be omitted or replaced by turmeric.

CHEESE AND DAIRY PRODUCTS

The Russians use large quantities of *prostokvasha* and *smetana*. The first is more or less equivalent to plain **yoghurt**, and may be bought easily or made at home. Avoid only those commercial varieties that are set with gelatine. The Georgians, Armenians and Soviet Asians also all use yoghurt-type preparations called variously *matsoni* (Georgia), *matsun* (Armenia), *katyk* (Azerbaijan), *churgot* (Tadzhikistan), and *egurt* (Turkmenistan), which may be replaced by yoghurt or in some recipes by buttermilk.

Sour cream: *Smetana* is the product of a culture introduced to cream, not the fresh variety allowed to go off! 'Sour' is not a very good translation and is not part of the Russian word. It has a very slight tang, is thicker than ordinary cream, and is as good to my mind on sweet things as it is in soups. Buy it in supermarkets, where it is cheaper even than single cream and lasts longer, or try delicatessens specializing in Eastern European or non-kosher Jewish food. Some of these and some supermarkets stock a very economical Polish *smatana* which is just right. An alternative is to sour fresh cream by stirring in a teaspoon of lemon juice and leaving it a few hours to thicken, but this is very much a second best.

The two cheeses that are essential to Russian cooking are *tvorog* (**curd cheese**) and *brynza* (goat's, cow's or ewe's milk cheese preserved in brine). Neither is matured. *Tvorog* comes, like all Russian dairy products, in specified degrees of fatness from fat-free to something close to cream cheese. Occasionally it may be replaced by cream cheese such as in making *paskha*, but in most cases this would be far too rich and deficient in *tvorog*'s slightly sour taste. Medium-fat unflavoured curd cheese which may be bought in some supermarkets and delicatessens is ideal, as is Italian *ricotta*. Or you can make your own by draining yoghurt in muslin to collect the curds overnight. The whey may be used in some cooking such as soda breads and scones and in making the dough for *khachapuri*. For *brynza* a crumbly mild white English cheese such as Cheshire or Lancashire is often suitable as a substitute, or you can buy its very close relative, Greek or Danish *feta*. The Danish Food Centre in London sells this cheese canned in brine, at a price which when I last bought it made it cheaper than Cheddar. Delicatessens sometimes stock these tins, and Greek food shops have *feta*.

BREAD

It is really worth making your own, but for emergencies Polish and other delicatessens often stock pumpernickel and dark unleavened wheat bread of a similar kind from Germany and Scandinavia. Both are useful for *zakuski*. Ask in good bakeries whether they do dark rye loaves and you may be lucky. Some Jewish and Polish delicatessens also stock black bread, but not all these loaves are as good as they look. Middle Eastern flat bread (*pitta*) goes well with Georgian and Armenian food.

FISH

Good fishmongers should be able to provide many of the less common fish to order, such as sea bass, carp, smelts and turbot. You will always find salmon and trout frozen or fresh at a price. Grivan, the London fish wholesalers and importers, can supply smoked **sturgeon** and **caviare** for *zakuski*, and frozen sturgeon. Harrods and Fortnum and Mason stock the best *beluga* black caviare, other lesser but still prized varieties such as *sevruga*, taken from the smallest sturgeon, and red freshwater salmon caviare which is considerably cheaper. For all but the most extravagant purposes any hard roe you can get hold of is worth trying as a substitute. At the lowest end of the scale comes Danish caviare which is actually lumpfish roe. It comes in two artificial colours to match the real thing. There is no difference between the two in either flavour or texture. Because of its pretensions and its name, many delicatessens are tempted to sell it at extortionate prices. Buy it at half the price from the Danish Food Centre.

Salt your own **herrings** or buy them ready salted from delicatessens. It is often easier to find and substitute marinated herring fillets or rollmops. Raw herring canned in a spiced wine marinade, on sale in the Danish Food Centre and other Scandinavian shops, is excellent on the *zakuski* table, or can be made at home (page 33). Portuguese **sardines** in oil, available from most supermarkets, are useful, as are tinned Baltic **sprats** (Skipper's Brisling) from delicatessens and some supermarkets.

MEAT

Continental sausages, especially German and Polish varieties available from most delicatessens, are similar to Russian sausages.

GAME

Rabbit, venison, and wood pigeon, being unprotected, should be available fresh or frozen all the year round, similarly guinea fowl and quail which are farmed. Other game birds and hare are on sale in season, beginning late summer/early autumn.

VEGETABLES AND FRUIT

Bottled or tinned **sauerkraut**, **pickled cucumbers** and dried **mushrooms** are generally available in delicatessens, and good supermarkets are gradually stocking more of these slightly unusual foods.

Supermarkets are generally the cheapest places to buy dried fruit too. Some Greek delicatessens keep *tkemali*, dried sour **plums/damsons**, which are useful in Georgian and Armenian cooking. Buy **chestnuts** in season when they are cheap just before Christmas, and store in a dry place for later use in *plov* and other Azerbaijani dishes. Spring or green **onions** and Welsh onions are available most of the year, but it is worth growing your own. Private enterprise is a necessity for **sorrel** and worth thinking about for **beetroot**. It is a lot easier than being faced with uncomprehending stares if you want to cook with young **beetroot leaves**. I find it hard enough to buy an uncooked beetroot, let alone its tops.

GRAINS, STARCHES AND PULSES

Italian delicatessens will certainly stock the best **rice** for *plov* (the highly absorbent Italian variety also used for making *risotto*). For the widest selection of other **grains**, including bulghur wheat, millet, cornmeal and buckwheat, go to a whole food shop. The same shops usually stock a range of **flours**, including barley, buckwheat, rice and potato flours, and rye flour. Supermarkets usually have wholewheat flour at a lower price, and also dried **yeast**. Chemists, as well as many delicatessens, stock **arrowroot**. Whole food shops are again the places to buy **beans** of many varieties, although for haricots and red kidney beans supermarkets are often cheaper. Small, shiny greenish-white flageolet beans stocked by delicatessens are excellent for use in salads.

MISCELLANEOUS

Malt extract: From chemists and whole food shops.
Molasses: From whole food shops.
Unrefined sunflower oil, poppy seed oil: From whole food shops.
Vinegar: Buy wine and cider vinegars from supermarkets or from the cask in whole food shops. Health food shops tend to be expensive. Check the proof of the vinegar before using it. Most Russian recipes assume it is 3–4 per cent, but many wine vinegars are as high as 7 per cent and may need diluting with a little water to soften their impact, especially in dressings.
Rassol: This is the liquid in which salted (dill) cucumbers are preserved.
Beetroot rassol: The liquid in which beetroot is preserved.

Cold Zakuski and Salads

A peculiarity of the Russian cuisine is the so-called *zakuska* resembling the Finnish *Smorgasbord*. In the larger restaurants there is always a sideboard or even a separate room for the *zakuska*, which consists of a caviare, different kinds of fish, patties (*piroshki*), pickled cucumbers and mushrooms, and so forth, along with vodka and other spirits.

KARL BAEDEKER, Russia 1914

One Christmas four of us – three old friends and a certain Georgy Ivanovich – were lunching together in the restaurant of the Grand Moscow Hotel.

Because of the holiday the Grand Moscow was empty and cool. We walked through the old dining-room, which was dully illuminated by the grey frosty afternoon, and paused in the doorway of the new one, looking for the most comfortable place to sit and running our eyes over the tables with their freshly spread, stiff, snow-white tablecloths . . . a minute later there appeared before us large and small glasses, bottles of different-coloured spirits, some pink salmon, some dark fillet of sturgeon, a dish with open shells on chippings of ice, an orange wedge of Cheshire cheese, a gleaming black block of pressed caviare and a white champagne bucket, smoking from the cold. We began with pepper vodka . . .

IVAN BUNIN, Ida

Zakuski, now one of the most characteristic features of the Russian table, were introduced to Russia in the eighteenth century by the great Europeanizing and modernizing Tsar, Peter the Great. They came from Peter's fact-finding tours of the civilized world west of Russia and his conquests to the North. He began his Grand European tour in the Baltic port of Riga, and travelled west across what is now Northern Poland, through Berlin, thence to Holland and England. His long war with the Swedes gave him control of the Baltic and a brief hold on Finland. Gastronomically speaking, this Swedish-dominated world was rich in salted and pickled fish, apples, potatoes, pickled cucumbers, cheese and dairy products, sausage and other preserved meats and dark rye bread. These preparations still characterize the attractive cold buffet that the typical *zakuski* table is today. You may quite legitimately search in Scandinavian delicatessens and stock up with a variety of tinned fish and wedges of Edam, Gouda and Cheddar to furnish your own spread. Here is a quick check list:

Any smoked or marinated fish, but particularly herring
    marinated in wine, sugar and spices, and Baltic smoked
    sprats (Skipper's Brisling)
Continental sausage, cold ham
Rollmops
Dutch, English, German and Scandinavian cheeses

To these may be added cold chicken, turkey or game, cold fish and shellfish dressed in vinaigrette, sour cream or mayonnaise, pâté, and fresh or pickled fruit and vegetables: apples, cucumbers, red cabbage, plums, cherries. Some recipes for pickling are given on pages 309–11. You may also prepare herrings in a sweet wine marinade at home (see page 33). Go for small quantities and variety, and serve the *zakuski* as a first course or buffet lunch with good bread (preferably brown or rye) and unsalted butter. If you are sitting down to *zakuski*, a pleasant change which turns them into a full meal is to serve boiled potatoes with them, especially when new potatoes are in season and can be served in their jackets. The only permissible drink is ice-cold vodka, served in tiny liqueur glasses and drunk down in one gulp between the different foods. If possible keep it in a freezer so that it steams with the ice on its sides when it comes to the table. The table should also include one or two bowls of sour cream to eat with plain cold meat, especially pork, and the spread could be eked out with hard-boiled eggs. Below are various home-prepared cold *zakuski* which will add an individual touch as well as being often more economical.

A word must be said about caviare, which is normally thought of as having pride of place on the *zakuski* table. The black eggs of the *beluga* and other varieties of sturgeon and the orange eggs of Siberian salmon did not become popular until the nineteenth century, when the fish were relatively common and inexpensive. The novelist Vladimir Nabokov recalled in his autobiography how his father set out to walk from St Petersburg to the Crimea, over 1,000 miles, to escape imprisonment or worse in the impending Revolution. The family chef gave him a packet of caviare sandwiches to see him on his way. Caviare generally was not so much a delicacy as highly nutritious. One variety of Volga sturgeon was nevertheless considered a particularly fine source of caviare, and its yield was much consumed by the Imperial family to whom it was sometimes sent in tribute. It was thus that the late nineteenth century began to associate caviare more and more

Urbain Dubois's elaborate interpretation of a Russian hors d'oeuvre *with caviare.*

with fine eating. But as Jane Grigson points out in *Fish Cookery* (Penguin, 1975), only under Soviet rule has the international caviare industry really been organized. The same Soviet industry has promoted caviare as a classic *zakuska*. It is a predictable feature of Soviet culture and ideology that what was considered an aristocratic delicacy under the Tsars should now be promoted as potentially available to the common man but mainly spun as a money-maker abroad. To be fair, caviare, or to give its Russian name, *ikra*, is not nearly as expensive in the Soviet Union as it is in the West, but the purchase of it is restricted to restaurants and to Western visitors using foreign currency. Restaurants are difficult to get into, and have long waiting lists and arbitrary doormen, so that all in all the closest many Russians come to caviare is to read in their only cookery book that the Soviet Union is the biggest producer in the world. There is a standard joke about the little boy who asks his father why there is no caviare to buy in the shops. He is told that the aristocracy took it all with them when they left Russia after the Revolution.

Ideology apart, if you like caviare particularly and can afford it, serve it in small dishes, chilled, with white, brown and black bread sliced thinly, unsalted butter or a bowl of sour cream, and wedges of lemon. One nineteenth-century variation was to mix it with very finely chopped spring onion and chill it for 24 hours before serving in the same way, which is particularly worth considering if you decide on a cheaper substitute like Danish lumpfish or any other hard roe. Caviare is also the classic filling for Russian buckwheat pancakes, *blini* (page 222).

HOME-PREPARED ZAKUSKI

ZAKUSKI ON BREAD

Traditional *zakuski* include small open sandwiches, *buterbrody*, and hot titbits on white toast, *tartinki*. As the German and French names suggest, there is nothing particularly Russian about either, except the habit of eating them. Make *buterbrody* with black bread cut into small squares, spread with one of the butters below, topped with a piece of herring, sardine or smoked fish and finished with a twist of lemon. Smoked sprats (*kilki*), a speciality of the Baltic states, are particular Russian favourites.

Herb butter

> 1–2 tablespoons fresh herbs (parsley, basil, tarragon, thyme)
> 100 g (4 oz) butter
> salt
> lemon juice

Wash the herbs, dry them and chop finely. Work into the softened butter with a pinch of salt and season to taste with lemon juice. Serve chilled and keep covered in the refrigerator.

Sardine or herring butter

> 1 small mild onion
> approximately ¼ pint milk
> 50 g (2 oz) sardines or salted herring
> ½–1 eating apple
> salt
> 120 g (4 oz) butter
> nutmeg

Soak the onion in warm milk for 30 minutes, then grate it, reserving both pulp and juice. Mash the sardines, mix with the onion, add the finely grated apple, salt and softened butter. Mix until smooth and chill. Serve with lemon wedges and black or brown rye bread. Sardine butter is also used as a dressing for plain boiled potatoes.

To make herring butter, soak the salted fish in weak tea for 3–4 hours, dry, cut into pieces and pound to a paste. Mix with the other ingredients until smooth and season with nutmeg.

Smoked fish butter

>300 g (11 oz) smoked fish (kipper, haddock, mackerel, etc.)
>2 hard-boiled egg yolks
>75 g (3 oz) butter
>lemon juice to taste
>salt and black pepper

Bone and skin the fish and put it through a fine mincer together with the two hard-boiled egg yolks. Add the softened butter and lemon juice. Season with freshly ground black pepper and salt if required. Chill.

Cheese base for buterbrody

>200 g (8 oz) brine cheese, or a crumbly cheese such as
>   Caerphilly, Cheshire or Lancashire
>⅔ small (5 fl oz) carton sour cream

Grate or crumble the cheese, and beat it with the back of a wooden spoon, gradually adding the sour cream, until you have a smooth mixture. Top with olives or sweet-marinated herring (see below).

FISH ZAKUSKI

Sweet-marinated herring

This is Jane Grigson's recipe for Danish pickled herring, slightly adapted. Made with red wine and a little extra vinegar, it exactly matches the delicious tinned product I was able to buy in Russia. My favourite way of eating it was on black bread with the cheese base given in the previous recipe, or simply on top of a piece of brine cheese.

'. . . the herrings must be soaked until they are mild in flavour.

>4–6 salted herring fillets
>milk and water for soaking
>225 g (8 oz) granulated sugar
>150 ml (¼ pint) red wine
>6 tablespoons cider vinegar
>6–8 peppercorns
>1 teaspoon pickling spice including a chilli
>2–3 onions
>a few bay leaves

Put the salted herring fillets to soak in milk and water. Simmer together the sugar, wine, vinegar, peppercorns and spices for 3 minutes. Leave to cool. When the saltiness of the herrings is reduced to a palatable level, drain and arrange them in a plastic box or glass jar, with slices of onion and bay leaves in between. Pour over the marinade and leave for at least 5 days in the refrigerator.' Serve cut into smallish pieces.

Lithuanian herring salad

There are many variations on this theme, which has been popular for the last two centuries in Russian cooking. The basic combination is salted herrings (soaked in milk to remove most of the salt), sour cream, onion and fresh herbs. For 3 herring fillets, which will provide a starter for 4 people, you will need ½ a small (5 fl oz) carton of sour cream or more to taste. I like to toss the herrings in a little olive oil and vinegar first, and then add the cream. Chopped spring onions, including the green parts, may be added, or finely chopped eating apple. Dress with parsley, dill and chervil. Cold boiled potatoes, sliced, may be included in the salad, in which case you will need more dressing, or you may serve the salad in larger quantities with hot boiled potatoes as a light meal. Cooked beetroot is a good accompaniment.

Smoked fish

Smoked sturgeon and smoked salmon are the most common *zakuski* in modern Russian restaurants. The sturgeon has a yellowish colour, a slightly rubbery texture and a strong flavour, and I regard it as an acquired taste! Good substitutes are smoked mackerel with grated horseradish and sour cream, or raw kippers, skinned, lightly beaten with a meat mallet, and served on black bread with a garnish of spring onion and a squeeze of lemon juice. Like their salted brethren, kippers also combine well in salads.

Kipper and broad bean salad

Dress cooked broad beans while they are still hot with lemon juice and olive oil, and season lightly with black pepper. When the mixture has cooled add chopped raw kipper and chill. Serve as a *zakuska* or with boiled potatoes to make a light summer lunch.

Sour cream fish salad

> 300 g (11 oz) cooked, filleted, firm white fish
> 1 chopped hard-boiled egg
> salt and pepper
> 3 tablespoons sour cream
> 3 tablespoons mayonnaise
> fresh parsley
> 1 lemon

Flake the fish or cut into small pieces, put in a bowl with the egg, and add salt and pepper to taste. Mix the sour cream and mayonnaise together, stir in the chopped parsley and pour this dressing over the fish. Decorate with lemon slices.

Fish salad with horseradish

A typical Russian combination of bland and sour pickled flavours to which a French mayonnaise has been added.

> 2–3 medium potatoes
> 250 g (9 oz) filleted firm white fish, cooked
> 2 pickled cucumbers
> 100 g (3½ oz) fresh horseradish root
> approximately 6 tablespoons mayonnaise
> salt
> 2 teaspoons vinegar
> 50 g (2 oz) spring onion
> parsley

Boil the potatoes in their skins, allow to cool, then peel and slice them. Cut the fish into bite-sized pieces and slice the cucumbers. Grate the horseradish into a bowl, add the mayonnaise, salt and vinegar, mix with the potatoes, fish and cucumber and turn into a salad bowl. Decorate with finely chopped spring onion and parsley. (If no fresh horseradish is available, replace 1 tablespoon of mayonnaise with prepared creamed horseradish.)

Fish in aspic

This is not strictly a *zakuska* but belongs to the collection of cold and versatile dishes which are close relations. (See Meat *studen'*, page 37.) Aspic dishes are old favourites in the Russian kitchen and were traditionally served as the second course of a meal, after a hot soup.

Today a whole fish, gleaming under a jelly coating and decorated with vegetables of every colour, is still served with delight by traditional diners after caviare *zakuski*. The most magnificent sturgeon I have ever seen was prepared this way by the Moscow patriarchy to celebrate Orthodox Christmas.

> 1 whole cod, sturgeon or sea perch (zander)
> 1 carrot
> 1 onion
> 1 bay leaf
> 1 parsley root
> a few allspice berries
> a few peppercorns
> 1–2 teaspoons gelatine for every 500 g (1 lb) of fish
> lemon slices

Clean, gut and fillet the fish, removing the fins and head but taking care not to damage the skin. Bring the fish trimmings, including the head, to the boil in enough water to cover them and add the carrot, onion, bay leaf, parsley root, allspice and peppercorns. Simmer for 20 minutes, strain the liquid, and reserve the head. Return the bouillon to a clean, preferably shallow, pan over a gentle heat.

Cut the whole fish into sections the size of a serving portion and lower into the bouillon. The fish is to be reassembled after poaching, so it is important to disturb it as little as possible in the pan. After 10 minutes remove the fish from the bouillon and place the sections in order on a serving place with a small space between each. Run the head under cold water to remove any debris and replace it on the fish. Cover with a damp cloth while you prepare the aspic.

Strain the stock and make up with water to a scant ¼ litre (⅓ pint) for every 500 g (1 lb) of fish. Dissolve the gelatine in water and add to the stock. (The stock may be clarified before adding the gelatine by bringing it slowly to the boil with a beaten egg white and a little vinegar or lemon juice. When the stock boils, remove it from the heat and set aside for 20 minutes. Then strain it carefully through a piece of muslin or cheesecloth.)

Decorate the fish with slices of lemon, and when the stock is just beginning to gel pour it over slowly so that it covers the outside of the fish thinly and leaves the lemon slices in place. Leave the fish in a cool place to set. Serve with mayonnaise or horseradish and vinegar, with potato salad and pickled and fresh cucumbers.

MEAT ZAKUSKI

The most traditional Russian meat dish served cold and dating back long before the era of *zakuski* is an aspic dish made with pig's trotters or ox cheek. It earned the name of *kholodets*, which simply meant cold dish, or *studen'*, derived from another word for cold or cool. It is traditionally served with a sweetish vinaigrette flavoured with mustard, which the nineteenth-century French gastronome Urbain Dubois immortalized as *sauce à la russe* (recipe given below).

Meat studen'

> 2 cow's feet or pig's trotters
> 1 carrot
> 1 onion
> 1 parsley root
> 5 black peppercorns
> 3 allspice berries
> 2 bay leaves
> salt and black pepper
> 1–2 thinly sliced pickled cucumbers plus a little *rassol* (see page 27)
> ½ head garlic
> 2–3 hard-boiled eggs

Clean the trotters, making sure no hair remains. Cover with cold water in a deep pan, bring to the boil, remove scum and simmer for 3–4 hours. Add the carrot, onion and parsley root after 2 hours and the peppercorns, allspice, and bay leaves after 3. When the trotters are done remove them from the bouillon and allow to cool. Strip the soft part from the bones and put it through the mincer. Return the bones to the bouillon and simmer until there is no more than ½ litre (scant 1 pint) of liquid. Add the seasoning, cucumbers and a little *rassol* to taste. Chop the garlic finely and add that. Spread the meat over the bottom of a shallow dish, slice the eggs thinly lengthwise and set them in the meat. Pour over the cool bouillon and allow to set in a cold place. Serve cut into slices, with *sauce à la russe* or sour cream dressing with dill (page 46), either as a *zakuska* or with boiled potatoes as a luncheon dish. For a short cut, buy brawn ready potted from a good butcher.

Sauce à la russe

> 1 tablespoon English mustard
> 8 tablespoons olive oil
> 2 tablespoons wine vinegar
> pinch of salt
> pinch of sugar

Mix all the ingredients together at room temperature. This dressing is also suitable for hard-boiled eggs and for smoked mackerel.

Stuffed pig's trotter or pâté of pig's trotter and liver

Old Russian cooking featured many recipes for what were known as 'subproducts' or offal. This one is a close relative of *studen'* which I have adapted. The original recipe required skinning the trotter before cooking (which I found impossible), removing the meat from the bones and making it into a pâté with the liver and breadcrumbs. The mixture was sewn inside the re-formed trotter and simmered in a stock made from the bones. I decided to cook the whole trotters first and dispense with the larger-than-nature presentation which smacks so much of the nineteenth century, though Russians do still seem to love it today. (Compare the Easter roast sucking pig on page 247, intended to come to the table crouching like a live beast, with a marinated apple in its mouth and cherries for eyes.)

For each pig's trotter (which you can get from the butcher for a few pence):

> 1 bay leaf
> 1 slice onion
> a few peppercorns
> 100 g (3–4 oz) pig's liver
> fresh white breadcrumbs equal in *volume* to the liver and the
>   meat removed from the trotter
> a little milk
> salt and pepper to taste

Simmer the washed trotter for at least 2 hours in water with the bay leaf, a slice of onion and a few peppercorns. Skim the froth from the top as it appears. Remove the trotter, allow to cool sufficiently to be easily handled, and remove the meat from the bones, including the skin. Return the bones to the pan and boil for another half an hour in the stock, topped up with water as necessary. Strain the stock and put on one side. It will cool into a firm jelly. Meanwhile lightly fry the liver and add it to the chopped meat from the trotter. Moisten the bread-crumbs with milk and allow to stand. Put the two meats once through a meat grinder, mix with the breadcrumbs and put through the grinder again until you have a smooth mixture. Discard any gristle. Season with salt and pepper and spoon out on to a piece of muslin which you can roll into a long sausage. Secure the ends and make sure the package won't leak. Simmer gently in the reserved stock, adding enough water to cover, for ½–1 hour. Remove and allow to cool. Remove the muslin and serve in slices with *sauce à la russe* (page 38).

Liver pashtet/pâté

> 500 g (1 lb) ox or pig's liver
> milk
> 1 carrot
> 1 small onion
> 1 parsley root
> 100 g (3½ oz) streaky bacon
> 1 tablespoon oil
> 1 bay leaf
> 2–3 allspice berries
> salt and pepper
> nutmeg, freshly grated
> a little brandy
> 100 g (3½ oz) butter

Soak the liver in milk for a few hours if necessary. Remove the film, clean and cut into small pieces. Slice the carrot, onion and parsley root thinly. Cut off the bacon rinds and sauté the chopped bacon in its own fat or with 1 tablespoon of oil. When there is enough fat to coat the bottom of the pan add the liver, sliced vegetables, bay leaf and allspice berries. When the liver is just cooked, remove it from the heat and put it through a food processor or grinder with the bacon and the dripping from the pan. Add salt, pepper, freshly grated nutmeg and a little brandy to the liver and bacon mixture, according to taste, and gradu-ally work in the softened butter with a wooden spoon. Transfer to a serving dish and chill.

BEAN SALADS AND BEAN ZAKUSKI

These relatively new ideas for *zakuski* have been imported to Russia from the Southern republics of Moldavia, Georgia and Armenia, and have become increasingly popular in the last 10 years. One method is simply to cook haricots, the smaller flageolet beans or green lentils in water until tender, drain them and dress while still hot with a mixture of sunflower or olive oil, wine vinegar, grated onion, parsley, and salt and pepper to taste. Leave for 24 hours if possible for the flavours to blend. Another method is to pound the beans to a paste with the oil and dress them with the remaining ingredients. I dislike the very solid texture that results from this, and the temptation is to add far too much oil to make it more elastic, but it is a standby if you have cooked the beans too long and they have gone mushy. A little of the cooking liquid added to the oil will lend a more liquid texture.

Bean salad with muzhdei
This is the classic Moldavian version of a bean salad, using fresh herbs and, instead of vinegar, *muzhdei*, a concentrated mixture of beef stock and garlic. If you like garlic it is astonishingly good.

> 200 g (8 oz) dried white beans (soaked overnight)
> 1 medium onion
> 1 tablespoon each chopped fresh parsley and dill
> 3–6 cloves of garlic, crushed with ½ teaspoon salt
> 3 tablespoons or more beef or chicken stock
> salt and pepper
> olive oil to taste (optional)

Cook the beans in water until tender. Chop or grate the onion and add it to the mixture with the chopped herbs. (If you grate the onion be sure to catch the juice and add that too.) Add the crushed garlic to the stock and stir into the beans. Season. More stock and a little olive oil may be added to taste. Allow to stand for several hours to allow the flavours to develop. Serve either chilled or at room temperature. Sweet tomatoes are an excellent complement.

Georgian bean salads
There are endless ways to dress a cold bean salad in the Georgian style, depending on the combination of herbs and spices selected and

what is chosen to bind the salad. Here are three variations, using (*a*) ground nuts, (*b*) a tomato purée or (*c*) a cheese mixture to hold the beans together.

500 g (1 lb) dried beans (soaked overnight)
4 tablespoons vegetable oil
4 tablespoons tarragon vinegar
2–4 onions, finely chopped
1–2 tablespoons each of 2–3 fresh herbs, chosen from
    coriander leaves, parsley, mint, thyme, basil
½ teaspoon each of 2–3 dry spices, chosen from coriander
    seeds, cinnamon, cloves, *suneli* (see page 24)
1 teaspoon black or red (cayenne) pepper
salt
2–4 cloves of garlic
(a) 50–100 g (2–3 oz) chopped walnuts *or* (b) 5 tomatoes *or*
    (c) 200 g (8 oz) brine cheese or *tvorog* (curd cheese)

Cook the soaked beans in plenty of water until just tender, and while they are still warm drain them, reserving a little liquid, and add the oil. Let it sink into the beans for a few minutes before adding the vinegar. (If tarragon vinegar is not available, plain cider or wine vinegar can be simmered with a small stalk of tarragon for a few minutes before using.) Add the chopped onions, herbs, spices, seasoning and crushed garlic to the vinegar and pour it over the beans.

(*a*) If nuts are used, they should be ground with the garlic and mixed with the vinegar before it is added to the beans.

(*b*) To make the tomato purée, dip the tomatoes in boiling water to remove the skins and crush them with a wooden spoon before adding to the beans.

(*c*) To make the cheese binder soak the brine cheese in cold water for an hour, then dry. (*Tvorog* (curd cheese) will not need soaking.) Pound smooth with red pepper, cloves and coriander seeds (from the recipe spice ration). Bring to the consistency of thick cream with a small amount of the reserved bean liquid. This makes a hot thick dressing for the beans.

Rasputin's red bean salad

This is my own name for a dish served by Rasputin's restaurant in London. It has no connection with the mad monk but is excellent in its own right. Rasputin's call it *lobio*, which is the Georgian word for beans.

> 200 g (8 oz) dried red beans (soaked overnight)
> 1–2 onions
> 8 tablespoons olive oil
> 1 tablespoon vinegar
> 5 tablespoons tomato purée
> 1 scant teaspoon red pepper or chilli powder
> a few peppercorns
> 1 bay leaf
> sugar to taste

Simmer the soaked beans in water until cooked, and drain. Sauté the chopped onions gently in olive oil, add the rest of the ingredients to the pan, and cook gently for 5–10 minutes. Add the beans to the sauce and simmer for another 5 minutes. Turn into a serving dish and allow to cool without refrigerating.

Armenian bean salad
This is another Rasputin speciality, a variation on a classic dish called *mshosh* which is a salad of cooked haricot beans and walnuts.

> 200 g (8 oz) dried white beans (soaked overnight)
> 1 fresh pomegranate
> 1 small (5 fl oz) carton single or sour cream
> salt and pepper
> a few chopped walnuts

Cook the soaked beans in water, drain, dress with a little pomegranate juice and allow to cool. Stir in the cream and test for seasoning. Arrange in a serving dish with pomegranate seeds and walnuts sprinkled over the top.

VEGETABLE IKRY (CAVIARES)

Apart from hard roe, the Russians use the word caviare to describe fine mixtures based on a single cooked vegetable. Vegetable *ikry* are for poor men and have no pretensions to high table. Russians eat them either tinned or freshly made in season.

Beetroot caviare

> 1 medium beetroot, cooked or raw
> ½ tablespoon sugar
> 2 tablespoons vegetable oil
> juice and rind of half a lemon
> pinch of salt

If using raw beetroot, wash and boil in plenty of water until tender. Rinse in cold water and peel. Chop the beetroot into small pieces and put it through a mincer or food mill, or purée it in a liquidizer, depending on how smooth you require the finished caviare. Add the remaining ingredients, turn the mixture into a pan and stir over a low heat for 5–10 minutes. Chill and serve with black bread and butter and other *zakuski*.

Aubergine caviare
Imported from Georgian, Armenian and Moldavian cuisine, the aubergine has been popular in Russia in the form of a caviare for over 100 years. The aubergines are baked in a medium oven until black, then the pulp is removed from inside the skins and beaten smooth with oil. Some recipes call for the addition of tomato pulp and sautéed onion as well as seasoning. Do not use metal implements to make this dish – they will discolour the aubergines.

Aubergine caviares are usually served chilled, although they are also worth trying hot, like *ratatouille*.

> 5 medium aubergines, about 650 g (1½ lbs) in all
> 6 medium onions, grated
> 4–5 tablespoons olive oil
> 6 tomatoes, skinned
> salt and black pepper

Bake the aubergines as above. Sauté the onions gently in the oil until transparent. Add the baked aubergine pulp and the chopped tomatoes, and stir the mixture over a low heat for 1–2 minutes. Season with salt and black pepper and turn into a serving dish.

(*a*) Another method is to sauté only the onion in enough oil to keep it from sticking to the pan, and then add it to the aubergine pulp with 2–3 raw, skinned, finely chopped tomatoes. Season the mixture, and add the rest of the oil plus a dash of wine vinegar to make a fairly firm caviare.

(*b*) If aubergine pulp alone is used, season it with oil, salt, black pepper and vinegar to achieve the same consistency.

(*c*) Yet another variety of aubergine caviare can be made by chopping the baked, skinned aubergines finely, and adding a chopped or grated onion and a few tablespoons of finely chopped walnuts pounded and mixed to a paste with 4 tablespoons of mild vinegar, 2 or 3 tablespoons each of fresh chopped parsley and coriander leaves, 2 crushed cloves of garlic, and a teaspoon of red (cayenne) pepper.

Mushroom caviare
(See page 210.)

CHEESE, BUTTERMILK AND YOGHURT STARTERS

The hard English cheeses were imported into Russia in the last century, when they were considered a luxury on the *zakuski* table. Dutch cheese had been brought in since the eighteenth century to be eaten the same way. The Russians never followed the French habit of eating these matured cheeses before pudding, or the English way of eating them at the end of a meal.

Tvorog, the national cheese product, did not appear on the classic *zakuski* table but was often the start of a simple family meal. At its simplest it was cottage cheese topped with sour cream and sprinkled with salt.

The Southern republics have their own tradition in cheese and dairy produce eaten as a first course. In Georgia and Armenia the local cheese is still basically *tvorog*, but pressed and preserved in brine. *Brynza* is the best-known of these brine cheeses. It is eaten as a starter with fresh basil leaves or other herbs, fresh cucumbers and tomatoes.

Ukrainian Mochanka

500 g (1 lb) curd cheese
1 small (5 fl oz) carton sour cream
3 tablespoons chopped spring onion
1 tablespoon dill weed

Combine all the ingredients and leave to stand for several hours in a cool place.

Belorussian Mokanka

> 500 g (1 lb) curd cheese
> 1 small (5 fl oz) carton sour cream
> 250 ml (½ pint) milk
> 125 ml (¼ pint) buttermilk
> 2–3 chopped spring onions
> 1 tablespoon dill weed
> ½ tablespoon caraway seed
> 1 medium potato, boiled and chopped into small pieces
> ¾ teaspoon salt

Combine the cheese with the sour cream, and the milk with the buttermilk, then slowly add the milk mixture to the cheese, stirring until completely blended. The result should be about the consistency of thick sour cream and very light. Stir in the remaining ingredients.

Georgian potted cheese

> 500 g (1 lb) brine cheese or crumbly English cheese
>   (Cheshire, Lancashire)
> 50 g (2 oz) butter
> 2 tablespoons fresh or 3 tablespoons dried mint
> 1 tablespoon fresh tarragon
> 1 teaspoon cayenne pepper

Soak the brine cheese in hot water for 10 minutes, take out and beat smooth with a wooden spoon, gradually working in the butter. Add the chopped herbs and pepper, place in a covered serving dish, and allow to stand for several hours or overnight in the refrigerator to let the flavours develop.

Beginning an Azerbaijani meal
The Azerbaijanis serve not cheese but yoghurt or buttermilk in a bowl or glass, accompanied by raw unchopped vegetables and herb greenery, such as spring onions, radishes, ridge cucumbers and cress, to start a meal. This is followed by fresh fruit, ideally a mixture of damsons and peaches, lightly sautéed in butter. The result should be slightly sour and may be sprinkled with a little lemon juice. The two preparations together are a wonderfully light way to start a summer dinner when the fruit and vegetables are easily available. Follow with *plov*, or roast lamb or chicken, or kebabs.

SALADS

Full Russian salads are more substantial than *zakuski* and are often served as a course in themselves. Other preparations closer to our own salads, and served with roast meat, game or fish, have come into being largely under foreign influence and are elaborate garnishes.

Traditionally Russian vegetables were served singly and alone, either pickled, salted or baked. The classic cold starters were cold soups and aspic (*studen'*). The soups were so abundant in raw and cooked vegetables, however, that they were in effect liquid salads.

When the French introduced salad dressings and mixtures of cold ingredients in the nineteenth century the ordinary Russian housewife seemed slow to learn the new art. As one cookery book writer early this century lamented:

> Unfortunately Russian housewives know very little about the different ways of making salads and in the majority of cases lose sight of the fact that salad can serve not only as a tasty accompaniment to a hot dish but can be a dish in its own right in summer.

Old habits die hard. In Russian restaurants today, even in season, a tossed green or mixed salad never appears on the menu. The preference is still for salads of one vegetable or of a single kind of meat or fish. What the West thinks of as 'Russian salad', a mixture of cooked vegetables and mayonnaise, was largely a French–Russian nineteenth-century creation called *vinegret*.

Basic sour cream dressing for salads and garnishes

    4 tablespoons sour cream
    2 tablespoons wine or cider vinegar
    salt, pepper and sugar to taste
    fresh dill or grated horseradish (optional)

Mix all the ingredients well. Equal parts of vinegar and sour cream may also be used to make a sharper dressing, and fresh dill or grated horseradish added. As a quick standby dressing Russians also simply blend equal parts of sour cream and mayonnaise.

A French version of sour cream dressing
This produces a light-textured mayonnaise.

1 raw egg yolk
½ teaspoon mustard
½ teaspoon sugar
1 small (5 fl oz) carton sour cream
1–2 tablespoons vinegar
salt and pepper
fresh dill or grated horseradish (optional)

Cream together the egg yolk and the mustard to make a smooth paste, and add the sugar. Stir in the cream gradually, and finish the dressing with vinegar when thick. Season to taste. Dill or grated horseradish may also be added.

Cucumbers in sour cream dressing
I like the basic Russian dressing (page 46) best with cucumbers. Peel them, slice thinly and salt lightly. After 30 minutes drain away the liquid, pat dry and coat with dressing.

Tomatoes in sour cream dressing
Slice the tomatoes thinly and coat with Russian sour cream dressing (page 46) to which dill and an extra pinch of sugar have been added. Top with a little chopped spring onion or grated onion, and freshly ground black pepper. Coat the tomatoes immediately before serving otherwise their juice will dilute the dressing and make the dish look watery.

Lettuce salad

1–2 medium heads of lettuce
2 hard-boiled eggs
6 tablespoons sour cream dressing with dill (page 46)
½ cucumber

Break the lettuce into smallish pieces and arrange in a salad bowl. Slice the eggs thinly and mix with the dressing. Just before serving add this mixture to the lettuce, toss gently, and arrange cucumber slices on top. Serve alone or with meat or fish.

Radish salad

> 2–3 bunches of radishes, weighing about 500 g (1 lb)
> 1 hard-boiled egg
> ¾ small (5 fl oz) carton sour cream
> salt and black pepper
> chopped fresh herbs

Wash the radishes, slice, salt lightly, and leave for half an hour. Meanwhile mix together the hard-boiled egg yolk and the sour cream to a smooth paste. Dry the radishes and add them to the dressing, together with the chopped egg white. Season to taste. Sprinkle chopped parsley, dill or any other fresh herb over the finished salad and serve. This is best as a course on its own.

Marinated beetroot with horseradish

> 500 g (1 lb) beetroot
> 6 tablespoons vinegar
> sugar to taste
> 1 bay leaf
> 6 peppercorns
> 2 horseradish roots
> oil or sour cream (optional)

Boil the beets in their skins until tender, cool, peel and slice thinly, or use cooked beetroot. Bring the vinegar to the boil with the sugar, bay leaf, peppercorns and enough water to make a marinade to cover the beetroot slices. Grate the horseradish coarsely or cut it in thin slices lengthwise. Arrange the beetroot in layers with a scattering of horseradish between each, pour over the marinade and refrigerate for 1–2 days. To serve, drain the beets and use either alone or coated with a little oil or sour cream. Serve with hot or cold meat.

Beetroot salad

A good example of how French chefs refined the basic Russian beetroot and horseradish combination, traditionally served alone as a Lenten sweet/sour dish, and transformed it into a smooth, elegant salad, rich in calories and relatively gentle on the palate.

400–500 g (about 1 lb) beetroot
1–2 teaspoons sugar
3 raw egg yolks
2 tablespoons olive oil
juice of 1 lemon
3–4 tablespoons grated horseradish
salt
chopped dill and parsley

Boil the beets until tender, cool, peel and slice thinly, or use cooked beetroot. Mix together the sugar and egg yolks and very gradually add the oil as for a mayonnaise. When the mixture thickens add the lemon juice, stir in the horseradish and check the seasoning. Pour the dressing over the beets and sprinkle with chopped herbs.

Spring onion salad

5 hard-boiled eggs
2 bunches spring onions, including green stalks
1 tablespoon made mustard
4 tablespoons olive or sunflower oil
salt, pepper and sugar to taste
red peppers or tomatoes to garnish

Chop the hard-boiled eggs, reserving one yolk for the dressing. Mix the chopped egg with the onion cut into small pieces about 1 cm (½ in) long. (Use all the green part of the onion that is fresh and not tough. It has a sharp taste, very popular with Russians, but is considerably mellowed by the dressing. Fairly thin, young onions are ideal for this salad.) Mix the reserved egg yolk with the mustard to make a smooth paste, and slowly add the oil. Season with salt, pepper and a sprinkling of sugar if liked. Coat the onion mixture thoroughly with the dressing and decorate with strips of red pepper or slices of tomato. Serve with plain grilled meat or fish, with an omelette, or alone with black bread.

Spring onions and hard-boiled eggs may also be served in a plain sour cream dressing (page 46).

Watercress and apple salad

Break 2 washed bunches of watercress into a bowl with olive oil, vinegar and seasoning, add a diced eating apple, toss, and serve with roast meat.

Red cabbage salad

Shred the cabbage, place in a saucepan, sprinkle with salt and cover with boiling water. Cook for 10 minutes, drain, and turn into a serving dish. Make a dressing with 6 tablespoons of mild vinegar, 2 tablespoons of sugar and a bay leaf brought to the boil together in a pan, and pour over the cabbage. Serve hot or cold. This salad was considered excellent in the last century as a garnish for rich roast game.

Salad-stuffed cucumbers

> 4–6 medium-sized ridge cucumbers or an equal quantity of
>   long cucumbers, total weight about 500 g (1 lb)
> 2 hard-boiled eggs
> 1 bunch radishes
> 250 g (8 oz) cooked tongue
> 1 tablespoon chopped spring onion
> ½ tablespoon fresh chopped dill
> sour cream to taste
> salt and pepper

Wash the cucumbers and cut them in half lengthwise, removing the seeds. Peel if desired. Mix together the chopped eggs, grated radishes and the tongue cut into small pieces. Add the onion and the dill. Bind with sour cream and add salt and pepper to taste. Fill the cucumbers with the mixture, and serve lightly chilled.

VINEGRETY

Here are four variations on the theme that eventually gave us our supermarket tubs of Russian salad.

> **(1)** 1 salted herring
>   500 g (1 lb) cold meat, poultry, game or fish
>   1–2 cooked fresh beets
>   1 tablespoon chopped gherkins
>   1 salt cucumber or 1 small fresh cucumber
>   2 hard-boiled eggs
>   a few marinated mushrooms (see page 211)
>   1 tablespoon pickles
>   5 cooked and diced potatoes
>   1 tablespoon capers
>   3 tablespoons sauerkraut
>   100 g (4 oz) cooked beans
>   20 pitted olives

Soak the herring to remove the salt, dice all the other ingredients and combine with a dressing of olive oil, vinegar, salt and pepper, mustard and sugar to taste.

(2) 7 or 8 boiled potatoes
2 medium cooked beets
100 g (4 oz) cooked white beans

Mix all the ingredients together and combine with a dressing of oil, vinegar, salt and pepper. Garnish with chopped parsley and serve with beef or on its own.

(3) Olivier salad
Olivier was a French chef who in the 1880s opened a restaurant in Moscow called the Hermitage (see page 293). Highly popular with the nobility, it became one of the most glamorous night spots in the city, with plenty of *fin de siècle* decadence in its mirror rooms, garden and private baths. Olivier, together with three compatriots working in Moscow and a Russian chef, also compiled an excellent book of Russian home cooking for economical housewives. The salad to which his name has been given should be made with cold game, but chicken or turkey may be substituted.

1 roast hazel hen (see page 165), grouse or partridge
½ roast chicken or the equivalent quantity of roast turkey
5 boiled potatoes
5 hard-boiled eggs
1–2 fresh cucumbers
1 large head of lettuce
a few shrimps (optional)

FOR THE DRESSING
1 raw egg yolk
1 teaspoon mustard
pinch of salt
½ teaspoon cold water
200 ml (⅓ pt) olive oil
3–4 tablespoons vinegar
salt and pepper
lemon juice (optional)

Cut the meat into bite-sized chunks and slice the potatoes thinly. Slice the eggs crosswise, reserving a few slices for garnish. Peel the cucumbers, reserve a few slices for garnish, and cut the remainder into small pieces. Mix together the egg yolk, mustard, salt and water. Add the olive oil to the egg mixture slowly, as for mayonnaise, and when it thickens add the vinegar. Add salt and pepper to taste, and a little more vinegar or lemon juice if liked. Mix well and add to the meat, potatoes, eggs and cucumber and the lettuce leaves, torn in half.

Serve Olivier salad in a mound on a large plate, smoothing the sides with a knife and decorating them with shrimps, and the reserved hard-boiled egg and cucumber.

(4) Lenten Parisian salad

An Olivier-type *vinegret* adapted to the constraints of the Russian Church calendar.

> 300 g (10 oz) or more fresh salmon
> ½ onion
> 1 bay leaf
> pinch salt
> a few peppercorns
> a few allspice berries
> a little vinegar
> 5–6 boiled potatoes
> 4 pickled cucumbers
> 1 large fresh cucumber
> 1 large head of lettuce
> small quantity of cooked French beans (optional)
> olives and tomatoes to garnish
>
> FOR THE DRESSING
> 1 teaspoon mustard
> 1 teaspoon salt
> 1 teaspoon sugar
> 1 teaspoon cold water
> 8 tablespoons olive oil
> 2–4 tablespoons vinegar
> pepper

Poach the salmon for 10–12 minutes or until tender, in water spiced with the onion, bay leaf, salt, peppercorns, allspice berries and a little vinegar. When it is cool cut it into pieces about the size of a walnut.

Slice the boiled potatoes and the cucumbers, and tear the lettuce leaves in half. Mix together the first 4 dressing ingredients. Add the oil slowly, and then the vinegar when the mixture thickens. Season and pour the dressing over the salad. Decorate with slices of tomato and slivers of olive.

A formal arrangement from Urbain Dubois called Russian eggs. Russians still like their guest tables to look grand and unnatural in this nineteenth-century manner.

Soups and Light Stews

Soup is the one part of a Russian meal in which the simple native tradition has never been superseded by richer or more varied foreign preparations. The classics, *shchi, ukha, borshch, rassol'nik, solyanka, okroshka* and *botvinya*, all held their own on the aristocratic, francophile tables of nineteenth-century Russia. Though they brought with them a range of new soups, French chefs were obliged to learn to make the staple Russian *potages*, as they called them, and the scores of dumplings, forcemeats, patties, *kashas* and pies that went with them. Vegetable brines, juices from marinades, the sweet-sour liquor from fermented rye, and the final whitening of sour cream gave them a unique richness of flavour. They were in addition inexpensive, simple to assemble, easily digested and sustaining.

No two recipes are the same for *shchi* and *borshch*, and all set instructions and measures are rightly regarded with scepticism by seasoned Russian cooks. Lack of money leading to lack of good ingredients has led to improvised 'hatchet soup' occasionally displacing both of them. What matters in the end is that magic dash of *rassol* or *kvas* which turns a soup without nationality into a Russian delight.

None of the classics are properly called *sup* (soup) in Russian. They are types of dish in their own right. The hot and cold soups which came to Russia in the eighteenth and nineteenth centuries gave the Russian language the European term. Most common among the new imports were various so-called *sup-pyuré*, incorporating a purée of the main ingredients in a béchamel sauce or with milk or cream, grain and a liaison of egg yolk. Other soups not strictly Russian came from the Baltics from about the seventeenth century.

To these outsiders have been added more recently soups from the Caucasus, the Balkans and the Middle and Far East, many of which could be more accurately described as light stews. Some of them have retained their local names in Russian use, like *bozbash* and *kharcho*.

Others have been adapted in name and in essence into something apparently simpler such as lamb, apple and quince soup.

The consequent variety in today's Russian soup kitchen is unbeatable!

THE CLASSIC RUSSIAN SOUPS

SHCHI

> Good people never turn down a bowl of *shchi*.

The one essential ingredient of real *shchi* is sauerkraut (*kislye shchi*). In Moscow's Central Market it is sold in huge enamel buckets, and Russians always taste before they buy in case the batch has gone too sour. It is easy to see why *shchi* became such an important part of the national diet. In winter Central Russia normally had no vegetables apart from cabbage, beetroot and a few other root crops. Certainly there was no fresh source of vitamin C. I write in the past tense ideally, but anyone who has visited Russia in February and March will know that much the same dearth of vegetables exists today, unless one has access to special imports by virtue of money or status. Cabbage in its fresh or marinated form is still the great standby in those grey months.

In the nineteenth century, when almost every issue in daily life – clothes, food, language, manners – came in for ideological interpretation, *shchi* was hailed as a great national dish. With Napoleon repelled from Moscow and suffering Russia triumphant, it mattered that a man should command his chef to cook something sound and native. For the sake of loyalty and national pride *sup-pyuré* was briefly cast aside. The cookery books which began appearing virtually for the first time were devoted solely to Russian dishes, although by mid-century the passion for things national had worn thin.

Waves of national feeling come and go. One seemed to hit Russia in the 1970s and there again, concurrent with it, was loyalty to *shchi*. I visited an excellent patriot in his seventies who had, after years in the restaurant trade, created Moscow's first Cookery Museum. It was devoted to the city's great old restaurants and, implicitly, to the demise of good cooking in the Soviet era. We wandered round the two floors of display cases of an old wooden house, painted inside and out the red, black, yellow and green of a lacquered souvenir box.

There were menus from the Slavyansky Bazar restaurant (see page 294), photographs of people eating and dancing in what looked to be the far more carefree twenties, fine silver and cutlery, crystal and porcelain from other hotels and restaurants. My host's favourite Russian dish was still *shchi*. An extremely patriotic modern Soviet cookery writer claims that *shchi* has existed for over 1,000 years and has never known social division. It is a dish for all classes at all times and will stand up to almost endless repetition.

Whatever the recipe, *shchi* is not normally thickened with flour or any other agent and it should always be left to stand, preferably for 24 hours after cooking, to bring out the flavour before eating. You will notice that *shchi* gets better from day to day. The traditional way of preparing it was to mature the cooked brew in its pot on a warm Russian stove. Certainly you should avoid using a pressure cooker to try to imitate it. Made with the quantity of meat given in all the standard recipes, *shchi* becomes almost a meal in itself. Make it with a good meat stock if you want something that fits the description of soup.

Full or rich shchi

> 750 g (1½ lb) beef (brisket, chuck or stewing steak, shin)
> 2 onions
> 1 carrot
> 1 turnip
> 1 large potato
> 1 parsley root or small parsnip
> 1 celery stick
> 500–750 g (1–1½ lb) sauerkraut
> 1 tablespoon butter
> 10 g (½ oz) dried mushrooms ⎫
> 2 tablespoons pickled mushrooms ⎬ OR 100–150 g (4–5 oz)
>   (see page 211) ⎭ fresh mushrooms
> 3 bay leaves
> 1–2 tablespoons fresh parsley or fresh celery leaves
> 8 peppercorns
> 1 teaspoon dried marjoram
> 5 cloves garlic
> 1 tablespoon fresh dill
> ⅔ small (5 fl oz) carton sour cream

Boil the beef with 1 onion and half the carrot, turnip, potato, parsley root and celery for about 2 hours in 1½–2 litres (about 3 pints) of water, skimming as necessary. Season, strain, and discard the vegetables. In a separate pan (not aluminium) pour ½ litre (about 1 pint) of boiling water over the sauerkraut, add the butter and cook over a medium heat, covered, until the sauerkraut begins to soften. Add the sauerkraut to the meat and stock. Dice the remaining potato and add that to the pan too. Bring the dried or fresh mushrooms to the boil in 400 ml (about ⅔ pint) of water. Cook for 15 minutes if the mushrooms are fresh, or until they are soft if dried. Remove them, reserving the liquid, and chop them finely. Add the mushrooms and mushroom stock to the pan, together with all the remaining vegetables and the bay leaves, parsley or celery leaves, peppercorns and marjoram. Season and cook for 20 minutes. Add the minced garlic and the dill. Now leave the pan to stand for as long as you can in a warm place, over the lowest heat on the stove, in a low oven, or in a hay box.

Bring to the required heat before serving with sour cream and, if you have them, diced pickled mushrooms. Eat *shchi* with black bread, with buckwheat *kasha* and chopped hard-boiled egg (page 174), or with stuffed eggs (page 96).

This is a dense mixture. You should end up with about 1½ litres (2½ pints) of liquid in the finished *shchi*.

VARIATIONS

(*a*) A mixture of beef and duck or goose stock is a traditional base for *shchi*.

(*b*) For a thoroughly vegetarian version use only mushroom stock, prepared with an extra 150 g (5 oz) fresh or 15 g (¾ oz) dried mushrooms. Not all the fresh mushrooms need go into the finished soup. Keep those extra to the basic recipe for a pie filling, or dress with sour cream and serve on rice or toast.

(*c*) Bacon or pork, haricot beans and tomato purée, either separately or combined, also find their way into latter-day *shchi*, changing its character completely in my view, but producing something not unpleasant.

(*d*) Lenten *shchi* used to be made with fish. Fish stock is worth trying with *Rakhmannye shchi* (page 59).

Shchi with fresh cabbage

SOUPE ALEXANDRINE

This is not true *shchi* in my view, but still a good soup. The apples (ideally unripe or crab apples) should make up for the lack of sourness in the cabbage. A little lemon juice may help the sourness along. Some nineteenth-century Franco–Russian chefs renamed it *Soupe Alexandrine*.

500–750 g (1–1½ lb) boiling beef as in previous recipe (or a
    vegetarian stock)
500–750 g (1–1½ lb) fresh cabbage, shredded
½ turnip, diced
2 onions, chopped
3 bay leaves
1 teaspoon marjoram
plenty of freshly ground black pepper and a few
    peppercorns
6–8 small unripe apples
2 tablespoons fresh dill
⅔ small (5 fl oz) carton sour cream

Boil the beef as in the previous recipe. Add the cabbage, turnip, onions, bay leaves, marjoram and pepper, and cook for 15 minutes. Add the apples, cored (peeled or unpeeled according to taste) and cut in chunks, and the dill. The *shchi* is ready when the apples have dissolved into a purée. Leave the *shchi* to mature as above. Serve with sour cream and black bread.

Green summer or lazy shchi

This *shchi* also earns the name *Rakhmannye* or *Rakhmanovskie*, meaning indolent, sluggish, or simple, by virtue of being prepared with green, summer vegetables. Young nettles, sorrel and spinach are used either alone or in combination, and the result is a soup which is cooked far more quickly and is much lighter in texture than its winter counterpart. Sorrel provides the necessary sourness. I have also come across old recipes that use half sorrel and half young caraway leaves.

500 g (1 lb) beef as in full *shchi* recipe (page 57), or vegetarian
   base, or stock made with a ham bone
1 onion
1 carrot
1 parsley or caraway root or ½ parsnip
1 stick celery
2–3 bay leaves
10 peppercorns
500 g (1 lb) sorrel *or* spinach, nettles and sorrel mixed as
   available
   OR
400 g (12 oz) nettles, sorrel and caraway leaves
   salt
4 cloves garlic (optional)
1 tablespoon fresh dill (optional)
⅔ small (5 fl oz) carton sour cream
chopped hard-boiled egg or poached eggs
1 tablespoon butter (optional)
1 tablespoon flour (optional)

Make a good beef stock as in previous two recipes with half the onion,
carrot, parsley root, celery, bay leaves and peppercorns. Wash the
greens, pour boiling water over them, drain, chop, and add to the hot
meat and stock with the remaining vegetables and seasonings. Cook
for about 20 minutes over a gentle heat. Add salt, minced garlic and
dill according to taste. Serve with sour cream and either chopped
hard-boiled egg or poached eggs. This *shchi* may be thickened with a
butter and flour roux, but it will not be the genuine thing! Turn it into
a vegetarian soup by using a vegetable stock, or use the following
specifically vegetarian recipe.

Green summer shchi (vegetarian version)

1¼ litres (scant 2 pints) water
salt
1 potato
1–2 onions
1 parsley or caraway root or ½ parsnip
1 stick celery
2 tablespoons buckwheat groats
1 tablespoon rice

8 peppercorns
750 g (1½ lb) nettles, sorrel or spinach, mixed as available
1 tablespoon fresh dill
up to 4 cloves garlic
2 tablespoons lemon juice or to taste (less if using sorrel)
⅔ small (5 fl oz) carton sour cream
poached, hard-boiled or stuffed eggs (page 96)

Bring the water to the boil and add salt, the chopped potato, onion, parsley root and celery, the buckwheat and rice, and the peppercorns. Cook for about 12 minutes, then add the nettles, sorrel or spinach which have been blanched in boiling water and chopped. Cook for a further 10 minutes. Remove from the heat, add the dill, minced garlic and lemon juice, and leave to stand. Serve with sour cream and poached, hard-boiled or stuffed eggs.

VARIATIONS
Franco-Russian chefs sometimes replaced the spinach/sorrel/nettles in both the meat and vegetarian versions with Savoy cabbage and young green pea pods. Garnish with asparagus if you can afford it, and eat with poached eggs.

BORSHCH

What *shchi* is to the Russians, *borshch* is to the Ukrainians. Food does not fit in with political boundaries, of course, and the home of *borshch* lies in a large area of Eastern Europe covered today by Western Russia, Poland and Lithuania. It is also claimed as a speciality of Jewish cookery, which has carried a number of originally Russian dishes to Europe and the United States.

Everything may vary in *borshch* except beetroot and sour cream. The stock may be made with beef, ham, chicken or duck. Spicy sausage may be added in cooking. There are also vegetarian versions based on mushroom stock. Vegetables include cabbage, potato, marrow, haricot beans, tomato, carrot, apple, turnip, pea pods, green and red peppers and sweet corn. Other flavouring comes from onions, garlic, pepper, lovage, angelica leaves, caraway, dill, marjoram, thyme, parsley and celery. Some varieties demand the addition of dumplings to the *borshch* before serving. The liquid base should be stock and beetroot *rassol* (see page 27), or stock and *kvas* (see page 300).

Ukrainian borshch (a basic recipe)

> 500 g (1 lb) beef (brisket or shin or flank) to produce 1¾–2
> litres (about 3 pints) stock
> 1 large raw beetroot, about 350 g (10 oz)
> 1 tablespoon vinegar
> 25 g (1 oz) bacon fat
> 2 teaspoons sugar
> 2–3 tablespoons tomato purée or 2 tomatoes
> 2 onions
> 1 carrot
> 1 parsley root or ½ parsnip
> 25 g (1 oz) butter
> ¼ Dutch cabbage, about 350 g (10 oz)
> 400–500 g (12 oz–1 lb) potatoes
> 5–6 peppercorns
> 3 allspice berries
> 3 bay leaves
> up to 1 head of garlic
> fresh chopped parsley
> salt to taste
> beetroot *rassol* to season (see page 27)
> ¾ small (5 fl oz) carton sour cream

Make a good stock with the meat and one or two extra root vegetables. Put the chopped raw beetroot in a pan with the vinegar, a little bacon fat or beef fat from the stock, the sugar and the tomato purée, and cook gently with a lid on. Chop the onions, carrot and parsley root finely and braise in the butter. Chop the cabbage, cut the potatoes into chunks, and simmer in the stock for 15 minutes. Add the beetroot, the braised vegetables, the peppercorns, allspice and bay leaves, and cook for 10 minutes. Finish with the minced garlic, the rest of the bacon fat and the chopped parsley. At this point I think *borshch* really needs to be allowed to mature slowly like *shchi*. It is best left to stand for 24 hours and reheated gently, or left in a low oven or a hay box for a good 8 hours. Before serving, season with salt to taste and add a tablespoon or more of beetroot *rassol*, which will heighten both taste and colour.

Borshch is eaten with a dollop of sour cream and with *pampushki*, onion *pyshki* or stuffed pancakes (pages 93, 94, 222), or sometimes with the addition of *galushki*, *ushki* or *kasha* (pages 93, 94, 174).

This recipe may be varied according to whatever vegetables and stock you have to hand, provided the beetroot is there. Don't leave out the bacon fat or the garlic, though. I find them both essential to a good *borshch*. Like *shchi*, you may find it more convenient to make *borshch* without including the meat. A good stock may be made with soup bones in this case, or, if brisket is used, follow the habit of many Russian families and serve the meat separately as a main course, dressed in any of the ways given for boiled beef (page 123).

Borshchok/Postnyi borshch

Originally *borshchok* was a Russian and Ukrainian soup served during the great Fast. Since meat and meat fat were proscribed, it was based on a mushroom stock and was served with a variety of vegetables – the most important being the young green leaves from spring beetroot. The actual beets were omitted! Another soup which also goes under the name *borshchok* or, wrongly, simply *borshch*, is a beetroot-flavoured bouillon, served clear with sour cream, dumplings and any of the accompaniments given above for *borshch* except *kasha*. *Pirozhki* (page 89) are also exceptionally good with this soup. It may be made with a mushroom stock, following the fasting tradition, or with meat stock. Its simplicity and elegance made it very popular with French chefs in the last century. Both recipes are well worth trying, and, because of their lean origins, are a boon to slimmers if the sour cream and dumplings are passed up.

Clear borshchok

250 g (8 oz) raw beets + 1 additional beet or 1 tablespoon
    beetroot *rassol* (page 27)
1½ litres (2¼ pints) good beef or other stock
1 teaspoon vinegar or lemon juice, or to taste
1 teaspoon sugar
1 wine glass medium sweet white wine (optional)
red (cayenne) pepper to taste
sour cream

Peel the beets, chop small and cook slowly in the stock for about an hour. Strain, and add the vinegar, sugar, wine and a little seasoning. Add the juice of 1 additional uncooked beet or a tablespoon of beetroot *rassol* to heighten the taste and colour of the *borshchok*. Serve with a dollop of sour cream. If a mushroom stock is used for this recipe, use the cooked mushrooms to make *ushki* or *pirozhki* (pages 89, 93) to serve with it.

Postnyi borshch

For the stock use about 20 g (¾ oz) of dried mushrooms to 2 litres (3 pints) of water, or substitute another vegetable stock or a chicken or ham bone stock from which all the fat has been removed.
To the stock add:

> 2 small turnips, peeled and chopped, or 1 small swede
> 4 handfuls leaves from young beets + 2 raw beets, chopped
> 2 medium onions, chopped
> 2 medium apples, chopped
> 2 sticks celery, chopped
> 2 slices of marrow, peeled, seeded and chopped
> 2 cloves garlic, peeled
> a handful of fresh parsley
> ½ teaspoon dried dill seed
> salt and pepper
> 50 g (2 oz) fresh mushrooms, chopped

If you cannot lay your hands on all the ingredients the essentials are beetroot leaves, celery, onion, apple, garlic, turnip and herbs. Cabbage may also be added, but it tends to dominate the soup.

Simmer the soup gently for 45 minutes, taste for seasoning, and dilute with water or more stock if it has become too thick. Add 1 tablespoon or more of lemon juice to give the soup a pleasant edge and balance its natural sweetness. Serve low-fat yoghurt separately and let each guest help himself to a spoonful in his soup. The yoghurt replaces the traditional sour cream 'whitener' used at the ordinary Russian table.

Cold borshch

A pleasant variation for summer. The base is a beetroot bouillon slightly fermented with black bread, called beetroot *kvas*. It should be made in advance.

> 500 g (1 lb) raw beets
> small piece black bread
> 2 eating apples
> ½ large fresh cucumber
> 75 g (3 oz) spring onion
> 2 hard-boiled eggs
> salt, sugar and vinegar or lemon juice to taste
> ¾ small (5 fl oz) carton sour cream
> fresh dill to taste

Boil the beets whole in their skins until tender. Peel, grate finely and pour over about 1 litre (1¾ pints) boiling water. Add a small piece of black bread to this mixture and leave to stand, covered, in a bowl for 1–2 days at room temperature. To make the soup strain this liquid, add the sliced or diced apples, chopped cucumber, chopped onion (including the green part) and the chopped hard-boiled eggs. Season with salt, sugar and vinegar or lemon juice, and serve with sour cream and fresh dill. A less sweet version may be made using boiled potatoes instead of apples.

Sup-kholodets/Khlodnik polskii

These are two names for a cold soup from the countries which created *borshch*. It is based on a mixture of sour cream diluted with *kvas* or water. My own preference is to use club soda here and either yoghurt or a mixture of yoghurt and sour cream.

> 500 g (1 lb) young beets with leaves
> ½ large fresh cucumber
> 75 g (3 oz) spring onion
> 1 litre (1¾ pints) liquid, made up of half sour cream or
>   yoghurt and half club soda
> 2 hard-boiled eggs
> 150 g (6 oz) peeled shrimps
> ½ lemon
> salt, pepper and sugar to taste
> fresh dill to taste

Peel the beets and cook in a little salted water, adding the finely chopped leaves after about 20 minutes. Simmer for another 10 minutes, and drain. Dice the beets and cucumber and chop the onions. Mix together the chilled liquids to make the soup base, add all the vegetables, the chopped hard-boiled eggs, shrimps and thin slices of lemon. Season with salt and pepper and a little sugar if liked. Sprinkle with dill. Chill again and serve in a large bowl with an ice cube to keep it cool.

RASSOL'NIK, KALYA AND SOLYANKA

These three classic Russian soups are flavoured with sour cucumber *rassol* (see page 27). The fullest and to my mind most impressive is *solyanka*, but *rassol'nik* is a wonderful light first dinner course if you like kidneys.

Rassol'nik with kidneys

> 500 g (1 lb) kidneys
> 1 onion
> 1 leek
> 1 stick celery
> 2 parsley roots with leaves *or* 1 parsnip + 2–3 tablespoons
>   fresh parsley
> 2 tablespoons butter
> 4 potatoes
> 1 litre (1¾ pints) stock
> a bay leaf
> a few peppercorns
> 2 pickled cucumbers
> cucumber *rassol* to taste (see page 27)
> 100 g (3½ oz) sorrel, lettuce or spinach
> 2 tablespoons single or sour cream, or to taste

Remove the fat and the film from the kidneys, wash them and bring them to the boil in a pan of cold water. Pour away the water, wash the kidneys again, add fresh water and leave to simmer gently for about an hour. (Calf's kidneys you may simply wash, season and fry in butter.) Chop each kidney into about 6 pieces when done. Chop the onion, leek, celery and parsley root or parsnip (reserve the parsley leaves), and braise in the butter. Remove from the heat, add the diced raw potatoes, the stock, the bay leaf and the peppercorns. Bring to the boil, add the sliced pickled cucumbers, and cook for 10 minutes. Add *rassol* to taste and the chopped sorrel and cook for another 5–10 minutes. Add the kidney, cream or sour cream and chopped parsley and serve.

♦ Less correctly, *rassol'nik* may be thickened with flour and butter cooked to a roux and the potatoes replaced by 2–3 sour (unripe or crab) apples, diced and added in the last 3 minutes of cooking.

♦♦ Following tradition strictly, the kidneys may be replaced by poultry giblets, cooked separately in salted water and chopped small.

Rassol'nik or kalya with fish

This ancient festive soup is very similar to *ukha* (page 70) except that it is made with a *rassol* stock, sometimes with lemon juice added, and with fish containing plenty of oil. It also contains potato, which strictly speaking *ukha* should not, and is more highly flavoured with herbs.

750 g (1½ lb) fish (halibut, John Dory, brill, angler-fish, Dover sole)
1 scant litre (1¾ pints) water
200 g (7 oz) pickled cucumbers
up to 500 g (1 lb) potatoes
1 carrot
1 parsley root
1 leek
10 black peppercorns
2 bay leaves
pinch of saffron
1 large onion
2 tablespoons butter or vegetable oil
1 teaspoon dried tarragon
1 tablespoon dill
salt and pepper
lemon juice (optional)

Make a fish stock with the fish trimmings and the water. Slice the cucumbers and cook them in the stock for 5–10 minutes. Remove the cucumbers and add the diced raw potato, carrot, parsley root, leek, peppercorns, bay leaves and saffron, and the onion chopped and lightly fried in the butter. Cook for 15 minutes and return the cucumbers to the pan. Add the diced fish and cook until just tender, about 8 minutes. Dress with the tarragon and dill, test for seasoning and add a squeeze of lemon juice if liked. Allow to stand covered for 5 minutes before serving.

Solyanka/Selyanka

Here the sourness of the dish is increased by adding olives, capers, lemon, and sometimes marinated mushrooms as well as cucumber *rassol* (see page 27). The basic meat, chicken, fish or mushroom stocks used should be strongly flavoured, and the taste enriched with tomato purée. Liquid *solyanka* is related to another dish of the same name without liquid, which is baked and served as a supper dish (page 194). I first encountered the soup on a train coming back from Karelia to Moscow. I was pleasantly surprised that railway food in the 1970s could be so good, which, though it does not flatter the chef on the train, goes to show how easy it is to make this soup well.

Solyanka with meat

1¼ litres (2 pints) good beef stock
6–7 tablespoons *rassol* (see page 27)
2 medium onions
3 tablespoons butter or oil
2 tablespoons tomato purée
2 pickled cucumbers
400 g (12 oz) boiled beef (from making stock)
200 g (7 oz) assorted cured meats, such as sausages, ham, continental sausage
1 tablespoon capers
1 bay leaf
10 black peppercorns
salt to taste
1 tablespoon chopped olives
¼ lemon
fresh dill or parsley
¾ small (5 fl oz) carton sour cream (optional)

Prepare the stock and let it simmer for 15 minutes with the *rassol* added. Chop the onions and fry gently in the butter or oil. Add the tomato purée and cook for a few minutes, then add the sliced cucumbers, the chopped meat and sausage, the capers, bay leaf and peppercorns, pour over the stock and cook for 10 minutes. Season with salt. Before serving, add the olives, slices of lemon, dill or parsley and sour cream if liked. I find *solyanka* one soup I actually prefer without sour cream. It needs no accompaniment. It is far from unpleasant with the meat omitted and just the stock used.

Solyanka with fish

500 g (1 lb) white fish
1–2 medium onions
2 tablespoons butter or olive oil
2 tablespoons tomato purée
2–3 pickled cucumbers

1 tablespoon capers
bay leaf
black pepper to taste
1 tablespoon olives
½ lemon
fresh parsley or dill, or spring onion
1–2 tablespoons *rassol* (see page 27) (optional)

Fillet the fish, cut into largish chunks and make about 1–1½ litres (1¼–2¼ pints) of stock with the trimmings and head. Chop the onions and fry lightly in the butter or oil. Add the tomato purée and cook for 5 minutes, then add the sliced cucumbers, the capers, a bay leaf and black pepper and stir in the stock. Cook for 10 minutes. Add the fish, and cook for another 5 minutes only. Add the olives, lemon slices and chopped fresh parsley or dill, or spring onion green. The *solyanka* may be seasoned with a tablespoon or two of *rassol* at the same time that the fish is added. Again, I think this soup is better alone than with sour cream. Made just with fish stock it has the uncommon advantage of being simultaneously tasty, elegant and extremely economical. It is a wonderfully easy first course and also Russian cookery's nearest equivalent to Mediterranean *bouillabaisse*, the latter being introduced to Russian cooks as French *solyanka*!

Mushroom solyanka

500 g (1 lb) fresh or 20 g (¾ oz) dried mushrooms
2 medium onions
2 tablespoons butter
2 tablespoons tomato purée
2 pickled cucumbers
bay leaf
a few peppercorns
1½–2 tablespoons capers
salt
½ lemon
8–10 olives
fresh parsley
sour cream to taste (optional)

Wash and simmer the dried mushrooms very gently in about 1¼ litres (2¼ pints) of water with one of the onions for about 50 minutes. For fresh mushrooms 30 minutes will do. Chop the other onion and fry lightly in the butter, then add the tomato purée, the sliced cucumbers, mushrooms and mushroom stock. Add a bay leaf, a few peppercorns and the capers, season with salt and simmer gently for 10 minutes. Bring to the boil once more and serve with slices of lemon and a few olives in each plate and a sprinkling of chopped parsley. Sour cream may be added.

UKHA

This is a fish stock in which the freshest of fish is poached lightly with a little onion, parsley root and celery which have first been sealed with butter. It has a long, distinguished history and was probably the finest way of showing off the great Russian river fish when they were easily available. Purists insist that the liquid should be clear, ideally just the fresh water and spices in which the fish is cooked immediately after it is landed. Certainly it should not be thickened with potato or grain or enriched with oil. For Russians who kept the Fast strictly it was an ideal soup for Lent. The little butter used was easily replaced by poppy seed or sunflower oil.

Ukha is a stranger word than the dish it now describes. It is actually a form of the word ear (*ukho*) and in the Middle Ages it meant a quick meat bouillon made of just that, plus the lips, innards and other boneless soft parts. Fish gradually replaced meat as the staple ingredient and *ukha* carried its present meaning by the seventeenth century.

The best recipes use a mixture either of river fish or of sea fish, but never the two together. Proverbially what makes *ukha* sweet and rich is the freshwater minnow or ruff. It should be combined with sterlet, sturgeon, burbot, perch, tench or pike. In a sea fish *ukha* the Mediterranean rascasse that graces the best *bouillabaisse* would be excellent, combined with any of the following: cod, halibut, turbot, sea perch, brill, red mullet, John Dory, gurnard, angler fish, Dover sole, flounder, horse mackerel, scad, eel, shark.

1 onion
½ carrot
1 parsley root
½ leek
1 bay leaf
a few black peppercorns
1½–2 litres (2½–3 pints) water
1 kg (2 lb) fish

salt
optional spices*: ginger *or* star anise *or* fennel seed *or*
   nutmeg *or* saffron
optional herbs*: parsley, chopped spring onion, dried
   tarragon
½ glass of white wine or champagne
butter
slices of lemon

Rarely does one have the chance to cook fish so fresh that the flavour
needs no enhancing. Cook the onion, carrot, parsley root, leek, bay
leaf and peppercorns in the water for a good half hour, adding some
fish trimmings half-way through for added flavour. This stock may be
strained and then clarified by adding beaten egg white and bringing it
to the boil. Pour off the clear liquid and add the fish cut in pieces.
Unfreeze frozen fish only enough to cut it before adding to the stock –
this will help preserve the freshness. Simmer for a bare 8 minutes
(slightly more for river fish) without a lid. Add salt, optional spices
and herbs, and the wine. Heat through gently and serve. A little
butter and a slice of lemon in each plate is a nice addition.

Serve *ukha* with black bread, fish-stuffed *pirozhki* (page 91) or *rastegai* (page 92). It is also the standard accompaniment to *kulebyaka*
(page 233), where a bowl alongside the dinner plate allows each
person to moisten the pie to his own taste as he eats it.

SUP-LAPSHA (RUSSIAN NOODLE SOUP)

Noodle soup, like the other pasta dishes, came to Russia from the East
as a result of the Mongol invasion in the thirteenth century. The
noodles are made either of white wheat flour or a mixture of wheat
and buckwheat. They are eaten in a chicken or mushroom stock or in
spiced milk.

FOR THE NOODLES
1 egg
200 g (7 oz) flour
4–5 tablespoons water
½ teaspoon salt

* The oilier the fish used for *ukha*, the more it will need spices and herbs.
Saffron and a pinch of ginger are recommended for sturgeon or salmon. Anise
or fennel are good with any river fish. Saffron, tarragon, parsley and dill are
best with sea fish.

Mix all the ingredients to a firm dough, leave for 10 minutes, then roll out very thinly on a floured board. Dust the surface of the dough with flour, wrap around a well-floured wide rolling pin, and cut into long, thin, narrow strips. Shake to separate and leave to dry a little in the air for a couple of hours before cooking.

FOR THE LIQUID BASES
(1) 1½–2 litres (2½–3 pints) good chicken stock
    1 onion
    a little butter
    fresh dill and parsley
    black pepper
    saffron
    minced garlic

Cook the noodles in the stock. 5 minutes before serving, add the other ingredients, softening the onion in the butter first.

(2) 500 g (1 lb) fresh or 20 g (¾ oz) dried mushrooms
    1½–2 litres (2½–3 pints) water
    a few root vegetables
    a few peppercorns
    1 bay leaf
    sour cream to taste
    garlic
    fresh dill

Make the stock with the mushrooms, water, vegetables, peppercorns and bay leaf. Cook the noodles in the strained stock and add sour cream, garlic and dill before serving.

(3) ½–1 teaspoon crushed coriander or anise seeds
    1½ litres (2¼ pints) full cream milk
    1 teaspoon salt
    butter
    powdered coriander or anise to taste

Boil the noodles in plenty of salted water with the crushed seeds in a muslin bag until half-cooked. Transfer, drained, to the simmering milk and finish cooking. Test for seasoning. Add butter, salt and powdered coriander or anise to taste.

OKROSHKA

About 15 miles outside Moscow, in the flat, birch-wooded countryside popular as a quick retreat from the city, the restaurant Russkaya Izba (The Russian Peasant Cottage) specializes in serving traditional Russian food. The waiters wear not strictly Russian but very colourful Caucasian tunics and loose trousers, and serve excellent *zakuski* and soups from wooden platters and bowls lacquered in the traditional *palekh* style. *Okroshka*, a refreshing cold summer soup made with *kvas*, chopped meat and vegetables and herbs and served with sour cream, is one of their best dishes. The Izba's secret, I decided, lay in its particular house brew of pale *kvas*, which was the golden colour of cider. It was slightly sweetened with honey and raisins and had something of the smooth texture and taste of barley water. Just a hint of yeast distinguished it. This brew was served on every table in large stone pitchers and turned out to be unexpectedly potent. In the serving of *okroshka* the *kvas* is mixed with sour cream to give a sharp, milky liquid. Make your own *kvas* (page 300) or replace it in *okroshka* with a blend of yoghurt and club soda.

Autumn vegetable okroshka

   3–4 potatoes
   1 carrot
   1 turnip
   6 chopped spring onions
   1 eating apple
   ½ medium cucumber
   200 g (7 oz) tin mushrooms in brine
   1¼ litres (2 pints) *kvas* or yoghurt and club soda in equal
      parts
   2 teaspoons French mustard (optional)
   100 ml (approx. 6 tablespoons) cucumber *rassol* (see page 27)
   1 tablespoon fresh dill
   1 tablespoon fresh celery leaves or chervil
   salt and freshly ground black pepper
   2 hard-boiled eggs

Boil the potatoes in their jackets until just cooked. Allow to cool, peel and dice. Boil the carrot and turnip until they are just cooked, and dice. Chop the spring onions, apple and cucumber, and drain and slice the mushrooms. Mix together the yoghurt and the club soda if using. Dilute the mustard with a little of this liquid, and blend in. Stir in the *rassol*. Add the fruit and vegetables, the fresh herbs, and the pepper. Leave to stand in the refrigerator for 30 minutes. Add the chopped hard-boiled eggs, and salt to taste. Serve chilled with an ice cube in the bowl and fresh black bread.

Meat okroshka

> 3–4 potatoes
> 1 swede
> 6 chopped spring onions
> ½ medium cucumber
> 1 pickled cucumber
> 1¼ litres (2 pints) *kvas* or yoghurt and club soda
> 2 teaspoons French mustard (optional)
> 6 tablespoons cucumber *rassol* (see page 27)
> 1 tablespoon each fresh parsley, celery leaves or lovage, and
> dill
> ½ tablespoon fresh tarragon
> 1 teaspoon sugar
> freshly ground black pepper
> 110 g (4 oz) chopped cooked meat (beef, lamb, ham, tongue)
> 2 hard-boiled eggs

Cook, dice and combine the meat and vegetables, and make the liquid base as above. Pour over and season. Serve chilled, with black bread.

BOTVINYA

The combination of fresh salmon, shellfish and white wine makes *botvinya* a luxury soup, ideal for a summer dinner party. The recipe is traditionally and wholly Russian. It takes its name from the green leafy part of young beets, *botva*, which only the Romans and the Russians have commonly used as a cooked vegetable. The beet leaves, cooked quickly and briefly, are combined with cooked spinach, sorrel or nettle leaves, finely diced fresh or pickled cucumber, and spring onions (bulb and stem), and the whole is seasoned with lemon juice, mustard, sugar, salt, pepper and dill. Genuine *botvinya* is then liquefied to the consistency of a thin soup by adding a liberal amount of pale *kvas*. The poached fish and shellfish are added to the bowl together with thin strips of fresh horseradish, and the whole brought to the table iced.

I confess to finding this original mixture overwhelming. Most Western cooks coming across the standard recipe have modified it to suit a blander but probably more refined modern palate. It has come under a different name according to whichever ingredients seemed prominent, that is 'spinach, sorrel and beetroot soup' or 'green vegetable soup with fish'. Some authorities swear by replacing the *kvas* with white wine. Better to my mind is a blend of yoghurt and club soda. The sourness of spinach and sorrel does not go well with any white wine I have tried.

To serve *botvinya* correctly, provide spoons for the liquids and a fork for the fish. Preference makes me keep the fish out of the soup tureen altogether. I serve it alongside.

In very hot weather, when *botvinya* is designed to stimulate the appetite gently, a bowl of ice cubes may be placed on the table and people invited to help themselves. At a formal Russian *obed*, *botvinya* would be followed by a second, hot, soup before the meal took its normal course.

350 g (12 oz) sorrel
250 g (8 oz) lightly cooked nettle tops
leaves from 3 young beets

OR
600 g (1¼ lb) spinach

1 pickled cucumber
4–5 chopped spring onions
fresh horseradish (if available)
½ litre (1 scant pint) white wine or yoghurt and club soda or
   enough to moisten the vegetables lightly, according to
   taste
1 teaspoon salt
1 teaspoon sugar
½ lemon
1½ tablespoons fresh dill
500 g (1 lb) cooked fish and shellfish (ideally poached
   salmon, crab, prawns)

Cook the green leaf vegetables in a very little water, drain well and chop finely. Chop the cucumber and the onions and grate a little fresh horseradish if available. Mix together the yoghurt and the club soda and add the salt, sugar, lemon juice and dill. Combine with the vegetables and chill. Serve with the fish.

A variation of my own invention to suit what is available in the shops is to use spinach and any lettuce, just blanched, instead of sorrel and nettles. Pour hot water over them, drain, chop very finely and use. The more I want to modify this dish the more it turns into a cool, sharp salad with fish. The 'dressing' may then be made of 2 parts yoghurt to 1 part soda.

OTHER RUSSIAN SOUPS

Fresh mushroom soup
Excellent when mushrooms are cheap.

> 500 g (1 lb) mushrooms
> 1–2 tablespoons butter
> 1 onion
> 1 tablespoon flour
> 1–1½ litres (2 pints) stock made with a ham bone, chicken stock, or a mixture of the two
> 750 g (1½ lb) potatoes
> 1 bay leaf
> 1 clove
> nutmeg
> ¾–1 small (5 fl oz) carton sour cream
> salt and black pepper
> chopped cooked ham (optional)
> fresh parsley or dill

Quarter the mushrooms and sauté them in the butter together with the chopped onion. Add the flour and cook for a few minutes before slowly adding the hot stock, stirring all the time. Add the diced raw potato with a bay leaf, a clove and a pinch of nutmeg. Cook slowly for 20–40 minutes, then purée by rubbing through a sieve or a food mill. Add the sour cream, heat through, season, and serve sprinkled with fresh parsley or dill. A little chopped cooked ham is an excellent addition.

Lemon and sour cream soup with mushrooms
This is an excellent, luxurious soup, light in flavour and texture, which shows off classic Russian ingredients at their best.

¾ litre (1¼ pints) water
2 carrots
1 onion
1 leek
1 parsley root or ½ parsnip
10 g (scant ½ oz) dried or 150 g (5 oz) fresh mushrooms
4–5 tablespoons pearl barley or rice
1 tablespoon butter
½ small (5 fl oz) carton sour cream
½ lemon
salt and black pepper
fresh parsley and dill

Make a vegetable stock with the water and the carrots, onion, leek, parsley root and mushrooms. Strain. Cook the barley or rice in slightly salted water until soft. Drain, add the butter, then add to the stock and vegetables (reserving the mushrooms). Put through a fine food mill or in the liquidizer until you have a smooth cream. Add the sour cream, lemon juice and grated peel, and the chopped cooked mushrooms. Bring to the boil once, test for seasoning, and serve sprinkled with chopped parsley and dill.

Haricot bean soup
This modern Soviet recipe provides what I have found to be the nicest way of eating haricot beans yet, though it is much more beans than soup.

250 g (8 oz) dried haricot beans (soaked overnight)
1–2 carrots
1–2 onions
1–2 celery sticks
1–2 parsley roots or parsnips
2 tablespoons butter, olive oil or sunflower oil
1½ tablespoons tomato purée
bay leaf
salt and black pepper
¾ small (5 fl oz) carton sour cream
fresh parsley or dill

Set the beans to cook in plenty of water. Chop the carrots, onions, celery and parsley roots and fry lightly in the butter or oil. Add the tomato purée to the vegetable pan. After the beans have cooked for about 50 minutes add the vegetable mixture, together with a bay leaf and a little salt. When the beans are tender, serve with a generous spoonful of sour cream to each helping, and sprinkle with fresh parsley or dill and black pepper.

Canned tuna fish soup

Don't be put off by the unattractive title. This soup is an excellent example of Soviet Russian cooking as it enters, some 20 or so years behind us, the age of instant cuisine. It retains basic Russian features of using fish in a thin but well-flavoured, slightly sharp, bouillon set off with fresh herbs and sour cream.

> 1½ litres (2¼ pints) water
> 3 tablespoons rice
> 1–2 medium onions
> 2 large carrots
> 1 parsley root or a bunch of stems
> 2 tablespoons olive oil or butter
> 200 g (7 oz) tin tuna
> 2–3 tablespoons fresh dill
> red (cayenne) pepper, salt and lemon juice to taste
> 2 fresh tomatoes, sliced
> sour cream to taste
> a little fresh parsley

Bring the water to the boil, add the rice and set to cook. Chop the onions, carrots and parsley root, fry gently in the oil or butter and add to the rice. When the rice is almost cooked (15–40 minutes depending on the type, and whether it is white or brown) add the tuna, flaked into smallish chunks, the oil from the can and plenty of dill. Bring to the boil. Season with salt, pepper and lemon juice. Serve with slices of fresh tomato and sour cream, and sprinkle with chopped parsley.

Tomato and apple soup

This soup may be made quickly with a beef stock cube, or turned into something more elaborate by making a stock from beef shin. Again this is a new Soviet recipe, but it follows so many traditional Russian soups and casseroles in combining savoury and sour ingredients.

500 g (1 lb) shin of beef
1 onion
1 carrot
1½ tablespoons butter
1½ tablespoons flour
200 g (7 oz) sour cooking apples
200 g (7 oz) fresh or canned tomatoes
salt
croûtons (optional)

Boil the beef slowly in water to make 1 litre (2 pints) of rich beef stock. Lightly fry the chopped onion and carrot in the butter. Sprinkle in the flour, cook for a couple of minutes, stir in a little bouillon and combine this mixture with the rest of the bouillon. Peel, core and slice the apples, and quarter the tomatoes. Bring the bouillon to the boil, add the tomatoes, apples and salt, and cook for half an hour. Purée the soup in a food mill or blender/liquidizer. Serve with croûtons. Eat the boiled beef as a main course, dressed with vinaigrette.

Soupe à la Dolgorouky/Litovsky soup

A wonderfully luxurious soup worked out in the nineteenth-century French–Russian kitchen. At once refined and sustaining, it represents the best the bi-national chefs were striving to achieve. These two recipes, the first incorporating a purée of onions, the second a purée of spinach and sorrel, are sufficiently similar to be thought of as one soup with variations.

500 g (1 lb) onions or 500 g (1 lb) spinach and 125 g (¼ lb)
    sorrel
butter or oil
½ litre (¾ pint) béchamel sauce
1¼ litres (2 pints) or more good chicken or veal stock
350 g (12 oz) chopped cooked ham or chicken and ham
4 egg yolks (optional)
cayenne pepper

Prepare one of the vegetable purées, either by stewing the onions slowly in a little butter and oil with the lid on the pan until they are completely soft, or by washing the spinach and sorrel and cooking them quickly with no more water than remains on the leaves after washing. Both mixtures can be put through a liquidizer or food mill. Add the vegetable purée to the béchamel, add to that the stock and simmer gently for 15 minutes. Add the chopped ham at the last moment, and if liked the egg yolks for extra richness, and gently heat through. Serve *soupe à la Dolgorouky* with a pinch of cayenne pepper. *Litovsky soup* calls for *kletski* (page 94) into which the ham added above is incorporated with a little onion and dill. Poach the *kletski* separately in boiling salted water, drain and serve in the soup.

Cherry soup with rice

Soups made either partly or wholly of fruit, either fresh or dried, and served hot or cold, are a traditional part of cooking in Western and North-western Russia, Poland and the Baltics. The Armenians also serve fruit soups, in rather a different manner, and Russian cooking has come under both these influences. Mrs Molokhovets also lists under soups many plates of sweetened and thickened fruit purée, chocolate and coffee purée which amount to a liquid *kisel*. Today these really belong in a chapter on sweet courses. One Russian friend told me she thought such concoctions were introduced to Russian households via the nursery by German governesses! Here is one I feel may appeal to adult tastes, particularly if the sugar is kept to a minimum or omitted altogether.

> 300 g (10 oz) cherries
> 2 tablespoons rice
> cinnamon to taste
> ½ glass red wine
> lemon juice
> 1–2 tablespoons sugar
> sour cream to taste

Wash and stone the cherries. Pour ½–¾ litre (1–1½ pints) of boiling water over the stones, bring to the boil, remove the stones, and cook the rice in the liquid for 15–20 minutes or until it is almost cooked. Add the cherries and cinnamon and cook for 5 more minutes. Add the red wine and season with lemon juice and sugar to taste. Liquidize and serve cold with lots of sour cream.

Chikirtma

This typical Caucasian soup claimed by both the Armenians and the Georgians makes an excellent light dinner soup. It is based on either lamb or chicken bouillon, thickened with egg yolks and seasoned with lemon juice and fresh herbs. No grain or vegetables are added, but the *chikirtma* may be served with the meat used to make the stock. I prefer it without meat. The stock should be well-flavoured since so much depends on it, but occasionally you might cheat and use stock cubes. With fresh herbs from the window-sill you can have ready rather an unusual dish within minutes.

2 medium onions
1 tablespoon butter
3 teaspoons flour
1½ litres (2¼ pints) water ⎫ OR 1–1¼ litres
500 g (1 lb) stewing lamb or ⎬ (about 2 pints)
   chicken or turkey on the bone ⎭ good stock
1 stick celery and leaves
1 parsley root
1–2 tablespoons fresh parsley
10 lightly crushed peppercorns
½ teaspoon cinnamon
½ tablespoon crushed coriander seeds
a pinch of saffron
2–3 eggs or 3 egg yolks
2–3 tablespoons lemon juice
2 tablespoons coriander leaves
1 tablespoon fresh basil (½ tablespoon dried)
½ tablespoon fresh dill weed
1 tablespoon fresh mint

Chop the onions, fry lightly in the butter, add the flour and cook, stirring, for a couple of minutes. Slowly add the stock, skimmed of fat. Add to this all the remaining ingredients except the eggs, lemon juice and fresh herbs. Cook for 10 minutes. Beat the eggs or yolks with the lemon juice, introduce a little hot stock (not boiling or the eggs will scramble) to the bowl and gradually return the mixture to the pan. Now add all the chopped fresh herbs and heat the soup through for a few minutes without allowing it to boil. If you are serving *chikirtma* with meat, add this chopped finely and continue to heat the soup gently for another 2–3 minutes before serving.

♦ Similar Armenian soups simplify the herb garnish and sometimes add a little rice, pearl barley or vermicelli to the stock. The barley and rice are added to the soup cooked. The lemon flavour is sometimes enhanced by including strips of peel and the flesh from one lemon.

♦♦ The Central Asian republics, particularly Uzbekistan and Tadzhikistan, make this soup, which they call *shurpa*, using lamb, potatoes, a few tomatoes and corn on the cob. No lemon juice or garlic are added, but plenty of onions and a pinch of turmeric. Dress with fresh herbs, especially lovage.

Spas/Tanabour

YOGHURT SOUP
Hot and cold yoghurt soups are to be found in all the Southern republics from Moldavia to Central Asia, and are particularly popular in Armenia. They are in a sense local equivalents of the Russian combination of stock and sour cream, or for cold soups *kvas* and sour cream. Use home-made yoghurt. It is creamier, more liquid and much more economical. This is an Armenian recipe.

> 60 g (2 oz) pearl barley (soaked overnight) or rice
> ¾ litre (1⅓ pints) yoghurt and the same quantity again of
>   stock or water
> 2 onions
> 25–50 g (1–2 oz) butter
> 2 tablespoons fresh mint or 1 tablespoon dried
> 2 tablespoons fresh parsley
> 1 egg, beaten
> salt to taste

Bring the soaked barley to the boil in plenty of water, skim, drain and cook in the water or stock until tender. Rice need not be soaked before cooking. Chop the onions, fry lightly in the butter, add the chopped mint and parsley and transfer the contents of the pan to the cooked barley or rice and stock. Beat the egg into the yoghurt and gradually stir in a little hot broth. Return to the pan and stir all the time over a low heat until warmed through. Serve either hot or cold, seasoned to taste. *Spas* is a great reviver of flagging appetites in hot weather.

LIGHT STEWS

Several of the recipes I have included earlier as soups could be counted as light stews if served in their fullest versions with plenty of meat. *Borshch* (page 61) and *shchi* (page 58) are particularly sustaining in their full form. Here are two more very good southern-influenced recipes which are almost a meal in themselves.

Kharcho

This is a Georgian speciality which has been assimilated into Russian cooking. It is distinctive for its use of walnuts as a major ingredient.

> 1 small chicken or 500 g (1 lb) stewing lamb
> 3 onions
> 4 cloves garlic
> oil or butter
> 1 tablespoon flour
> 1–2 bay leaves
> pinch of turmeric
> 2 teaspoons *suneli* (optional) (see page 24)
> ½ teaspoon crushed coriander seeds
> 100 g (3½ oz) shelled walnuts
> 10 fresh damsons or 200 g (7 oz) stewed prunes plus lemon
>   juice or pomegranate juice to taste (the fruit may be
>   partially or wholly replaced by up to 400–500 g (1 lb)
>   tomatoes)
> 1 tablespoon fresh coriander leaves
> fresh parsley and basil to taste
> salt and red (cayenne) and black pepper

Cook the chicken or lamb in plenty of water until tender. Remove the bones, and return the meat to the pan together with the strained stock. Fry the chopped onions and garlic in a little oil or butter, sprinkle over the flour, cook for a few minutes and dilute with stock. Add to the pan with the bay leaves, turmeric, *suneli* and coriander seeds and the walnuts pounded in a mortar. Cook for 10–15 minutes. Soften the fruit and/or tomatoes in a little stock separately and add to the soup. Cook for 5 minutes, then add the fresh coriander, parsley and basil and cook for another 5 minutes. Season with salt, cayenne and black pepper. Allow the *kharcho* to stand covered for a final 5 minutes before serving.

BOZBASH/BOZARTMA/PITI (LAMB STEW WITH SOUR FRUIT)

Caucasian cooking boasts so many variations on this theme that it is an idea of a kind of dish that has been brought back to Russia rather than a named soup with a definite recipe. I was given a lamb, quince and apple soup recipe which could have been adapted from any of a number of Armenian recipes. Sometimes the characteristic sour effect is achieved by adding natural pomegranate juice to a simple combination of chicken or lamb, tomatoes, potatoes and herbs. The Armenians tend to be elaborate, adding apricots, damsons, apples and quince. The recipes that follow will all stand considerable adaptation according to the fruit and vegetables available.

Piti

Best-known as an Azerbaijani speciality, but also cooked in neighbouring Armenia.

> 40 g (1½ oz) chick peas (soaked for 24 hours)
> 500 g (1 lb) stewing lamb
> ¾ litre (1⅓ pints) water
> 2 onions
> 4 damsons or stoned prunes with a dash of lemon juice
> 6 black peppercorns
> 1 tomato or ½ tablespoon tomato purée
> 1–2 potatoes or 5 chestnuts
> salt and black pepper
> 1 tablespoon coriander leaves
> 1 tablespoon fresh parsley
> ½ tablespoon fresh thyme
> few pinches saffron or turmeric

Cook the chick peas in *unsalted* water for 2–3 hours or until tender. Drain and reserve the liquid. Place the lamb in a pan with the water, bring to the boil and simmer for 1 hour or until tender. Remove any bones. Put the cooked chick peas in a pan with the chopped onions, damsons, peppercorns, boned meat and stock. Cover and cook for 20–30 minutes. Add the tomato, and the chopped potatoes or peeled chestnuts cut in quarters, season with salt and plenty of black pepper, and cook for another 30 minutes, adding the reserved chick pea liquid as necessary if too much of the stock evaporates in cooking. Towards the end of the cooking time add the fresh herbs, and saffron, and simmer for a further 3 minutes. Leave to stand off the heat but covered for 5 minutes more, then serve.

Armenian bozbash

This is a light stew of lamb, potatoes and/or chick peas, tomatoes and onions to which are added in various combinations red peppers, okra, aubergine, quince, apples, damsons, apricots, plums.

Boil 500 g (1 lb) lamb in water for a good hour, bone it, skim the stock and remove the fat. Braise the meat in butter with the chopped raw vegetables and fruit (see below), then add the strained stock with red and black pepper and fresh basil, coriander and parsley. Simmer gently until the vegetables are soft and all the flavours well blended. 5 minutes before serving add a tablespoon of lemon juice or more, or up to half a cup of pomegranate juice. Here are some classic combinations of fruit and vegetables. (All quantities given are suggestions rather than rules.)

(1) *Winter bozbash*

> 4 potatoes
> 4 tablespoons cooked chick peas
> 1 tablespoon tomato purée
> 2 medium onions
> 3 tablespoons dried apricots

(2) *Summer bozbash*

> 5 tomatoes
> 2 onions
> 2 red peppers
> 10 fingers of okra
> 2 sourish eating apples or 1 large cooking apple

(3) *Shushinsky bozbash*

> 3 potatoes or 4 tablespoons cooked chick peas
> 2 tomatoes
> 2 medium onions
> 1 quince
> 2 sourish eating apples or 1 large cooking apple
> 3 tablespoons dried apricots (or double the quantity of
>   tomatoes)

(4) *Echmiadzin bozbash*

> 4 potatoes
> 5 tomatoes
> 2 onions
> 2 handfuls string beans
> 2 medium red peppers
> 8 fingers of okra
> 1 medium aubergine

(5) *Full bozbash*

> 4 potatoes
> 3 tablespoons cooked chick peas
> 3 tomatoes
> 2 onions
> 1 medium red pepper
> 6 fingers of okra
> 2 sourish eating apples or 1 cooking apple
> 8 damsons or prunes
> 2 tablespoons dried apricots

CHORBA

This is another savoury-sour southern soup or light stew, originally from Moldavia, which I have seen adapted and simplified in Russian kitchens. Unlike *chikirtma* it contains plenty of vegetables, above all green beans and tomatoes. The traditional souring agent was a *kvas* made with bran. Most modern recipes suggest simply water in its place, with lemon juice to taste. Make it with fresh spring/early summer vegetables for ideal results.

Country chorba with beef or chicken

> 500 g (1 lb) stewing beef or 1 small chicken
> 1–2 new potatoes (optional)
> 300 g (10 oz) tomatoes
> 1 onion
> 1 leek (or double quantity of onions)
> 1 carrot
> 1 parsley root
> 150–200 g (6–7 oz) string beans
> 1 tablespoon fresh dill

2 tablespoons fresh lovage or 1 tablespoon dried
2 tablespoons fresh parsley
salt, red pepper (cayenne), garlic and lemon juice to taste

Make a good stock with the beef or chicken and about 1¾ litres (2½ pints) water which will reduce to 1½ litres (2–2¼ pints) in cooking. Bone and reserve the meat. Cook the potatoes in the skimmed fat-free stock for 10 minutes, then add the remaining raw vegetables, chopped, and cook for a further 10 minutes. Add the fresh herbs, garlic, pepper, salt and lemon juice to taste. For a summer stew include all the meat and double the quantities of carrots, beans and potatoes. Otherwise serve *chorba* as a light spring vegetable soup. If you have not tried fresh lovage before you will find it a very pleasant surprise – it has a taste somewhere between celery and fenugreek, the spice which gives curry powder its distinctive flavour as opposed to its hotness. It is excellent in salads.

◆ A variation of this soup which some people would claim is another dish altogether goes under the name of *zuma*. Follow the recipe above, using chicken, twice the quantity of string beans and omitting the tomatoes and garlic. Add a raw egg, beaten, with the lemon juice before serving.

A NOTE ON STOCKS

Fish stock
A good fish to use is flounder (megrim, plaice) or even just flounder trimmings. Otherwise the trimmings from any white fish, especially a cod's head, will yield a good stock. Avoid mackerel and tunny fish and make sure you do not use an aluminium pan otherwise your fine creation will be disgustingly metallic. Start off by sweating or lightly sautéing in oil a little chopped onion and carrot, then add the fish trimmings and pour water over so that they are well covered. Add a bay leaf, a few peppercorns and a few parsley stems and simmer for half an hour. Strain, and the stock is ready for use.

Meat stock
Nowadays, sadly, one has to pay for soup bones from the butcher and I have sometimes even been told there are none available, but they are worth chasing and buying. Beef gives the best flavour, or, if you want a stock for *borshch*, a ham bone. The bones should be simmered in plenty of water for a couple of hours with a bay leaf, onion and peppercorns.

Chicken and poultry stock
Chicken is always a winner where stock-making is concerned. You can hardly fail to have a well-flavoured stock using just a carcass, boiled in plenty of water for an hour with the usual vegetables and spices and then strained. Turkey bones may be used in the same way and also duck, although personally I find the taste of duck stock too distinctive for it to have a use beyond *borshch*.

Vegetable stock
No hard and fast rules apply here, except to beware of using more than 1 medium parsnip per 2-litre (3-pint) brew, otherwise the stock will be too sweet. Similar care should be taken with turnips, which add a strong, slightly bitter flavour to stock. Otherwise, leeks and celery are particularly good, along with washed potato peelings, carrots, one or two tomatoes and fresh herbs. A little swede may be added in season and also one or two sprouts. In my most hard-up days I used to make vegetable stock almost entirely with well-washed vegetable peelings, the root stems and outside leaves of cabbage or celery, wilting lettuce, cauliflower greens and any liquid left after cooking vegetables or pulses. This is Russian hatchet soup style, but

with care and experiment you can work wonders. The liquid from cooked dried beans is especially valuable. Don't throw it away if you don't have to. Add extra flavour to a bland stock with tomato purée or juice and a dash of tabasco sauce.

Mushroom stock

This is best made with dried mushrooms, about 20 g (¾ oz) to 2 litres (3 pints) of water. Soak them for 30 minutes in water, then bring them slowly to the boil with an onion and simmer for at least an hour. The mushrooms themselves may be used again in a soup or pie filling. The taste of this stock is very rich when made with dried morels, but you can achieve a passable imitation for everyday soups by using about 450 g (1 lb) of fresh mushrooms. It is probably only economical to do this when mushrooms are fairly cheap, otherwise you might as well lash out on a small packet of dried *cèpes*, sold by most delicatessens, and get a better flavour into the bargain. Fresh mushrooms left over from stock-making may be used in the same way as cooked dried mushrooms.

ACCOMPANIMENTS TO SOUP

These are essential Russian eating and fall into three categories:

(*a*) Those served in the soup, like *galushki* and *pel'meni* (pages 94, 228).

(*b*) Those served with it like *pirozhki, rastegai* and *kasha* (pages 92, 174 and below).

(*c*) Substantial pies which serve as a main course and are moistened by the soup, e.g. *kulebyaka* (page 233).

Accompaniments to soup will be found in this chapter and in the chapters on vegetables, vegetarian and grain dishes (page 173) and hot *zakuski* and supper dishes (page 215). Those included here are generally too small to be served as a course or dish in their own right. The larger pies and dishes of grain on the other hand can be a course or even a meal in themselves. One need only bear in mind that they are usually the better for being served alongside a bowl of well-flavoured stock. Certainly this is the ideal way to serve miniature pies or *pirozhki*.

Pirozhki

For these tiny pasties, usually eaten with a clear meat, chicken or mushroom broth or a *borshchok*, use a raised dough (page 232). Cut it out in small circles in which you can enclose the filling in a semi-circle or canoe shape. Choose from any of the combinations given below, and seal the edges carefully with a little milk. Either brush with egg and bake in a moderate to hot oven for about 10 minutes until golden brown, or fry them uncoated in deep fat.

Meat filling

>   1 medium onion
>   1 tablespoon oil or butter
>   250 g (8 oz) minced beef or veal or chicken
>   seasoning: salt, pepper, nutmeg, chopped herbs to taste
>   optional: 2 teaspoons beef suet or jellied stock, chopped
>   hard-boiled egg
>   1 egg for binding

Lightly fry the onion in the oil or butter, add the meat and cook for 5 minutes. Combine in a bowl with the seasoning and herbs and allow to cool. *Pirozhki* often come out rather dry because of the small quantity of filling which cannot, as with a pie, be moistened by the last-minute addition of stock. Both suet and frozen stock in little chips have been recommended to me by conscientious Russian pastry cooks to cure this fault. My objections are that suet makes the *pirozhki* undesirably fatty while the ice chips need forethought and a sledge-hammer, both of which go missing when I am in a hurry. A better solution, I think, is to use stock either naturally or artificially jellified with gelatine. Add 2 teaspoons, finely chopped, to the mixture when it is absolutely cold from the refrigerator, bind with egg and use straight away.

Brain filling

>   1 pair of brains
>   60 g (2½ oz) butter
>   ½ tablespoon flour
>   salt, pepper, nutmeg, chopped herbs to taste
>   2 tablespoons stock or sour cream

Prepare the brains as on page 135, and cook in plenty of salted boiling water with a little vinegar added for about 40 minutes. Remove, allow to cool and chop finely. Make a roux with the butter and flour, add the brains, seasoning, herbs and stock or sour cream, and stir until the mixture is smooth and well blended. Allow to cool a little before use.

Mushroom filling

Chop 350–500 g (¾–1 lb) fresh mushrooms into quarters and cook gently in butter with finely chopped herbs for 15 minutes. Season, add a little chopped onion, chopped hard-boiled egg or rice or both, and enough sour cream to make a fairly moist filling.

Fish filling

Any white fish, though preferably firm, is suitable here. You will need 250–350 g (½–¾ lb), weighed after boning. If the fish is cooked specially for the purpose, bring it to the boil once in a court-bouillon, remove and bone it. Combine with 50–60 g (2–3 oz) rice or cooked unsweetened semolina or sago, add seasoning and chopped herbs, especially dill, to taste, and chopped hard-boiled egg. A little anchovy essence or jellied fish stock will add greatly to the flavour of these *pirozhki* and keep the filling moist. Traditionally Russian cooking made great use of *vyaziga*, dried sturgeon's spinal cord, to flavour fish pie fillings. Chopped anchovies or anchovy essence are possible substitutes.

Millet and curd cheese filling

Bring the millet to the boil in plenty of water. Drain and rinse with boiling water, then cook for about 20 minutes in enough milk to give a not too firm consistency when cold. Combine with curd cheese in any proportion, seasoning including a few pinches of sugar, chopped herbs to taste and a raw egg. Add milk if the filling is too stiff, otherwise the *pirozhki* will be dry when cooked.

Buckwheat, egg and mushroom filling

Cook the buckwheat in salted water for about 15 minutes until soft but not mushy. Drain well and combine with chopped hard-boiled egg, chopped fried onions, and chopped mushrooms sautéed in butter. Add seasoning and herbs to taste. Allow the mixture to cool thoroughly in the refrigerator and add little pieces of very cold butter. Use straight away.

These are basic traditional fillings but there is plenty of scope for invention along non-Russian lines, for example bacon, egg and mushroom filling, moistened with butter. I have not included fillings of cooked cabbage and carrots here because they seem to me rather insipid, but chopped cooked vegetables may be added to any filling in moderation.

Rastegai

These are small fish pies also made with a yeast dough but somewhat bigger than *pirozhki*. An English traveller to Russia at the beginning of this century described them as 'circular, with a little round hole at the top for the gourmet before he eats it to put some fresh caviare there'. It was of a size that allowed it to be cut and eaten in four mouthfuls. For the filling, use slices of fresh raw herring cut to a length to fit the pie and sprinkled with plenty of sautéed onion, pepper and dill. A little sour cream and nutmeg would also not go amiss. Layers of white fish and fresh salmon, combined with sautéed onion and seasoning, may also be used, Allow the *rastegai* to rise for 20 minutes in a warm place before baking in a hot oven for 15–20 minutes. Serve with or without caviare to delight the gourmets at your table, and with any fish soup.

Vatrushki

These are open-topped curd cheese buns made with raised dough and traditionally eaten with *borshch* or *borshchok* (pages 61–3). Recipes date back to medieval Russia, and the name *vatrushka* derives from an ancient Slavonic word for oven or hearth.

FOR THE DOUGH

6 tablespoons milk
1 teaspoon sugar
25 g (1 oz) fresh yeast
300 g (10 oz) flour
30 g (1¼ oz) butter
1 egg
2–3 tablespoons water

FOR THE FILLING

250 g (½ lb) curd or cream cheese
½ beaten egg
1 tablespoon butter
pinch of salt, pinch of sugar
beaten egg and melted butter for glazing

Warm the milk and water slightly, dissolve the sugar and the yeast in it and add a third of the flour. Leave to rise for 15 minutes before adding the remaining ingredients for the dough. Knead and put on one side to rise again while you make the filling. Beat the cheese till smooth, then add the egg, melted butter and seasoning. Form the dough into 12 equal pieces and then into rounds about a finger thick, and about 5 cm (2 inches) in diameter, Make a well in the centre of each round with the sharp end of an egg, and fill each well with about a tablespoon of the filling. Plump up the edges of the rounds, pushing the dough towards the middle, and allow the *vatrushki* to rise on a greased baking tray for 15 minutes in a warm place. Prick with a fork in several places, then glaze with beaten egg and melted butter. Bake in a hot oven for 15–20 minutes. The dough is cooked when you can insert a matchstick and it comes out clean. The *vatrushki* should be golden brown in colour. To stop them drying up during cooking, lower the heat for the last 5 minutes. When they are done put them on a wooden board, brush again with melted butter and cover with a clean tea towel for 15 minutes. In Lent the cheese filling used to be replaced with a vegetable mixture such as onions, sweated in oil.

Ushki, pyshki and ponchki
These crisp-fried little patties with their endearing diminutive names belong to a family of sorts. *Ushki* are made of noodle paste, filled with finely chopped onion and mushroom, folded over into a semi-circular shape (the word means 'little ears'), sealed with milk and deep fried. They are eaten with mushroom soup or *borshchok*. For the noodle paste see page 228. In effect they are deep-fried *pel'meni* or ravioli.

Pyshki or *ponchki* are made with the same raised dough used for *pirozhki* and using any of the fillings, but are always deep-fried and in the form of a square of dough containing a small quantity of stuffing. Roll out the dough in two strips about 2 cm (1 inch) wide. Place a little ball of filling on one of the strips at 2-cm (1-inch) intervals, cover with the second strip and cut into 2-cm (1-inch) squares. Close the edges and fry in deep fat. Drain on greaseproof paper and serve in pyramid form garnished with fresh dill. *Pyshki* should be swollen, well browned and as light as air. Those filled with brains are considered the lightest and most delicate.

GALUSHKI, PAMPUSHKI AND KLETSKI

These are varieties of dumplings of Ukrainian and Western Russian (Belorussian) origin. The Ukrainians traditionally eat them in *borshch*, the Belorussians eat them either by themselves with oil or butter and fried onions, or in hot milk flavoured with caraway and dill and thickened to the consistency of a thin soup with oatmeal (*zhur*). They are homely, uncomplicated recipes which have no special rules except that they combine flour or a grain with butter or fat, egg, milk and seasoning and are cooked in boiling salted water.

Plain galushki/kletski

> 300 g (10 oz) white flour
> 1 egg
> 2 tablespoons melted butter
> 2–3 tablespoons water or milk
> ½ onion (optional)
> ½ teaspoon caraway seed or 1 tablespoon dill weed or other
>   fresh herbs to taste (optional)

Mix together all the ingredients to a smooth dough, knead and leave to stand for about 20 minutes covered with a tea towel before forming into small balls and cooking in boiling salted water. The *galushki* are done when they rise to the surface. Onion may be added, finely chopped, and either caraway or dill. Eaten the Belorussian way, plain *kletski* with onion and caraway are excellent with butter, fried onion and crumbled crispy bacon. You can also experiment with different kinds of flour. Barley, rye and buckwheat, either alone or in combination, have all been used in the past to make these dumplings, as inevitably have leftovers of cooked rice and mashed potato. Bind potato *kletski* with a little flour.

Curd cheese galushki

> 300 g (10 oz) curd cheese
> pinch of salt
> pinch of sugar
> 30 g (1¼ oz) butter
> 3–4 tablespoons flour
> 2 egg whites

Mix together the cheese, salt, sugar, melted butter, flour and finally the beaten egg whites. Form into little balls and drop into boiling salted water. When they rise to the surface, remove, drain, and serve either in a bowl with sour cream or with soup.

A more luxurious French adaptation adds 2–3 tablespoons of sour cream and 2 egg yolks to the basic recipe, triples the quantity of butter and adds in all 150–200 g (6–7 oz) flour.

Pampushki with garlic

> 25 g (1 oz) yeast
> 150 ml (¼ pint) water
> 400 g (14 oz) buckwheat flour
> 1 teaspoon salt
> 4 tablespoons sunflower oil or butter
> ½ head of garlic

Dissolve the yeast in the warm water, then add the flour and salt to form a stiff dough. Knead and leave in a warm place for about 2 hours to rise. Form into little balls and drop into boiling salted water. When cooked, drain and transfer to a pan containing the oil or melted butter. Pound the garlic with the salt and add to the pan. Stir over a low heat until the *pampushki* are well coated and start to brown. Eat with or in *borshch*.

A richer recipe for kletski

> 6 tablespoons milk or water
> 20 g (¾ oz) butter
> ½ teaspoon salt
> 50 g (2 oz) flour or semolina
> 2 eggs
> pinch of nutmeg
> chopped parsley or any other fresh herbs (optional)

Put the milk, butter and salt in a pan and bring to the boil. Add the sifted flour. Mix well and beat with a wooden spoon over a low heat until the mixture comes away from the sides of the pan. Remove from the heat, add the egg yolks one at a time, then the beaten whites and the nutmeg and herbs. If you are using grain you may find it easier to add the grain to the liquid before it boils to avoid lumps. Allow the mixture to thicken over the heat and then put it in a medium oven for 5 minutes to swell. Allow to cool a little before adding yolks, whites and flavourings. To assemble the *kletski*, drop the mixture teaspoon by teaspoon into rapidly boiling salted water about 10 minutes before serving. Dip the spoon in hot water each time you return it to the mixture. The *kletski* are done when they float to the top. Remove with a straining spoon, put in a serving bowl and cover with bouillon or soup as required.

OUTSIDE INFLUENCES

As if Russian traditions did not provide enough varieties of patties, dumplings and other titbits to eat in or alongside the great soups, there has also been a great deal of borrowing from the French. Many different kinds of forcemeat were prepared in the last century. Meat and fish forcemeats were either rolled into a sausage shape, poached, cooled and put into the soup in slices or appeared as little round poached *kneli* (quenelles). The panada base was invariably French white bread. Bread-based forcemeat balls also appeared under their russified German name, *frikadel'ki*, meat *frikadel'ki* with *borshch* and cheese *frikadel'ki* in plain bouillon. Vol-au-vents (*valovany*, *valovanchiki*) were fashionable in some Russian–French restaurants. Finally there were a variety of croûtons (*grenki*, *grenochki*), plain or flavoured with a meat, cheese or fish spread, which could also be served with almost any soup, Russian or foreign.

Eggs
Poached eggs were the most refined accompaniment to soups made with spinach and sorrel, or, for variety, stuffed eggs. The French-influenced chef Khlebnikov at the end of the last century left the latter in their shells for elegant effect and recommended serving them with green or summer *shchi* or with *borshchok* (pages 59, 63).

Stuffed eggs in their shells

> 5 eggs
> fresh parsley or dill
> 3 handfuls fresh breadcrumbs
> pepper and salt
> 1 tablespoon butter

Hard-boil three of the eggs, cool them in cold water, and cut lengthways in half with a sharp knife so as not to break the shell.
Scoop out the insides, chop finely with the herbs, and mix with

about half the breadcrumbs, seasoning and $\frac{1}{2}$ a lightly beaten raw egg. Restuff the shells with this mixture and lay them carefully in a greased baking dish, open side up. Cover the tops of the eggs with the remaining $1\frac{1}{2}$ raw eggs, well beaten, then the rest of the breadcrumbs, and dot with butter. Bake in a medium oven for 5 minutes.

Fish

The great Russian fish are freshwater fish, headed by the celebrated sterlet from the river Volga. They include several varieties of sturgeon and over a dozen different salmon. The finest tribute Russian cooking paid to any of them was to stop short of elaborate sauces and just to poach them absolutely fresh in water and spices. French chefs in Russia refined the technique to poaching in white wine, insisting that the only way to do justice to sterlet was to simmer it in Chablis or champagne in a silver saucepan.

In the last century when fish cookery reached its height, fish was prized all the year round but came into its own during Lent. The week of *Maslenitsa* which preceded the forty-day Fast was an annual fish feast in which vast quantities of caviare, smoked sturgeon and smelts were consumed, accompanied by pancakes. During Lent itself much was made of salt cod and salted herring, and poppy seed oil was used to fry fish. The ban on meat led to such combinations as fish and sauerkraut and fish *borshch* and *shchi* to replace daily dishes. One of the most highly esteemed and useful small fish was the ruff, with its delicate white flesh. Gourmets would buy it live and eat it cooked in white wine or incorporated in *ukha* or a *bouillabaisse* of freshwater fish. Freshwater smelts and *ryapushki* (small fish of the *sig* family, a variety of salmon) also went into the best soups and stews. *Piscari* (small freshwater carp like goldfish) were a Moscow restaurant delicacy. Of the extensive salmon family the *sig* was the most sought after. It is still known to some people as 'the Tsar's fish'.

The nineteenth-century writer Sergei Aksakov wrote a small treatise on some Russian fish and on fishing which makes delightful reading. He was particularly enthusiastic about burbot, a freshwater fish which was, he said, excellent in *ukha* or with its liver used to make pies. Everyone knew the taste of these dishes to be first-rate. About carp he was more circumspect. The meat on a large fish could be coarse, and it was best to look for small ones. Freshwater pike, a favourite fish with Russians, impressed him primarily by its size and longevity. It could live 100 years, and the biggest he had seen weighed over 25 kilograms (50 lb). One of the best fish for the Russian table was pikeperch, which was particularly valuable during Lent. It could be frozen successfully, was healthy, had few bones, was very adaptable and could usually be bought cheaply. Aksakov called it 'Lenten beef'.

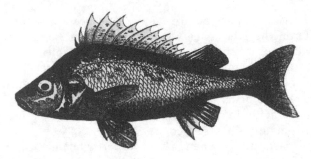

The ruff, a small freshwater fish named in Russian according to its prickly body. In the last century it was still easily available and prized for its delicate white flesh, eaten hot or cold or in ukha. *The illustration is taken from the 1886 edition of S. T. Aksakov's essay on Russian fish and fishing.*

Supplies of most fish were guaranteed all the year round by deep freezing in ice or by salting. The Russian rivers, particularly the Volga and the Neva, were plentifully stocked, as were the Karelian lakes Ladoga and Onega. Salmon came frozen from Siberia, and trout was often available fresh from the environs of St Petersburg. The most exquisite trout came from the near-by Imperial estate at Gatchina, which Catherine the Great built for one of her lovers, Grigory Orlov. Sea fish were imported salted or smoked from the Baltic coast, while shrimps, prawns and crayfish, which were used lavishly to decorate French–Russian poultry dishes, were brought from Finland.

The nineteenth century was thus rich enough and free enough to allow a golden age of simple fish cookery to flourish in Russia. The decline since that time has been marked. Restaurants can rarely offer more than a rubbery piece of sturgeon by way of fresh fish. Shoppers are at the mercy of a mass market supplied by sea trawling in the Pacific, the Atlantic and the North Sea. Cod and mackerel are good, but no substitute for the freshwater classics.

Poached or steamed fish
Try this with freshwater fish if you can get it: sturgeon, roach, wels, freshwater pike, burbot, bream, salmon, otherwise use cod, skate, halibut, turbot, hake. The secret is to get just the right cooking time. Err on the underdone side – about 15 minutes for freshwater fish, no longer than 8 minutes for sea fish. The fish should be gutted but not skinned. It need not be boned but should be cut into good sized chunks for cooking. Poach in just enough court-bouillon to cover, or steam over a pan of water containing slices of onion and a bay leaf. For 1 kg (2 lb) fish make a court-bouillon with:

> ½ onion
> ½ parsley root or a small bunch of stems
> 6 black peppercorns
> 500 ml (1 scant pint) cucumber *rassol* (see page 27) or a
>   mixture of water and *rassol* or, as a last resort, water with
>   a tablespoon of good vinegar and ¾ teaspoon salt
> a pinch of saffron (optional)
> butter to taste

Serve the fish with boiled potatoes sprinkled with chopped fresh dill and onion or spring onion. Grated horseradish, stoned olives, salted cucumbers and mushrooms in sour cream are all possible extras.

Plaice in a Polish sauce
I was first served this sauce in Karelia with fresh pike, but it suits plaice or any flat fish (sole, turbot, brill) very well. Prepare 750 g–1 kg (1½–2 lb) plaice fillet as you prefer. I think short steaming is ideal if the fish is fresh. Serve dressed with the following sauce, which is Polish only in name.

> 2 hard-boiled eggs
> 100 g (3½ oz) butter
> finely chopped fresh dill
> lemon juice and salt to taste

Chop the eggs very finely. Melt the butter gently in a saucepan, or in whatever jug or dish the sauce is to be served in, placed in hot water. Add the eggs and dill and finish with lemon juice and salt to taste. Keep the sauce warm and pour over the fish as it is served. Boiled potatoes and green beans are the best accompaniment.

Baked cod and onions
Do try this simple recipe.

> 2 large onions
> 3 tablespoons olive oil and a little extra oil or butter for
>   frying onions
> 500 g (1 lb) cod fillet
> 1 tablespoon flour
> salt and pepper
> chopped fresh dill, parsley or spring onion

Slice the onions in rings and soften in the extra olive oil or butter. Roll the cod fillets in flour and place in a deep baking dish, cover with the onions, pour over the 3 tablespoons of oil and 2–3 tablespoons hot water, and season. Bake for 15 minutes in a pre-heated medium oven. Serve in its own juices, sprinkled with chopped fresh dill, parsley or chopped spring onion, with boiled potatoes or buckwheat. It is especially good with buckwheat *krupenik* (page 176).

Fish baked in sour cream
Use a firm white fish for this recipe, such as John Dory, sea bass, Dover sole, brill, angler fish or red mullet if you cannot get hold of the pike or perch for which the recipe was intended. If you use a fish that has little characteristic taste or aroma the dish will be too bland.

> 1 kg (2 lb) filleted fish
> freshly ground black pepper
> 1–2 tablespoons sunflower or olive oil
> 1 lemon
> 2–3 small (5 fl oz) cartons sour cream
> nutmeg

Rub the fish with plenty of pepper and brown it lightly in the oil, either in whole fillets or cut into smaller pieces. Transfer to a baking dish, pour over the lemon juice and the sour cream so that the fish is half covered, cover the dish and bake in a low oven for 45–60 minutes. Sprinkle with grated nutmeg and serve. If the sauce seems too thin it may be poured into a separate pan and reduced before pouring back over the fish.

Zrazy or Tel'noe

ROLLED FISH FILLETS WITH DILL
Suitable for cod, sea perch, sole, whiting, pilot fish and other sea fish.

> 700 g (1½ lb) skinned fish fillets (not steaks)
> 1–1½ cups fresh breadcrumbs
> melted butter
> 2 tablespoons dried dill weed
> salt
> a little vinegar or lemon juice
> dill sauce (page 130)

Choose fillets thin enough to roll up and about 15 cm (7 inches) long. Soak the breadcrumbs in enough melted butter to bind, and mix with the dill. Sprinkle the fillets with salt and half the dill mixture, roll up and secure with a wooden cocktail stick. Poach the roulettes in salted water with a dash of vinegar or lemon juice for about 10 minutes. Remove the sticks, place in a serving dish, and coat with dill sauce. Serve with boiled vegetables, boiled potatoes or rice, and raw tomatoes.

Riga Tel'noe

ROLLED FISH FILLETS WITH MUSHROOMS

> 700 g (1½ lb) whiting or sole fillets
> 4 tablespoons olive oil
> 2 tablespoons lemon juice
> juice from ½ onion
> ½ teaspoon dried thyme
> 1 bay leaf
> 200 g (7 oz) mushrooms
> 75 g (3 oz) butter
> 1–2 teaspoons anchovy essence or 4 anchovy fillets,
>   pounded, or 1 sardine, pounded
> salt and pepper
> beaten egg and breadcrumbs for coating
> fresh parsley

Marinate the fish fillets in the oil, lemon juice, onion juice and herbs for 1–2 hours in the refrigerator, turning to make sure all the fish absorbs the flavours. Lay the fillets flat and spread with a layer of forcemeat made by chopping the mushrooms, previously boiled in water or fried in butter, very small, and mixing them with the butter, anchovy essence or pounded anchovies or sardine, and seasoning. Roll up the fish fillets and secure with a wooden cocktail stick. Dip twice in egg and breadcrumbs and deep fry. Serve sprinkled with parsley.

Fish stuffed with buckwheat

> 100 g (3½ oz) buckwheat (uncooked weight)
> 1 fish weighing about 1 kg (2 lb) (sea bass, sea perch, grouper)
> salt and pepper
> 1 large onion, chopped
> 2 hard-boiled eggs
> 1 tablespoon flour
> 3 tablespoons butter
> a little oil
> 1–2 small (5 fl oz) cartons sour cream

Cook the buckwheat in water until tender (see page 174). Clean the fish by cutting off the head at the gills and removing the innards that way. Do not cut open the belly. Wash and dry the fish, season inside and out with salt, and stuff with the buckwheat mixed with the lightly fried onion and the finely chopped eggs. Pepper the outside of the fish and coat it in flour. Brown the fish in the butter and a little oil in a pan for 5 minutes, then transfer to a medium oven, with the sour cream poured over it, to cook for 25 minutes, or until tender. Serve in the baking dish with salted cucumbers or a fruit and vegetable salad.

Bream with apple and horseradish

> 600 g (1½ lb) filleted fish
> vinegar
> court-bouillon with 1 carrot, 1 parsley root, 1 onion, 1 bay leaf and 5 allspice berries
> 2 large cooking apples
> 50 g (2 oz) fresh horseradish, grated
> 1 teaspoon sugar
> 1 tablespoon lemon juice

Divide the fish into serving portions, sprinkle them with vinegar, and leave in the refrigerator for 30 minutes. Prepare the court-bouillon, simmering until it is well flavoured. Place the fish in a pan, pour over the strained court-bouillon, and simmer the fish for about 10 minutes until it is just cooked. Grate the apple and the horseradish together, and sprinkle with the sugar and lemon juice. Add stock from the cooked fish to make a pouring sauce and serve with the fish.

Tuna fish, red snapper or pompano with marinated vegetables
This dish demands good, firm-fleshed fish and was once considered best made with salmon or *beluga* sturgeon. Some modern recipes recommend lufer, a fish caught in the Bosphorus and prized throughout the Balkans as a table fish. Tuna fish, which is increasingly available deep frozen in this country, red snapper or pompano are acceptable substitutes. It is a step up from what I feel is the unimpressive, lowly combination of fish and sauerkraut which is to be found in Balkan and Russian cooking.

    1–2 onions, lightly fried
    2 tablespoons butter
    2–3 tablespoons olive oil
    750 g (1½ lb) fish fillets
    salt and pepper

as many of the following as you can muster:

    5 marinated mushrooms (see page 211)
    5 marinated cherries (see page 310)
    5 gherkins or 1 pickled cucumber
    5 tablespoons sauerkraut
    6 tablespoons *rassol* (see page 27)

Fry the onions until soft in 1 tablespoon of butter and 1 tablespoon of olive oil, and set aside. Add the other tablespoon of butter to the pan and brown the fish lightly on both sides. Transfer to an ovenproof serving dish, season well, cover with the sliced marinated vegetables and the fried onions, and pour over the *rassol* and the remaining oil. Cover and cook in the oven at 375 °F for about 30 minutes. Cover the fish with a light parsley sauce and serve the vegetables alongside, with buttery mashed potatoes into which you have mixed a few tablespoons of chopped fresh herbs.

Fish kchuch

FISH WITH MARINATED RED PEPPERS
An Armenian dish, originally made with trout.

750 g (1½ lb) tuna or firm white fish fillets
2 tablespoons butter
150 g (5 oz) marinated or canned red peppers
2 large onions
2 tomatoes
2 pinches cayenne pepper
freshly ground black pepper
3 crushed allspice berries
¼ teaspoon dried basil
¼ teaspoon salt
½ teaspoon sugar
4 tablespoons white wine

Divide the fish into serving portions, brown them lightly in the butter
and remove from the heat. Drain the peppers and cut into strips.
Chop the onions and tomatoes and put half of them in a buttered
baking dish with the peppers. Sprinkle with the cayenne, black
pepper and allspice, and add the fish. Cover with the remaining
vegetables, add the herbs and sprinkle with salt and sugar. Pour over
the wine, cover tightly, and bake in a medium oven for 35 minutes.
Serve with rice, bulghur wheat or boiled potatoes.

Fish with potatoes and bacon

This is a hearty, unsophisticated and very satisfying combination,
originally from the Baltic states. Use unsmoked streaky bacon with
cod, salt cod, coley (or its salted equivalent, saithe) or pike. Smoked
bacon should be used only with freshwater fish. Heap up the quantity
of potatoes in relation to fish on frugal days.

100 g (3½ oz) bacon
1 large onion
up to 750 g (1½ lb) potatoes
salt and pepper
750 g (1½ lb) fish
fresh chopped parsley

Chop the bacon into small pieces and fry with the sliced onion until
transparent. Add the potatoes, cut into thin slices, season and add a

cup of water. Cover and cook for 15 minutes over a low heat. Add the fish, cut in good size pieces, and cook until this is tender, not more than 8 minutes. Garnish with chopped parsley and serve with cabbage dressed with sour cream:

Cabbage with sour cream

> 750 g (1½ lb) white cabbage
> salt
> sour cream to taste
> 1 teaspoon caraway seeds
> freshly ground black pepper

Chop the cabbage, salt it and cook in a covered pan without water over a low heat until it is cooked to taste. Add sour cream, caraway seeds and plenty of freshly ground black pepper and heat through.

Forshmak

BAKED CHOPPED HERRING IN CREAM

Forshmak comes from the archaic German word *Vorschmack*, meaning literally a foretaste, and variations on this dish, usually combining herring and meat, used to be common hot *zakuski* (see page 217). Prepared in larger quantities it is a useful lunch or supper dish when served with boiled potatoes, lemon wedges and a green vegetable or pickled cucumbers. Its home is again the Baltics.

> 600 g (1¼ lb) filleted salted herring
> milk or weak tea for soaking
> 2 medium onions
> 70 g (2½ oz) fresh breadcrumbs
> 1–2 grated apples (optional)
> black pepper
> 200 ml (⅓ pint) milk and 200 ml (⅓ pint) cream (or all cream if you are feeling rich)
> 2 tablespoons butter
> 1 tablespoon toasted breadcrumbs
> nutmeg

Soak the herring in milk or weak tea to remove most of the salt, skin and bone it, and put it twice through a mincer together with the lightly fried chopped onion and the fresh breadcrumbs soaked in milk and squeezed out. Add the apple, if using. Mix well with a wooden spoon, season with pepper, and add the cream and milk and the melted butter. Place the mixture in a greased dish, dot with butter, sprinkle with the toasted crumbs and a little grated nutmeg, and bake in the oven at 350°F for 20 minutes or until bubbling and brown on top. You may use fewer breadcrumbs and beat in an egg if you wish.

Herring fillets may also be baked in a buttered dish covered with a layer of chopped raw onion and a layer of sour cream, and sprinkled with dill. Use fresh or salted and soaked fish. Serve with a wedge of lemon and boiled potatoes.

Fish poached with horseradish

Any firm white fish may be poached in a fish stock strongly flavoured with vinegar (1 tablespoon for each 200 ml (⅓ pint) of stock) and fresh grated horseradish. When it is cooked strain off the stock, thicken with flour and butter cooked to a roux, and add a few tablespoons of sour cream. Pour the sauce over the fish, cook for a further 5 minutes and serve. Cheat when there is no fresh horseradish by introducing a teaspoonful of creamed horseradish at a time to the thickened stock and cream until you have the right flavour.

Baked or poached carp

Carp is not a classic fish in the Russian kitchen. It belongs to Germany and to Eastern Europe and is a mainstay of the Jewish cooking which originated there. When the Russians cooked it in the last century they either baked it and served it with marinated vegetables and fruit (mushrooms, cherries, dill cucumbers) or with horseradish, or they borrowed a Jewish recipe such as the one given by Mrs Molokhovets. Fresh, small fish are essential if this dish is to taste good.

> 1 kg (2 lb) fish, skinned, boned and cut into pieces
> 200 ml (⅓ pint) cider vinegar
> 2 cloves
> salt and black pepper
> 1 tablespoon oil
> 6–7 tablespoons beer
> 2 tablespoons fresh breadcrumbs
> 2 tablespoons raisins, soaked in warm water
> ¼–½ teaspoon grated lemon rind

Marinate the fish in the vinegar, cloves and seasoning for at least an hour, turning once. Put the oil in a pan, and add the beer, fish, vinegar and breadcrumbs. Cover and simmer until cooked. Add to the sauce in the pan the raisins plumped out in warm water and the lemon rind. Bring the sauce to the boil once and serve.

Cod, turbot or brill in cherry and red wine sauce

750 g–1 kg (1½–2 lb) fish fillets
court-bouillon for poaching fish
1–2 tablespoons vinegar or white wine
7 tablespoons cherry purée
1 clove (optional)
pinch of cinnamon
sugar to taste
½ tablespoon flour
1 tablespoon butter
4 tablespoons red wine
1 tablespoon chopped gherkins or capers

Simmer the fish in a court-bouillon with 1–2 tablespoons vinegar or white wine until just tender, about 8 minutes. Serve in a sauce made with the cherry purée, the clove, cinnamon, bouillon and sugar to taste, thickened with the flour and butter cooked to a roux. Bring to the boil, add the red wine and the chopped gherkins or capers, heat through and coat the fish on a serving dish.

Fish cutlets

This is the fish equivalent of *bitki*, consisting of a forcemeat of flaked fish, bound with egg and either flour, fresh breadcrumbs or cooked grain, flavoured with onion and herbs, and either poached or fried in breadcrumbs. The equivalent is to be found in many cuisines. What distinguishes the Russian dish is the habit of serving these cutlets cold with marinated cucumbers or horseradish, whence almost certainly Jewish *gefillte fisch*. To my taste, however, fish *bitki* are much better hot, served with dill sauce (page 130) or parsley sauce.

1–2 medium onions
1 tablespoon each fresh dill and parsley
1 egg

1 tablespoon flour or 1 heaped tablespoon fresh
  breadcrumbs
500 g (1 lb) flaked fish
salt to taste
½ teaspoon ground black pepper
flour or breadcrumbs for coating
oil and butter for frying

Chop the onions and herbs finely and mix with the egg, the flour or the breadcrumbs soaked in milk and squeezed out, and the fish. Season well. Either form into a long sausage, dust with flour, wrap in muslin tied at both ends and simmer in salted water or fish stock for about 15 minutes, or make cutlet shapes, dust with flour or breadcrumbs and fry in oil and butter for about 10 minutes.

A variation on this second method which ensures that the cutlets keep their shape is to put them in a baking dish with a little hot butter and oil, scatter chopped parsley and very thinly sliced lemon over them, cover with buttered paper and a tight lid and bake in a hot oven for 10 minutes.

Fish plov
South-west Turkmenia borders on the Caspian sea, and in that small area fish rivals lamb in popularity. The two classic Central Asian dishes borrowed by the Russians, *shashlyk* and *plov*, are both made with bream from the Caspian. There is no recipe for the *shashlyk*. The fish need only be freshly caught and cooked in a heavy pan in its own juices, basted with a little lamb fat. In other words there's no imitating it in the suburbs of London, though it's worth a try with shark. With *plov* one can get away with more. Use bream, carp or pike, or failing that, catfish, brill, angler fish, John Dory or halibut.

salt to taste
2 bay leaves
1 parsley root or ½ parsnip
a few black peppercorns
4 onions
500–750 g (1–1½ lb) filleted fish
2 teaspoons ground black pepper
3 tablespoons fresh parsley
2 tablespoons fresh dill
1 teaspoon crushed fennel seeds

2 pinches saffron or turmeric
1 small (5 fl oz) carton sour cream
2–3 carrots
7 tablespoons vegetable (preferably olive) oil
400 g (14 oz) Italian rice
juice of ½ lemon

Bring just under a litre (1½ pints) of water to the boil and add salt, the bay leaves, half the parsley root, a few crushed peppercorns and half an onion. Add the fish, cut into smallish pieces, and simmer for 10 minutes. Remove the fish, transfer to a serving dish, and cover with two finely chopped onions, the remaining grated parsley root, half the black pepper, the parsley, dill, fennel seeds and half the saffron. Sprinkle with salt and pour over the sour cream. Set to cook very slowly on the stove or over steam.

In a separate pan soften the remaining onion and the carrot, both finely chopped, in the oil, add the strained fish bouillon, bring to the boil and add the rice which has been washed and soaked for 30 minutes in hot water. Allow to come to the boil uncovered over a medium heat, add the remaining pepper and saffron, stir, cover, and leave over a very low heat to cook for 8–10 minutes. Leave to stand without removing the lid for another 5 minutes. Serve the rice sprinkled with the lemon juice in one bowl and the fish in another.

Trout stuffed in the Armenian style

750 g–1 kg (1½–2 lb) trout (2 large fish)
½ teaspoon ground black pepper
6 prunes (soaked for a few hours), fresh damsons, or dried
  or fresh sourish apricots (soaked if dried)
1 pomegranate or 1 eating apple and 1 teaspoon lemon juice
2 large onions
1 teaspoon dried basil
150 ml (¼ pint) white wine or oil and butter for frying

Clean the fish by cutting off the heads at the gills and removing the insides through the opening. Wash, dry and season the inside of the fish. Fill the fish with a stuffing made of the chopped fruit, onions and basil. Simmer in the wine for 8–10 minutes, and serve with rice or bulghur wheat. The pomegranate, of which the seeds and juice are used, may be replaced by one finely chopped eating apple and a teaspoon of lemon juice. The stuffed fish may also be fried in olive oil and butter, which I think is tastier.

Another stuffing worth trying is called *kutap*.

> 60 g (2½ oz) rice (uncooked weight)
> 75 g (3 oz) butter
> 3 tablespoons fresh parsley
> 1 teaspoon ground ginger
> 50 g (2 oz) raisins (soaked for a few hours)

Cook the rice in boiling water and drain. Mix with the softened butter, parsley, ginger and soaked raisins and stuff the fish as above. Bake in a buttered dish in the oven at 350°F for 10–15 minutes per lb of fish, or fry in olive oil and butter.

Cold walnut sauce for baked or boiled fish (particularly bream or carp)

> 200 g (7 oz) shelled walnuts
> 1 teaspoon prepared mustard
> salt to taste
> 2 hard-boiled egg yolks
> 1 tablespoon olive oil
> 1 tablespoon fresh breadcrumbs
> 7 tablespoons wine or cider vinegar
> 2–3 teaspoons sugar

Moisten the walnuts with a little water in a mortar and crush into fine pieces. Mix with the mustard, add a little salt, the hard-boiled egg yolks beaten with the oil to a paste and the breadcrumbs. Warm the vinegar, dissolve the sugar in it, and allow to cool before adding to the other ingredients. Serve with hot fish.

Trout Lake Sevan style

The *ishkhan*, a magnificent salmon trout native to Armenia's Lake Sevan, was the finest fish I ever tasted in the Soviet Union. On the shores of the lake, not far from the capital city of Erevan, there is a restaurant which specializes in serving these fish freshly caught. The *ishkhan* was served grilled flat, brushed with oil, red pepper and basil. To imitate it, take a large river trout, or better still a salmon trout, cut it along the belly, clean and dry it, and remove the backbone so that it lies flat. Sprinkle with salt, paprika or cayenne pepper, and a little dried or fresh chopped basil, and dot with butter or olive oil. Put under a hot grill for 10 minutes and serve with lemon wedges and a sprinkling of more fresh basil if you have it.

Meat, Poultry and Game

In Moscow an American friend of mine was astonished to find Russians commonly referring just to meat, as if whether one ate pork, beef or lamb, or which cut of the animal was served, were merely decorations.

This attitude has something to do with the undeniable scarcity of meat in many parts of Russia today, in cities and particularly in the Northern and Central provinces. The problem of meat supply is tied to grain, and thus to the success of the harvest and the amount of extra wheat and barley the Soviet Union can and will import to feed its people and livestock. Such imports are a drain on highly valued foreign currency reserves which the State would ideally wish to spend elsewhere. Lack of meat causes much grumbling among the population while grain is bought abroad at a political as well as an economic cost. Meat then is a politically sensitive issue.

This explanation will not, I hope, be taken as propaganda. It is not for everyone a criterion of a modern, or even of an affluent, society that meat should be available for daily eating. On the other hand Soviet shops undoubtedly run short of nutritionally acceptable substitutes, particularly outside the big cities.

Shortages of meat are not new to this century, and the Russian peasant diet has the hallmarks of a successful search for substitutes. That said, probably the primary reason for the prevalence of non-meat dishes for consumption at more affluent Russian tables was the strong influence of the Orthodox Church. Meat was allowed neither in Butter nor Carnival Week nor throughout the 40-day Lent Fast. Mushrooms were the best substitute, and highly valued for their taste as well as their nourishment. Fish was another important standby. Tales are told of recalcitrant fasters cooking themselves meat and trying to pass it off as fish so that they did not lose face in public. Russian cooking also mixes beef and herring in classic homely dishes like *forshmak* (page 217), and one wonders if the root of the habit is not to be found in the ease with which one might exclude the meat during Lent and still apparently eat the same dish.

Today, outside the influence of the Church, grains and dairy products combined provide some protein and fat in the low meat diet, while the Soviet State has greatly encouraged and increased poultry farming to make up for the shortage of red meat. It is probably no coincidence that the 'traditional' dishes most favoured by international Russian hotels today are Pozharsky cutlets (page 152) and chicken Kiev (page 151), the latter being the only Soviet gastronomic product to my knowledge to have won recognition in foreign restaurants. Tradition favours beef and pork in northern and western Russia, and lamb in the South, the Caucasus and Central Asia.

The basic Russian way with meat is either to roast it or to boil it on the bone. The French were thus in a position to introduce to the aristocracy in the nineteenth century many new ways of cutting and cooking meat off the bone, a fact borne out by the invasion of French terms: *antrekot, eskalop, filé*. Other ways with filleted meat came from Germany (*shnitzel*) and as early as the sixteenth century from the Baltics (*zrazy*, page 128).

During the summer months, there was good meat available to French chefs in St Petersburg in the middle of the last century. Petit liked beef from the Caucasus, but disliked the frozen beef that was offered from October till spring. The best lamb also came from the South and then from Central Asia. Moscow had excellent veal. Pork was generally of a very high quality, especially milk-fed sucking pig which, as Petit informed his fellow chefs working in Russian households, was much sought after by Russian gourmets. Lady Londonderry commented on beef being generally good in Russia but mutton being bad. She disliked a dish she was offered as Torzhok cutlets in the town of the same name on the route from Moscow to St Petersburg. 'At Torzhok we stopped to taste the famous cutlets of this place and thought them remarkably nasty.' Perhaps they were made with the frozen meat abhorred by Petit!

It is difficult to have an overall picture today, but much good beef is imported from France and South America. Meat on sale in private enterprise markets, produced on farms and brought in in small quantities for quick sale, is of a markedly better quality than what is commonly available in State shops.

PORK

Marinated roast pork
This recipe is suitable for any roasting joint.

> 1 joint of pork weighing 1–1½ kg (about 2 lb)
> 16 tablespoons vinegar
> 8 tablespoons olive oil
> 8 tablespoons madeira or sherry
> 1 bay leaf
> a little fresh or dried tarragon
> a few black peppercorns
> ½ teaspoon salt
> 1 onion
> black breadcrumbs (optional)
> ½ tablespoon grated lemon peel

Large joints are marinated most economically in a leakproof plastic bag. Wipe the joint and put it inside a bag in a large bowl. Mix together the vinegar, oil, madeira or sherry, bay leaf, tarragon, peppercorns, salt and chopped onion, and add to the pork in the bag. Tie loosely and leave to stand for 2–3 days. Turn the joint regularly so that the meat is evenly marinated. To cook, roast in a hot oven for 1–1½ hours, basting frequently with the marinade during the first half hour. Sprinkle with black breadcrumbs and grated lemon peel and finish cooking. Serve with either redcurrant sauce (see below) or a gravy made with the skimmed juices from the pan, thickened with a little flour and seasoned with lemon juice.

Redcurrant sauce

> 200 g (½ lb) redcurrants, cooked to a purée
> 8 tablespoons wine
> juices from the roasting pan after the fat has been removed
> sugar and cinnamon to taste
> 1 teaspoon cornflour

Place all the ingredients except the cornflour in a small pan on the heat. Dissolve the cornflour in a little cold water and add. Bring gently to the boil stirring all the time.

Sucking pig

Roast sucking pig is a classic festive dish on the Russian table, and one which has priced itself out of the modern repertoire. The traditional method was to roast the pig on a spit, or on a platform of birch twigs on a baking tray in the oven. It was cooked whole with the head left on, basted frequently with oil or butter, and served with buckwheat and sometimes a hot sauce. On Easter Sunday roast sucking pig was served cold with a stuffing of liver and raisins. Both the stuffing and the sauce lend themselves to more common cuts of pork.

Stuffing for a festive loin of pork

> 450 g (1 lb) liver (pig's liver may be used, but the film should
> be removed and it should be soaked for several hours in
> milk first)
> 60 g (2½ oz) butter
> 2 eggs
> 2–3 teaspoons sugar
> 5 cloves, crushed
> 4 tablespoons raisins
> 2 tablespoons fresh white breadcrumbs
> a little milk
> salt
> ground white and black pepper

Simmer the liver in boiling water until cooked, then cut into pieces and pound until smooth in a mortar. Add the butter, eggs, sugar, cloves and raisins, and the breadcrumbs soaked in milk and squeezed out. Season well with salt and pepper. Mix well and beat with a wooden spoon until smooth.

Sour cream and caper sauce for pork fillet or cutlets

> ½ tablespoon butter
> 2 teaspoons flour
> 300 ml (½ pint) stock
> 2 tablespoons sour cream
> squeeze of lemon juice
> 1–2 teaspoons capers
> a little dry sherry (optional)
> a pinch of sugar (optional)

Make a roux with the butter and flour and gradually stir in the warmed stock. When the mixture is smooth and thick add the sour cream and the remaining ingredients. Test for seasoning, pour over the cutlets and serve with plain boiled potatoes.

Vereshchaka

A casserole of pork and beetroot, thickened with rye breadcrumbs or oats. It is probably of Ukrainian origin and very much a classic peasant mixture.

> 500 g (1 lb) pork (spare rib, loin)
> 50 g (2 oz) bacon fat or streaky bacon
> 2 onions
> 400 ml (⅔ pint) beetroot *rassol* (see page 27) or *kvas* (see page 300) or a mixture of both
> 1 tablespoon sugar
> salt to taste
> 5–6 black peppercorns
> 2–3 allspice berries
> 2 tablespoons rye crumbs, oats or barley
> fresh chervil or lovage
> sour cream (optional)
> 1 tablespoon chopped parsley

Cut the meat into cubes and brown it in the bacon fat or with the streaky bacon. Remove the meat from the pan and lightly brown the onions in the remaining fat. Transfer the meat, onions and bacon to a casserole, add the beetroot *rassol* or other liquid, sugar, salt, peppercorns, allspice and grain, and set covered in a medium oven to cook for about an hour. If after half an hour the casserole seems too dry, water may be added until a satisfactory consistency is achieved. Serve sprinkled with fresh herbs and a little sour cream if liked.

Bigos

Another classic pork casserole from western Russia, also to be found in Polish cooking.

> 500 g (1 lb) stewing pork
> 150 g (5 oz) bacon in chunks
> pork, bacon fat or oil

10 black peppercorns
2 medium onions
1 head of garlic
3 bay leaves
1 small white cabbage – about 750 g (1½ lb)
2 medium cooking apples
water or light stock
1–2 tablespoons cucumber *rassol* (see page 27) (optional)

Cube the meat and bacon and brown it in a little lard or oil. Transfer to a casserole and add the crushed peppercorns, chopped onion and garlic, bay leaves, the cabbage cut into strips and the sliced apples. Pour over a little water or light stock and one or two tablespoons of cucumber *rassol* if available. Cover tightly and cook in a slow oven for 1½–2 hours, checking periodically to see that the casserole has not become too dry. Serve with boiled potatoes.

Kostitsa

PORK WITH GARLIC SAUCE
Spare rib or loin of pork are best for this Moldavian dish, but belly of pork may also be used if you do not find it too fat.

500 g (1 lb) boneless pork
salt and pepper
½ glass dry white wine (optional)
a little oil for frying if liked
muzhdei sauce (see below)
fresh chopped parsley and dill

Have the meat divided into serving-size cutlets, beat them lightly with a meat mallet, season with salt and pepper, and if wine is used, pour over and allow to stand for 15 minutes. The cutlets should then be fried for 4–7 minutes each side, depending on their thickness. The cutlets may be transferred to a shallow baking dish, coated with *muzhdei* sauce, wine and chopped herbs and baked in the oven for a further 5 minutes, or they may be cooked a little longer in the frying pan until they are done. Add the wine for the last few minutes of cooking and coat with *muzhdei* sauce as they are served. Serve with raw or cooked whole tomatoes, baked onions, and boiled potatoes.

Muzhdei sauce

> For every 100 ml (about 6 tablespoons) bouillon (vegetable, chicken, beef or the liquid left over from cooking white beans):
> 1 head garlic (or the equivalent in garlic powder)
> ¼ teaspoon salt

Pound the garlic and salt in a mortar until smooth and dilute with the warm bouillon. This classic recipe makes a very strong sauce indeed and may be diluted further with bouillon according to taste. It is also an excellent accompaniment to plain roast chicken and to cooked haricot beans.

Pork casserole with mushrooms
A hearty, economical dish from the Ukraine.

> 500 g (1 lb) stewing pork
> lard or oil for frying as required
> 3 tablespoons tomato purée
> 500 g (1 lb) potatoes
> 1–2 carrots
> 2 onions
> salt and black pepper
> 5 dried mushrooms or 300 g (10 oz) fresh
> 2 bay leaves
> 3 cloves of garlic

Chop the meat into cubes, brown it on all sides in a little lard or oil, add the tomato purée to the pan and cook for a few minutes. Dice the potatoes and carrots and fry lightly in a little oil or fat separately. Remove from the heat, add the raw onion cut in rounds and season with salt and pepper. Put the meat and tomato and the vegetable mixture into a deep casserole in alternate layers, beginning and ending with vegetables. If using dried mushrooms, bring them to the boil in 200 ml (⅓ pint) of water, chop them finely and reduce the stock by half. Add both to the casserole with the bay leaves. Fresh mushrooms should be diced and added raw with 100 ml (about 6 tablespoons) water or stock. Bake, covered, in a medium oven for about an hour, or simmer gently on top of the stove. Check seasoning. Before serving, sprinkle with the chopped garlic and allow to stand with the lid on for 5 minutes.

Spiced pork fillet with prune sauce

750 g (1½ lb) fillet of pork
½ glass white wine
6 tablespoons wine vinegar or cider vinegar
salt
4 bay leaves
a few peppercorns
a few juniper berries
250 g (8 oz) prunes or 150 ml (¼ pint) thick cherry juice
½ tablespoon butter
1 tablespoon fresh white breadcrumbs
1–2 teaspoons sugar
a generous pinch of cinnamon

Flatten the fillets with a meat mallet, place in a heavy pan and add the wine, vinegar and 6 tablespoons of water. Season with salt, add the bay leaves, peppercorns and juniper berries and simmer with the lid on until the meat is tender. The fillets should be turned several times during cooking. Meanwhile bring the prunes to the boil in enough water to cover them and cook until soft. Purée the mixture in a liquidizer or rub through a sieve. Melt the butter in a pan and cook the breadcrumbs in it for a few minutes without letting them brown. Add the buttered crumbs to the purée with sugar to taste and the cinnamon. Dilute to the consistency of a pouring sauce with cooking juices from the pan, and bring the whole mixture to the boil before pouring over the cooked fillets.

BEEF

Roast beef Russian style

1 prime rib joint weighing 1–1½ kg (2–3 lb)
1 small carrot
1 small onion
½ stick of celery or parsley root
2 bay leaves
a few black peppercorns
1 teaspoon ground ginger
150 ml (¼ pint) beef stock
1–2 tablespoons cucumber *rassol* (page 27)
    or 1 tablespoon lemon juice

2–3 tablespoons sour cream
½ teaspoon salt

Wipe the meat, trim off the fat, melt a little of it in a heavy, shallow pan and brown the joint lightly on all sides, sprinkling it with the finely chopped vegetables, the bay leaves, peppercorns and ginger. Roast in a medium to hot oven for about an hour, basting the joint every 10 minutes with a mixture of stock and *rassol*. About 5 minutes before the joint is cooked, drain off the stock and juices from the pan, add a couple of tablespoons of ice-cold water, and put it in the refrigerator until the fat has solidified on the surface and may be removed easily. Return the juices to a pan, bring to the boil, strain if desired, and add the sour cream. Keep the sauce warm. Remove the beef from the oven, sprinkle with salt and allow to stand for 15 minutes before carving. Serve with the sour cream sauce, roast or boiled potatoes, boiled carrots, turnips or swede, or mushrooms.

Boiled beef

Largely replaced in insipid modern international cuisine by the ubiquitous piece of tasteless steak (Russia has *bifshteks, rompshteks* and *antrekot*), boiled beef is quickly becoming a forgotten delicacy. It demands long slow cooking and cannot be thought of now as a particularly economical dish. But it is worth every penny it costs. It was a staple in Russian middle-class households before the Revolution and lent itself to infinite variation by way of sauces. The following description was given to me by a Russian friend now living in England:

A dish we had often which must be Ukrainian was a cheap bit of beef boiled carefully and slowly and eaten with hot boiled potatoes and raw tomatoes. A French dressing would be poured over the tomatoes and the meat. The taste of oil and vinegar on boiled beef is for me a taste of childhood.

500 g (1 lb) brisket, shin of beef or flank (skirt)
2 carrots
1 onion
1 turnip
1 stick of celery
1 small parsnip
2 bay leaves
5 peppercorns
salt

Place the meat in a large saucepan and pour over hot water until it is just covered. Cover and bring to the boil, skim and leave to simmer on a low heat for about 2½ hours. Half an hour before the meat is cooked, add the peeled and sliced vegetables and the seasonings. When the meat is done pour off the cooking liquid and reserve for making a sauce. The vegetables may be served separately. The meat should be left to stand in the pan with the lid on until it is required. It may be served with boiled potatoes and any vegetable, though particularly Russian accompaniments are the hot sweetish mixtures of vegetables and fruit called *vzvary* (see pages 190, 195, 197), hot beetroot (page 188), or baked sauerkraut with mushrooms and sour cream (page 196).

Try any of the following sauces instead of gravy:

Hot horseradish and sour cream sauce

> 3 tablespoons butter
> 2 tablespoons freshly grated horseradish or horseradish
>   sauce
> 1–2 tablespoons vinegar
> 200 ml (½ pint) +1–2 tablespoons beef stock
> 1 bay leaf
> a few peppercorns
> 1 scant tablespoon flour
> ½ small (5 fl oz) carton sour cream

If fresh horseradish can be found prepare it in the following way. Melt 2 tablespoons butter in a small pan, add the horseradish, grated, and cook it gently without browning. Add 1–2 tablespoons vinegar and the same quantity of water or stock, a bay leaf and a few peppercorns, and allow the mixture to simmer until all the liquid evaporates. Make a roux with 1 tablespoon butter and the flour, add the stock and allow to thicken into a smooth sauce over a gentle heat. Stir in the prepared horseradish or made horseradish sauce and the sour cream, and test for seasoning. Dilute the sauce with more stock if it is too thick, and add a splash of vinegar if the flavour needs sharpening. The sauce may also be served cold.

Mushroom sauce

> 2 tablespoons butter
> a slice of lemon
> 400 ml (⅔ pint) stock

150 g (5 oz) mushrooms
1 generous tablespoon flour
salt
1 small wine glass of sherry
1–2 tablespoons sour cream

Melt ½ a tablespoon of butter in a pan. Add the juice from a slice of lemon, a quarter of the stock and the cleaned mushrooms. Bring the liquid to the boil, remove the mushrooms and chop them into small-ish pieces. In another pan make a roux with the remaining butter and the flour, add 2 cups of stock, the mushrooms and the liquid in which they were cooked. Add salt and the sherry and bring to the boil. Remove from the heat and add 1–2 tablespoons of sour cream.

Onion and caraway sauce

500 g (1 lb) onions
1 tablespoon oil
500 ml (¾–1 pint) stock
1 tablespoon butter
1 tablespoon flour
1½ teaspoons caraway seeds
pinch of brown sugar
½ teaspoon mustard (optional)
splash of vinegar (optional)

Slice the onions finely and cook very slowly in the oil in a heavy-bottomed pan with the lid on until they are soft. This will take about 45 minutes. Make sure they do not brown or stick to the pan, especially at the beginning of cooking. Purée the cooked onions with about 300 ml (½ pint) stock. Make a roux with the remaining butter and the flour, add the remaining stock and then the onion purée, the caraway and the sugar. The mustard may be blended with a little water and a splash of vinegar and added to the pan. Bring to the boil and cook for a few minutes before serving. This is also a good sauce for lamb.

Beetroot sauce

½ tablespoon butter
¼ tablespoon flour
a little hot water or stock
½–1 small (5 fl oz) carton sour cream
500 g (1 lb) cooked beets, finely chopped
salt and pepper

Make a roux with the butter and flour, add a little hot water or stock, and mix to a smooth paste before adding the sour cream and the chopped beets. Season, bring to the boil stirring constantly, and serve.

Braised beef
Another way of cooking the cheaper joints of beef.

500 g (1 lb) shin, brisket or flank
1 carrot
1 medium onion
1 parsnip
1 stick celery
1 tablespoon tomato purée
1 bay leaf
2 cloves or a little lemon peel
8 peppercorns
salt and pepper
½ tablespoon vinegar
½ wine glass red wine (optional)
300 ml (½ pint) stock or water
a little flour

Salt the meat and brown it quickly on all sides in a shallow pan. Transfer to a casserole and add the diced vegetables, the tomato purée, the spices, bay leaf, cloves, peppercorns and seasonings, the vinegar and the wine, with about 300 ml (½ pint) stock or boiling water. Bring to the boil, put a lid on the pan, and leave to cook slowly for a couple of hours. Serve in its own sauce, thickened with a little flour. Baked apples and haricot beans are favourite Russian accompaniments.

Stewed beef with fruit
For an all-in-one dish stewing beef may be cubed, browned and braised slowly in a little stock, with the same quantity of apples, prunes or quince added half-way through cooking. Add a small chopped onion softened in butter or oil at the same time, and salt and pepper to taste. Prunes may need extra liquid – water or stock – added to the pan.

Beef Stroganov

Alexander Grigorievich Stroganov, if my Russian history sources are correct, gave his name at the end of the last century to a dish to which almost no one takes exception. Personally I would add that it needs little skill or imagination to cook and is without nationality! Stroganov's chef, if he was not French, was certainly French-trained. But the original dish, served on the numerous occasions when the master held open house in the Black Sea port of Odessa, was probably better than all the misnamed *beef à la Stroganov, in Stroganov sauce* and *Stroganovsky* I have seen on menus from London to Kathmandu. It aspires to being more than a quick, expensive beef and cream scramble.

500 g (1 lb) fillet steak*
salt and pepper
1 tablespoon tomato purée or 2 tablespoons tomato juice or
    1 heaped teaspoon French mustard
1 onion, cut in rings
3 tablespoons butter or oil
1 tablespoon flour
¾ small (5 fl oz) carton sour cream

Beat the meat with a wooden mallet until it is about half a finger thick, and cut it into thin strips about 5 cm (2 inches) long. According to the classic recipe it should then be ready for cooking, but a Russian friend of mine finds beef today so poor in quality that she insists on marinating it for 24 hours beforehand. In that case put the strips in a dish, season them with salt, pepper and the mustard if used, cover with the onion rings and leave covered in a cool place until the next day. Then continue to follow the traditional recipe. It is said the meat should not come in direct contact with the pan and for this reason the onions are first lightly fried in the oil or butter, then the strips of beef placed on top of them. As soon as the meat is in the pan turn the heat up high and cook for 5 minutes until the meat takes on a lacquered look. Sprinkle it with flour, reduce the heat, cook for 2–3 minutes and add

---

* Cheaper cuts of steak than fillet may be used, but in this case marinating is essential, and the cooking time should be extended by adding about 200 ml (⅓ pint) stock after the flour and allowing the meat to simmer covered for 20–30 minutes. The sour cream may be added with the stock or just before the dish is served.

the sour cream and tomato purée if used. Bring gently to the boil, stirring carefully, and serve with matchstick potatoes if you want to be correct, and with sauté potatoes and baked or raw tomatoes otherwise. Salted cucumbers go well with *beef Stroganov*.

Liver Stroganov is an adulteration well worth trying. Substitute calves' or lambs' liver for the steak. These may be soaked in milk for a few hours or used straight away, depending on how mild a flavour one likes. The liver strips and onion rings should be cooked together in oil or butter over a high heat for no more than 5 minutes. Add the flour, cook for a couple of minutes and finish with the sour cream and tomato purée. There is no tradition to follow here – I would serve *liver Stroganov* with plain rice.

Zrazy

These are *roulades* of beef or veal which found their way into popular Russian cooking through Poland and the Baltic States. They are made either with whole slices of beef, stuffed with egg, breadcrumbs and seasonings, or with chopped raw beef mixed with egg and beaten flat. *Zrazy* made with chopped meat are spread with a filling like a sandwich and cooked flat. To my mind they make the more interesting dish.

Open zrazy with horseradish
A Lithuanian recipe.

> 500 g (1 lb) best minced beef
> 1 egg
> 2 teaspoons marjoram
> salt and pepper
> 2–3 tablespoons flour
> 6 tablespoons brown breadcrumbs
> 2–3 tablespoons butter
> 1 large horseradish root or 2–3 tablespoons creamed
>   horseradish
> 2 onions
> 1 small (5 fl oz) carton sour cream
> 6 tablespoons stock or water
> 2 tablespoons vegetable oil

Mix together the minced meat, egg and marjoram, season with salt
and pepper, and form into thin flat cakes about the size of a hamburger. Coat them on both sides in a little flour and fry over a high
heat for a few minutes on both sides. Place in a buttered baking dish
and spread with a thick layer of forcemeat, made by adding 1½–2
tablespoons of flour and the breadcrumbs to the melted butter in a
separate pan and blending in the grated horseradish root or creamed
horseradish to make a stiff mixture. Over this place a layer of chopped
onion, and finish with a layer of sour cream. Pour over the stock or
water mixed with the oil, and bake in a medium oven, covered, for
about 40 minutes. Serve the *zrazy* in their own sauce, with boiled
potatoes. Follow with a plain green salad.

Bitki and Kotlety
Somehow the Russian versions of the hamburger and the meatball
have acquired a gastronomic reputation above their station. Would I
dare leave out *kotlety*? asked one devotee, while *Larousse Gastronomique* gives the humble *bitok* an entry all of its own. The two differ to my
mind only in shape: *kotlety* are oval-shaped, *bitki* are smaller and
round. They are essentially plain, homely dishes.

> 500 g (1 lb) lean beef, veal or lamb
> 125 g (4 oz) fresh white breadcrumbs
> 150 ml (¼ pint) milk
> salt and pepper
> beaten egg and breadcrumbs or flour for coating
> 2 tablespoons butter or oil for frying

Mince the meat finely. Soak the breadcrumbs in the milk, squeeze out
and mix with the meat, season with salt and pepper and put twice
through the mincer or grinder to make the mixture completely
smooth. Coat with egg and breadcrumbs or flour and fry in butter or
oil for about 8 minutes on each side. Serve with sour cream or any
tomato sauce. Lamb *kotlety* are especially good with baked onions or
with onion and caraway sauce (page 125).

These are the basic ingredients but every Russian family has its
special recipe. *Kotlety* and *bitki* are transformed for me from humble
dishes into delicacies by the liberal addition of the following dill sauce
or sour cream and spring onion sauce.

Dill sauce

> 2 tablespoons butter
> 2 tablespoons flour
> 2 cups stock and milk
> 2 tablespoons lemon juice
> dill (2 tablespoons dried or 4 tablespoons fresh)
> 1–2 egg yolks
> seasoning

Make a roux with the butter and flour, add the warmed stock and milk gradually, stirring all the time, then the lemon juice and the dill. Add the egg yolks off the heat and blend in. Reheat carefully and cook for a few minutes without allowing the sauce to boil. Season and serve hot. This recipe appeared in Mrs Molokhovets's classic *Gift to Young Housewives*, published in the 1860s. An almost identical dill sauce without nationality is given in Anna Thomas's *The Vegetarian Epicure* (Penguin, 1974). Dry sherry replaces the lemon juice.

Sour cream and spring onion sauce
Make a white sauce in the same proportions as above, omitting the lemon juice and adding 1–2 finely chopped spring onions, including the green stalks. Simmer for a few minutes, add 2 tablespoons sour cream, reheat gently and serve. (Two egg yolks are optional.)

As one travels south, *kotlety* and *bitki* become Moldavian *kiftelutse* and Armenian *kokony* and *kololak*. The mixture changes to include garlic, plenty of onion, black pepper, fresh parsley and coriander, mint, caraway, red pepper, walnuts and raisins. The meat may be lamb, veal or beef.

Armenian kokony

> 500 g (1 lb) beef
> 2 red peppers
> 1½ teaspoons caraway seeds
> ½ teaspoon cayenne pepper
> 1 head of garlic, peeled and finely minced
> ¼ tablespoon fresh mint
> beaten egg white and breadcrumbs for coating

Mince the beef, blanch the peppers and chop fine, add all the remaining ingredients except the egg white and breadcrumbs and put the whole mixture twice through a mincer or grinder. Form into burger or meatball shapes, coat in beaten egg white and breadcrumbs twice over and fry for about 8 minutes each side, depending on size. Serve with a tomato sauce (page 132) or cooked tomatoes.

Kololak gekharkuni

500 g (1 lb) minced beef
60 g (2 oz) butter or margarine
1 tablespoon flour
150 ml (¼ pint) milk
2 tablespoons fresh coriander
   leaves   OR 3 tablespoons parsley
1 tablespoon fresh parsley
½ teaspoon ground black pepper
¾ teaspoon salt
2 medium onions, chopped
2 tablespoons vodka or brandy
1 egg
stock for cooking meatballs

Traditionally the meat for *kololak*, lamb or beef according to the various recipes, is beaten with a mallet until it becomes soft and almost like a dough. It is then seasoned and further beaten until it begins to look whitish. The process can be cut short and made effort-less if you have an electric meat grinder or food processor. Melt the butter in a pan, add the flour, cook for a couple of minutes, stirring, then slowly add the milk until you have a smooth thick sauce. When it has cooled slightly, add this to the meat with the herbs, seasoning, onion, spirits and egg. Put the whole mixture into the liquidizer for a minute, adding a couple of tablespoons of water if the mixture is too thick. A processor will deal more easily with a thick mixture. You should have a fairly uniform, elastic, soufflé-like mass when you have finished.

    Drop the meat mixture a heaped tablespoonful at a time into sim-mering stock and cook gently. The meatballs are done when they rise to the surface. Serve the *kololak* with bulghur wheat cooked separately in stock.

Tomato sauces vary from Central Russia to the Caucasus and from one Southern republic to another, mainly in their use of local herbs. Russian recipes used to rely on easily available crops such as carrot and parsley root, but nowadays southern herbs and spices are easily obtained outside their natural habitat. Tomatoes were introduced to Russia only in the eighteenth century, whereas they have always played an important part in Caucasian cooking.

Tomato sauce (1)
An Armenian recipe.

> 2 onions
> 1 tablespoon butter
> 1 tablespoon flour
> 200 ml (⅓ pint) stock
> 3 tablespoons tomato purée
> 1 teaspoon wine vinegar
> ½ teaspoon black pepper
> 2 tablespoons chopped fresh parsley and basil (half quantity if dried)

Soften the onions in the butter, sprinkle with the flour and cook for a couple of minutes. Gradually add the warm stock, stirring all the time, and the remaining ingredients. Simmer gently for 10 minutes. Serve with plain *kotlety*.

Tomato sauce (2)
A Georgian recipe.

> 1 kg (2 lb) tinned or fresh tomatoes
> ½–1 head of garlic, chopped
> 2 teaspoons cayenne pepper
> 3 teaspoons *suneli* (see page 24)
> 2 teaspoons crushed coriander seeds
> salt and sugar to taste

Cook the tomatoes over a gentle heat until soft, pass through a sieve, return to the pan with the other ingredients and season with salt and a little sugar if liked. Cook for a further 5–10 minutes, reducing the sauce to the thickness required. It is usually served as a thick purée.

Tomato sauce (3)
A Moldavian sauce. Make meatballs by following the recipe for *bitki* (page 129) and adding onion and garlic to taste. The sauce is made with wine.

½ carrot
½ leek
1 tablespoon fresh parsley plus a few stalks, finely chopped
1 tablespoon fresh celery leaves and 1 tablespoon chopped
  celery
1 tablespoon oil or butter
1 tablespoon flour
6 tablespoons stock
200 ml (⅓ pint) tomato juice or 3 tablespoons tomato purée
salt to taste
6 black peppercorns
red (cayenne) pepper to taste
1 teaspoon sugar
½ teaspoon wine vinegar
4–5 tablespoons white or red wine

Soften the carrot, leek, parsley and celery in the oil or butter, sprinkle with the flour, then add the stock, tomato juice or purée, season with salt, and add all the remaining ingredients except the wine. Cook gently for 10–15 minutes. Add the wine, remove from the heat and serve.

SAUSAGES AND SAUSAGE-TYPE MIXTURES

Like all cuisines with a strong peasant element, Russian cooking makes great use of offal. Russian sausages of the continental variety are known collectively as *kolbasy*. Small sausages to be eaten hot have a name like our own word, *sosiski*. Both are mainstays of the quick food trade and the basis of packed lunches, snacks and suppers at home and on the move.

The idea of stuffing chopped meat and grain or meal into some part of an animal's gut or gullet we owe to the Romans. Russian cookery has a recipe as old and revered in this tradition as the haggis and faggots of our own island. Whereas the Scots stuff the paunch and pluck of a sheep into a sheep's stomach and the Welsh use pig's liver and lights stuffed into a pig's caul, Russian *sal'nik* stuffs a sheep's caul (the fatty membrane around the intestines) with sheep's (lamb's) liver and adds three classic local ingredients: buckwheat, dried mushrooms and sour cream. Another recipe, *nyanya*, stuffs a sheep's stomach with meat stripped from the head and trotters, and buckwheat. A third, *perepecha*, is liver baked in a sheep's stomach, but contains no grain or meal. It is highly flavoured with garlic.

To make these recipes viable today I have assumed that most people will not have the time or inclination to procure the necessary innards from the butcher. I suggest instead baking two of these excellent, homely mixtures in a baking dish. *Sal'nik* makes a tasty hash and *perepecha* an excellent liver soufflé.

Sal'nik

> 500 g (1 lb) lamb's liver
> milk for soaking
> 150 g (5 oz) buckwheat (uncooked weight)
> 2 medium onions
> butter or oil
> 2 eggs
> 100 g (3½ oz) fresh mushrooms
> ⅔ small (5 fl oz) carton sour cream

Soak the liver in milk for a couple of hours. Simmer it in boiling water until just cooked, remove and chop finely. Cook the buckwheat in boiling water until tender (see page 174). Mix the liver with the onions, softened in butter or oil, the cooked buckwheat and the chopped mushrooms, also softened in butter. Bind with the sour cream, season and pile into a buttered baking dish. Bake in a slow to medium oven, covered, for 1–1½ hours. Serve with a plain vegetable.

Perepecha

> 750 g (1½ lb) lamb's liver
> 100–150 ml (⅛–¼ pint) milk
> 1 onion
> ½ head of garlic
> black pepper to taste
> 2 eggs

Soak the liver in the milk. Drain, reserving the milk. Simmer in boiling water until just cooked, chop finely and pound to a smooth paste with the finely chopped onion and garlic and the pepper. Beat the eggs into the reserved milk and stir into the liver mixture. (A good liquidizer will do all this in one go and relieve you of the pounding.) Pour into a buttered soufflé dish and bake uncovered in a slow oven for 2–3 hours or until set. I find this dish is best complemented by a good tomato sauce (no. 1 or no. 3, page 132).

BRAINS

Brains are a delicacy that seems to have gone out of fashion in Britain. They were once very popular in Russia as the most refined of offal dishes. The standard preparation followed the French model and is given below.

> 2 pairs of brains (calf's, lamb's or sheep's)
> 2 tablespoons vinegar
> salt
> 2–3 bay leaves
> a few black peppercorns
> seasoned flour for coating
> 4 tablespoons butter
> 1 lemon
> chopped parsley or dill

Soak the brains in cold water for 40 minutes, remove the film and place them in a saucepan. Cover with cold water, add the vinegar, salt, bay leaves and peppercorns, and bring to the boil. Simmer for about 30 minutes. Allow to cool in the bouillon, remove, dry gently and divide the pairs in two.

Coat in seasoned flour and fry in butter for a few minutes each side. Serve with more melted butter, lemon juice and chopped parsley or dill. Accompany with plain boiled potatoes, tomato purée and boiled carrots.

Fried brains may also be served in dill sauce (page 130).

VEAL

Boiled veal in sour cream sauce

> 500 g (1 lb) stewing veal
> a court-bouillon containing 1 carrot, 1 parsnip or parsley
>   root, 1 chopped onion, a bay leaf and a few peppercorns,
>   a little salt
> 1 tablespoon butter
> 1 tablespoon flour
> ⅔ small (5 fl oz) carton sour cream
> 1 teaspoon sugar or to taste
> salt and pepper
> chopped fresh parsley

Simmer the veal in the court-bouillon until tender. Make a roux with the butter and flour, reduce the liquid in which the veal was cooked to about 200 ml (⅓ pint), strain and add gradually to the pan, stirring all the time to make a smooth sauce. Add the sour cream and sugar and test for seasoning. Pour over the veal and gently beat through. Sprinkle with chopped parsley and serve with boiled potatoes.

Veal escalopes with brains
These are open *zrazy* with a luxurious cream and brain filling.

> 1 pair of brains
> 4 veal escalopes
> a handful of fresh white breadcrumbs
> butter
> ½ onion
> fresh parsley to taste
> 2 teaspoons flour
> 2 tablespoons sour cream
> a little milk if necessary
> 1 egg yolk

Prepare the brains in a court-bouillon as above (page 135). Beat the veal into very thin slices and lightly cook on one side until just done (no longer than 5 minutes). Place the veal cooked side down in a buttered baking dish. Divide the brains in two, cut one half into slices about half a finger thick, and lay these on top of the escalopes. Follow the brains with a sprinkling of breadcrumbs, dot with butter and put in the oven to keep warm. Meanwhile soften the onion and parsley in butter, rub the remaining brains through a sieve or pound until smooth, add them to the pan, sprinkle with the flour and stir in the sour cream. Allow the mixture to thicken, adding more cream or milk to bring it to the consistency of a thick sauce, and remove from the heat. When it cools slightly add the beaten yolk, pour the mixture over the cutlets and bake in a medium oven for 15 minutes.

Galya (Azerbaijani veal stew)

> 500 g (1 lb) stewing veal
> 1 head of garlic
> 3 medium onions
> 50–75 g (2–3 oz) butter
> 200 ml (⅓ pint) water

100 g (3½ oz) lentils, preferably green or brown (soaked
   overnight)
200 g (7 oz) shelled chestnuts
4 tablespoons almonds, hazelnuts or filberts
2 teaspoons dried thyme
1 tablespoon dried mint
200 g (7 oz) dried cherries or apricots (soaked overnight)
stock
1 tablespoon fresh parsley

Brown the cubed meat and chopped garlic and onions in the butter.
Add 200 ml (⅓ pint) of water and the soaked lentils. Leave to cook in a
slow oven or on the stove. After 45 minutes add the peeled and
cooked chestnuts, the chopped nuts, the dried thyme and mint and
the soaked dried fruit. Add stock as required and leave to cook for
another 40 minutes. Add the parsley for the last 5 minutes of cooking.

KEBAB, SHISH KEBAB AND SHASHLYK

All these terms mean meat, either lamb or beef, on a skewer and
served with a rice *plov* (pilaff). The cooking of meat this way was
introduced from the Caucasus in the mid nineteenth century. By that
time the area covered by the three modern republics of Georgia,
Armenia and Azerbaijan had all been absorbed into the Russian
empire. Enterprising chefs set up special restaurants in Moscow to
introduce the new cuisine and its wines. From these beginnings are
descended the *shashlychnayas* common in Russian cities. They are
generally quick, cheap cafés that sometimes specialize in *shashlyk* and
do not always produce very memorable dishes. The best *shashlyk* is
cooked over open fires in the countryside, and is a great attraction for
Russian city dwellers in summer.

   The *shish* in *shish kebab* and the *shash-* in *shashlyk* mean that the
cooking is done over a spit. *Kebab* is a Turkish word. *Shashlyk* is a
Russian word derived from the Arabic, and it was from Russian that it
passed into French. Meat cooked this way is popular throughout the
Balkans and the Middle East, but not all kebabs are cooked over a spit.
Caucasian versions also include meat, usually lamb, cooked delici-
ously in its own juices in a heavy iron pan. The meat is usually
marinated before cooking.

   It is a myth that *shashlyk* was originally served in the Caucasus on a
sword. Use skewers.

Mtsvadi-Basturma
This is one variety of Georgian *shashlyk*, made with marinated beef.

> 500 g (1 lb) fillet steak
> 1–2 tablespoons wine vinegar
> 2 onions
> salt and black pepper
> 1 tablespoon crushed coriander seed
> lemon and spring onions to garnish

Chop the meat into cubes, place in an enamel dish and cover with the vinegar, chopped onions, seasoning and coriander. Leave for up to 3 days in the refrigerator, turning the meat occasionally to make sure it marinates evenly. Thread the meat on metal skewers and cook over hot charcoal or under a hot grill for 8–10 minutes. Do not overcook, especially if using a grill where the heat is likely to be fiercer. Turn the skewers once or twice during cooking. The meat should be slightly crisp on the outside but succulent inside. Garnish with chopped spring onion and a wedge of lemon, and serve with raw tomatoes.

Shashlyk po karski
Lamb *shashlyk* as cooked in the Caucasian and Central Asian republics is basted with *kurdyuk*, fat from the so-called fat-tailed lamb native to the region. Slices of this fat are also placed on the skewer alongside the meat to keep it from becoming dry. No other lamb or mutton fat compares with it:

> Unlike ordinary mutton and lamb fat, which tends to be tallowy, the fat of this sheep does not completely liquefy when it is rendered, but retains a residue of minute, wonderfully flavoured grains of crackling. The rendered fat can be used for cooking and as a spread it equals – and some would say, surpasses – butter.
> HELEN AND GEORGE PAPASHVILY, *The Cooking of Russia*

Regrettably we must do without. *Shashlyk po karski*, probably named after the ancient Armenian city of Kars in what is now north-eastern Turkey, close to the Soviet border, remains one of the best kebab recipes.

> 500 g (1 lb) lamb fillet
>
> FOR THE MARINADE
> juice of 2 small onions
> ¼–½ lemon (juice and pulp)

2 teaspoons brandy
¾ teaspoon salt
½ teaspoon black pepper
a few crushed dill seeds
1 teaspoon crushed coriander seeds
½ tablespoon dried or 1 tablespoon fresh basil
2–3 allspice berries, crushed
1 clove
½ tablespoon wine vinegar

Combine all the marinade ingredients. Chop the lamb into cubes, combine in a bowl or inside a plastic bag in a bowl, and leave for about 8 hours or overnight. Cook on skewers as in the previous recipe. Brush with oil from time to time if liked, though I do not find this necessary provided the kebabs are cooked quickly and the meat is good. Serve with fresh herbs (coriander, parsley), chopped onion, tomatoes and flat bread, plain rice, or fruit *plov* (page 179).

Kazan kebab

This is an Uzbek speciality, named after the heavy-bottomed cast iron pan, *kazanka*, in which the lamb is cooked in its own fat and juices.

500 g (1 lb) lamb
350 g (12 oz) onion, sliced in rings
1 teaspoon red (cayenne) pepper
salt
fresh herbs (coriander, parsley, thyme, mint) to taste

Season the meat, cut in cubes and mix with the onions. The mixture should half fill the pan, which must have a heavy bottom and preferably be made of iron otherwise the dish will stick. It should also have a lid which can be tightly closed. *Kazan kebab* is cooked slowly for about an hour, adding the herbs for the last 10 minutes.

Lyula-kebab

Kebabs are also made with ground lamb, flavoured with parsley, onion and ground coriander, moistened with water or milk and bound with fresh breadcrumbs to make *lyula-kebab*. The mixture is formed into small sausage shapes, fried in butter or oil, and served immediately with spring onions and a slice of lemon.

STUFFED CABBAGE LEAVES AND OTHER VEGETABLES

Stuffed vegetables are popular all over Russia and are considered national dishes to the north-west in Lithuania and to the south in Armenia. Stuffings resemble the mixtures of grain, meat and seasonings given for *kotlety* and *bitki*, and are wrapped in whatever vegetables and fruit are plentiful locally. The North acquired the dish from the Tartars as early as the fourteenth century, using cabbage leaves to prepare *golubtsy*. The South made *dolma* (Moldavia) or *tolma* (Armenia) in the original tradition by stuffing vine leaves, aubergines, tomatoes, peppers, marrow, onions and apples with a delicious mixture of minced lamb and spices. Central Russian cooking has happily reabsorbed this southern influence with the greater availability of exotic vegetables. The smaller vegetables, such as tomatoes, onions and peppers, make ideal hot or occasionally cold *zakuski* with a meat or purely vegetable filling, while the larger vegetables stuffed have given way to some excellent vegetarian dishes.

Golubtsy
Choose large fresh Dutch or Savoy cabbage leaves. Gently flatten the stalks by beating them with a meat mallet, then either blanch them by dropping them into boiling salted water for 3 minutes, or wrap them together in tin foil and put them in a medium to hot oven for 5–7 minutes. (The latter method results in tastier, more elastic leaves and is to be recommended.) For the filling, lamb, beef or pork are suitable with rice, millet, barley or bulghur wheat and chopped onion. The meat need not be too lean, as this tends to make the stuffing dry. Herbs vary from recipe to recipe and region to region. Cook the grain, drain it and combine with the minced meat, lightly fried onion and seasoning. The stuffing is placed on the flat leaf which is then rolled up tightly like a sausage. It should be big enough to allow several turns. Sauces, which are essential accompaniments to *golubtsy*, also vary from region to region.

Basic recipe for golubtsy

> 500 g (1 lb) lamb, beef or pork
> 90 g (3 oz) grain (uncooked weight)
> 1 onion
> 1 egg
> 1–2 teaspoons dried or 1–2 tablespoons fresh herbs

Mince the meat and cook the grain in boiling water till tender. Combine the minced meat, cooked grain and other ingredients, roll up in the leaves, and cook uncovered in a medium oven for 30–40 minutes in a tomato and sour cream sauce (see below).

For Lithuanian *golubtsy*, which are made with pork, add 150 g (5 oz) boiled and chopped mushrooms and a scant teaspoon of marjoram to the filling, and cook the cabbage rolls in a mushroom and sour cream sauce (see below).

Tomato and sour cream sauce

> 1 tablespoon butter
> 1 tablespoon flour
> 200 ml (⅓ pint) water
> 2 tablespoons tomato purée
> sour cream to taste

Make a roux with the butter and flour, add the warm water, and when the mixture thickens add the tomato purée and sour cream. Season, bring to the boil gently and pour over the *golubtsy* before baking in the oven.

Mushroom and sour cream sauce

> liquid from boiling 150 g (5 oz) fresh or 10 dried mushrooms
>   in 500 ml (¾ pint) water reduced to about 200 ml (⅓ pint)
> ⅔ small (5 fl oz) carton sour cream

Mix the two ingredients together and pour over the *golubtsy* before baking in the oven.

In Armenia stuffed cabbage leaves are steamed, surrounded with sourish fruit, such as damsons, and served with plain yoghurt or yoghurt and garlic.

Dolma/Tolma

> 2–3 tablespoons cooked rice or bulghur wheat
> 3 onions, chopped
> 1–2 eggs (optional)
> 500 g (1 lb) lamb
> up to 1 head of garlic, minced
> 1 tablespoon each fresh coriander, parsley and basil

2 tablespoons fresh thyme (or 1 tablespoon dried)
3 teaspoons fresh mint (or 1½ tablespoons dried)
black pepper to taste

Prepare the vegetables and fruit in the following ways:

Cabbage – as for *golubtsy* (page 140).

Tomatoes, peppers – cut off a 'lid' that can be replaced. Scoop out the seeds. Blanch peppers in boiling water.

Aubergines – cut lengthways to provide a long lid. Remove the seeds and some of the flesh from the bottom half to make a hollow.

Marrow – cut in half lengthways, scoop out seeds, blanch.

Onions – blanch, wiped but unpeeled, in boiling water for 2 minutes and remove the centre.

Apples and quinces – cut off a replaceable 'lid' and scoop out a hollow inside, leaving the walls of the fruit fairly thick. Cook quinces in boiling water for 5 minutes.

Combine the cooked grain, onions, beaten egg (if used), minced meat, garlic and herbs, season well, and stuff the vegetables with the mixture.

Most stuffed vegetables are cooked in a little bouillon in a pan or casserole, either mixed or all of one kind. The spaces between them may be filled with slices of apple, quince, apricot, onion and sour prunes (plums, damsons). Marrow, however, should be cooked alone in a tomato sauce or bouillon.

Serve with the fruit and bouillon from the pan, and a little yoghurt if liked. A plain stuffed marrow cooked in bouillon is excellent with yoghurt and garlic.

CHANAKHI AND CHAKHOKHBILI

These are simple, typical and very tasty Georgian stews which have become favourites with Russians. They vary only in the way they are cooked, though *chanakhi* is restricted to lamb while *chakhokhbili* may be made with lamb, beef or chicken. Fresh herbs are used liberally.

Chanakhi

500 g (1 lb) stewing lamb
500 g (1 lb) onions
500 g (1 lb) potatoes
500 g (1 lb) aubergines

500 g (1 lb) tomatoes, fresh or tinned
2 tablespoons butter or olive oil
1 tablespoon fresh basil
2 tablespoons fresh coriander
salt and freshly ground black pepper
½ teaspoon red pepper
200 ml (⅓ pint) tomato juice

Cut the meat into cubes, slice the onions and potatoes finely and cut the aubergines and tomatoes into largish pieces. (The tomatoes can be left whole if preferred.) Place the meat in a buttered casserole and cover with the vegetables, the butter or oil and the herbs and black and red pepper. Pour over the tomato juice, season lightly, and bake covered in a medium oven for 1½–2 hours. Add water if the dish becomes dry during cooking.

Chakhokhbili with lamb or beef

500 g (1 lb) lamb or beef, cubed
400 g (12 oz) onions
salt and black pepper
500 g (1 lb) tomatoes
1 tablespoon each fresh parsley, thyme or savory, coriander
   and basil
1 teaspoon red (cayenne) pepper
½–1 head garlic

FOR LAMB ONLY

3 potatoes
½ tablespoon each fresh dill, mint and tarragon

Fry the meat without additional oil or fat in a heavy-bottomed pan for 10 minutes, stirring to prevent it sticking, then add the chopped onions, cook for a further 5 minutes and season lightly. Skin the tomatoes and cook until soft in a separate pan. Parboil the potatoes, if using. Put the meat, tomatoes and potatoes together and cook for another 15 minutes, covered. Add the fresh herbs and red pepper and cook over a gentle heat for another 5 minutes. Add the finely chopped garlic, replace the lid and allow the *chakhokhbili* to stand for 5 minutes before serving.

For *chakhokhbili* made with chicken see p. 158.

Lamb with apricots
Another Armenian dish which is very simple to prepare.

500 g (1 lb) lamb
75 g (3 oz) butter or oil
200 g (7 oz) onion
200 g (7 oz) dried apricots (soaked for a few hours)
1½ tablespoons tomato purée
fresh green herbs to taste
freshly grated black pepper

Boil the meat in water on or off the bone for an hour, then remove from the pan, reserving the liquid. Bone the meat, cut it into smallish pieces, and fry lightly in butter or oil with the chopped onion. Add about 200 ml (⅓ pint) of the strained liquid left over from the first cooking, and the remaining ingredients. Cook gently, covered, for 15–20 minutes or until the meat is tender. Add more stock if the dish becomes dry. Check the seasoning and serve.

Boiled lamb with turnips
A homely, very economical Russian family dish.

1 kg (2 lb) lamb
salt and freshly ground black pepper
4–5 medium-sized turnips
1 leek
1 onion
1 parsnip or parsley root
½ tablespoon butter
½ tablespoon flour
fresh dill and parsley, chopped

Cut the lamb into two or three large pieces, bring to the boil in a pan of water, remove the scum from the surface, and cook for 50 minutes. Reduce the stock, add salt and the vegetables cut into smallish pieces, and cook until tender. The stock should just cover the meat and vegetables. Make a roux with the butter and flour, dilute with a little of the cooking liquid and add to the pan. Bring to the boil once, stirring all the time. Serve in one dish, sprinkled with dill, parsley and black pepper.

Boiled lamb with cumin or caraway sauce

Bring the lamb (shoulder or leg) to the boil in a pan of water, skim the surface, add a bay leaf, peppercorns, a little salt, a carrot and a small onion, and cook gently until the lamb is tender (about 1 hour). It may be boned or served as it is with the following sauce.

1 tablespoon butter
1 tablespoon flour
1 dessertspoon cumin or caraway seed
1 teaspoon sugar or to taste
1 teaspoon vinegar or to taste
salt and black pepper

Make a roux with the butter and flour, thin with 200 ml (⅓ pint) of the liquid in which the lamb was cooked, and add the remaining ingredients. Adjust the seasoning and serve poured over the lamb. Dill sauce (page 130) is also excellent with lamb.

Lamb with chick peas and tomatoes

An Uzbek dish that reminds me of cassoulet.

500 g (1 lb) chick peas (soaked for 24 hours)
500 g (1 lb) lamb
150 g (5 oz) butter or oil
500 g (1 lb) tomatoes
salt and freshly ground black pepper

Cook the soaked chick peas in boiling water without salt for 2–3 hours until almost tender. Drain, reserving the liquid. Cut the meat into small pieces and brown in butter or oil and butter. Add the chick peas to the pan and continue cooking for 10 minutes. Add about 6 table-spoons of water (or reserved chick pea liquid) and cook until the peas are tender. Add the quartered tomatoes and continue cooking, covered, for 10–15 minutes over a very low heat. Season and serve.

The same kind of dish is made in Armenia, using haricot beans and adding 4 chopped onions to the pan as the meat is browned.

PLOV

This is the Russian name for the rice dish popular from the Balkans to the East, known also as Pilaff, Pilau and Pilaw. One can be pedantic about the cooking of it and speak of it as an art, but I think Robin Howe has the right idea in his *Balkan Cooking* when he labels the technique 'basic principles and do as you please'. The important thing is not to end up with soggy, sticky rice which appeals neither to the eye nor to the palate. The *plov* served in Moscow restaurants specializing in Azerbaijani and Central Asian dishes (the Baku, the Uzbekistan) does not often make the grade.

For good results use Patna or Italian rice. The latter is particularly absorbent. The aim is to have the rice take in just the right amount of liquid, so that the pan is dry at the end of cooking. Cooking times vary with the different kinds of rice, but those given below should serve as a rough guide. Err on the dry side. Wash the rice thoroughly before cooking to remove the starch from the grains – this will help avoid stickiness. Some Azerbaijani recipes also advocate soaking the rice in cold salted water after washing, about 5 hours for Italian-type rice and 7 hours for Patna.

Here are three classic cooking methods:

(1) Add the washed, soaked and dried rice to a heavy-bottomed deep pan in which you have melted butter or oil according to the recipe in which you are going to use the rice. Cook, stirring for a few minutes until all the grains are coated, then add 3 times the volume of the rice in cooking liquid. Cover tightly and cook over a medium heat for 10 minutes. Turn off the heat and allow the pan to stand without removing the lid for a further 10 minutes.

(2) Boil the washed and soaked rice for 8 minutes in plenty of salted water or until the outside of the grains begin to soften. Drain, pour cold water over, drain well again and complete the cooking by putting half the recipe quantity of oil or butter in the bottom of a heavy pan, then the rice, then the rest of the oil or butter, and closing the pan tightly. Cook over a medium heat for 5–10 minutes. Turn off the heat and allow the pan to stand without removing the lid for a further 5–10 minutes.

(3) Simmer the washed and soaked rice uncovered for 8 minutes in 2–3 times its volume of water or stock and half the recipe quantity of oil or butter until all the liquid is absorbed. Add the remaining oil or butter, cover the pan and cook for a further 5–10 minutes. Turn off the heat and allow the pan to stand without removing the lid for another 5–10 minutes.

A *kazmag*, a thin layer of dough which prevents the rice sticking to the pan, is prepared with noodle dough in the following proportions: 180 g (6 oz) flour to 1 egg, ½ teaspoon salt and 2–4 tablespoons cold water. Mix until smooth. Roll out thinly and cut with a saucepan lid into a round to fit the bottom of the pan. Do not forget to oil the pan before you put in the *kazmag*. It will absorb the butter and juices and should be served with the *plov*. It can be used with either the second or the third method above.

In an Azerbaijani meal *plov* is considered the centrepiece, served after soup and a main meat or game dish, and before the sweetmeats, sherbets and tea. It is made with a different meat from whatever was served before it. For this reason the proportion of meat to rice in the recipes below may seem skimpy. It may be increased and the amount of rice (and correspondingly, other ingredients) reduced to serve as a single dish for supper.

Lamb plov (1)

200 g (7 oz) rice
pinch of saffron
500 g (1 lb) lamb
50–75 g (2–3 oz) butter or oil
3 onions
1 pomegranate
150–200 g (6–8 oz) sour plums (or prunes, soaked in water
     with 1 tablespoon lemon juice)
2 tablespoons raisins
fresh mint, watercress, spring onions, garlic shoots for
     garnish

In Azerbaijani recipes the meat and rice are cooked separately, with the meat left on the bone and the rice cooked in water. Cook the rice with the saffron according to any of the methods given above. Chop the meat on or off the bone into smallish pieces, and brown it in a little butter or oil in a heavy-bottomed pan over a high heat. Add the chopped onions, the pomegranate juice, the stoned fruit, the raisins and a little boiling water, and simmer, covered, over a low heat for 30–45 minutes or in the oven. About 100 ml (⅛ pint) of unsweetened apple juice or grape juice may be used instead of the pomegranate juice.

Serve the lamb and the rice together, garnished with fresh mint, watercress, chopped spring onions (including the green part), and, if you grow your own garlic, the young green shoots, chopped.

VARIATIONS

The lamb may be cooked without fruit, but with the addition of chopped garlic to taste and fresh herbs. Pumpkin and/or cooked chestnuts may also be added. Yoghurt is used as a dressing for *plov* in Armenia.

Lamb plov (2)

The Uzbek way of preparing *plov* cooks the meat and the rice together with an unusual combination of spices – red pepper, caraway and dried barberries – and a pinch of turmeric to colour the rice.

250 g (8 oz) or more lamb off the bone
250 g (8 oz) carrots
3 onions
125 g (4 oz) oil/butter (usually a combination of vegetable oil and animal fat such as rendered beef or lamb fat)
500 g (1 lb) rice
1 cup raisins (optional)
1 teaspoon turmeric
½ teaspoon red pepper
½ teaspoon caraway seed
½ teaspoon dried barberries (if obtainable)
½ teaspoon salt
about 300 ml (½ pint) water

Chop the meat into smallish pieces, dice or cut the carrot into thin strips and chop the onions. Braise the meat, carrots and onions quickly in the oil over a fairly high heat, stirring regularly. Lower the heat gradually and cook for 20–30 minutes, then add the washed and soaked rice, the raisins which have been previously soaked in water, turmeric, pepper, caraway, barberries, salt and the water. In theory the rice is not mixed in with the meat but is left to cook as a separate layer for another 20 minutes. Check that the pan does not become too dry, adding more water if necessary. Turn off the heat and leave the pan to stand without removing the lid for 15 minutes. This is probably easier to achieve in a casserole in the oven than on top of the stove. Serve the meat and vegetables on the rice.

In Armenia and Uzbekistan *plov* is also prepared with bulghur wheat, which may be substituted in equal quantity for the rice in the above recipe

For chicken *plov* see (page 150).

For Vegetarian *plovs* see *Vegetables, Vegetarian and Grain Dishes* (page 173).

For other lamb dishes see *Soups and Light Stews* (page 55).

POULTRY

Poultry ranks second to game in the best Russian cooking of the past, but being one of the richest and most nourishing ingredients in the peasant diet, it has encouraged some excellent simple dishes like goose and cabbage and duck with apples. Goose and duck were most popular in Western Russia and the Baltics, where the fat was considered good protection from the cold. Under French and Caucasian influence the repertoire was considerably extended to include more chicken and turkey dishes. Cream, tomatoes, herbs and more exotic fruits than the humble apple were excellent complements for the lean, dry flesh of these birds. The Soviet era has also seen culinary invention where chicken is concerned, partly at least because it is cheap to mass-produce and a good substitute for scarce red meat. Chicken Kiev turns up on almost all international Russian hotel menus.

I have a suspicion nevertheless that nineteenth-century Russian connoisseurs liked their chicken above all to taste like game. In the older cookery books there are instructions for feeding pullets on juniper berries in the last few weeks before killing to give them a rich flavour. Other gastronomically-minded landowners fed their pullets on corn and killed them young, sometimes as early as 6 weeks old and not later than 13 weeks. According to one source these very young birds, boiled according to the favourite Russian way with young, tender meat, were eaten in large quantities in early spring. They were called 'the great martyrs', and were prepared with juniper berries or served with crayfish.

Roast chicken or turkey
Roast the bird in the manner preferred. Serve with chopped green onion and sour cream salad, with a savoury fruit salad, with pickled cucumbers, or with fresh green herbs and a slice of lemon.

Chicken, lemon, chestnut and nut plov

> 250 g (9 oz) rice
> pinch of saffron or turmeric
> 180 g (6 oz) shelled chestnuts
> 2 large onions, chopped
> 30 g (1 oz) chopped almonds
> 180 g (6 oz) sour plums or prunes (previously soaked)
> 1 head of garlic with the green shoots if available
> 150 g (5 oz) butter

½ tablespoon dried thyme
½ teaspoon salt
1 roasting chicken
½ teaspoon red or black pepper
1 teaspoon cinnamon
150 ml (¼ pint) pomegranate, grape or apple juice
fresh watercress, tarragon and mint
1 egg
lemon juice to taste

Cook the rice with the saffron according to one of the methods given for *plov* above (page 146). Peel the chestnuts and simmer in water for about ½ hour. Lightly fry the onions, almonds, plums or soaked prunes, chestnuts and garlic (reserve the shoots) in the butter, add the thyme and season with salt. Season the chicken inside with salt, the pepper and the cinnamon, and stuff with the fruit and nut mixture. Sew up and roast, basting with the pomegranate juice and the juices in the pan several times during cooking. Divide the chicken into serving portions, with the rice and the stuffing in separate dishes, or alternatively arrange the three components on a large plate, the chicken on the rice surrounded by the stuffing. Sprinkle with the chopped fresh garlic shoots, watercress, tarragon and mint. Pour the juices from the pan including the fat over the chicken and rice, followed by the raw egg well beaten with one or more tablespoons of lemon juice.

Chicken Kiev

This is a Soviet hotel and restaurant classic which has no pre-revolutionary history as far as I have been able to discover. It is simple, perhaps a little too simple and bland for many tastes, but can be improved by serving with lemon wedges and a good salad and a fresh herb garnish.

4 chicken fillets
150 g (4–5 oz) butter
seasoning to taste
beaten egg
fresh breadcrumbs
oil for frying

Prepare the fillets by removing the breast portions from 2 chickens, with the wing bones attached. This is not as difficult if you use a skinned fresh chicken. Cut with a sharp knife close to the bone, starting at the breast bone and working back. The fillet divides naturally into one large and one long thin 'mignon' fillet. Beat the larger fillet with a meat mallet as you would veal escalope. Use the mignon fillet to patch up any tears or just roll it in with the butter.

Cut the butter into 4 fingers, wrap each finger in a cutlet which has been well seasoned, seal the edges as best you can with a little extra butter, and refrigerate. The cutlets should be chilled for an hour or so, or put briefly in the ice box or freezer after they have been rolled around the butter. That way they keep their shape and their butter. Dip the cutlets twice in egg and breadcrumbs and deep fry in the oil for 3 or 4 minutes. Serve immediately with fresh chopped herbs, fresh green peas, and raw tomatoes.

The butter may be garlic, dill or parsley butter. The herbs and a little salt are mixed into the butter when it is soft, but *not* melting, and the butter then reshaped and put to harden in the refrigerator before use.

Chicken cutlets with cashew nuts
A variation on Chicken Kiev.

> 4 chicken breasts + 150 g (5 oz) chicken flesh
> 1 onion, chopped
> 50 g (2 oz) cashew nuts, chopped
> 50 g (2 oz) butter
> salt and black pepper
> 1 egg
> breadcrumbs for coating
> butter for frying

Flatten the chicken breasts with a meat mallet until they are quite thin. Mince the rest of the chicken with the onion and the chopped nuts, add the butter and seasoning and mix well. Spread the mixture on to the fillets and roll them tightly. Leave them in the refrigerator for a couple of hours to harden, then dip them in egg and white breadcrumbs and fry in butter. Serve with rice, or a sweet *plov* and fresh herbs.

Pozharsky cutlets
A man called Pozharsky apparently kept a hotel on the road from Moscow to St Petersburg in the middle of the last century and made his reputation with chicken and partridge cutlets which he served

with sliced mushrooms. A contemporary French chef set down the following recipe:

> about 500 g (1 lb) chicken flesh (from a 3 lb chicken)
> butter equal in volume to ¼ of the chicken
> white breadcrumbs
> a little milk
> salt, pepper, nutmeg to taste
> flour, egg and fresh breadcrumbs for coating
> butter for frying

Mince the chicken finely by putting twice through the grinder or mincer. Mix with the softened butter, and the breadcrumbs soaked in milk and squeezed out. Season with salt, pepper and nutmeg, form into a dough, roll in flour and divide into smallish portions in the shape of cutlets. Roll again in flour, dip twice in beaten egg and fresh breadcrumbs, and cook in hot butter for about 5 minutes each side. Serve around a plate of diced, cooked mushrooms in sour cream.

Boiled chicken with sour cherry and raisin or gooseberry sauce

> 1 small boiling fowl
> 1 onion
> 1 carrot
> 1 *bouquet garni*
> 200 g (8 oz) fresh cherries ⎫   OR
> 50 g (2 oz) raisins ⎪   200 g (8 oz)
> 2–3 tablespoons chopped fresh parsley ⎬   gooseberries or
> 1 tablespoon chopped fresh dill ⎭   plums
> 25 g (1 oz) flour
> 25 g (1 oz) butter
> 1 wine glass table wine (optional)

Boil the chicken until tender in a court-bouillon of water, onion, carrot and a *bouquet garni*. Remove, skin, and cut into portions either on or off the bone. Keep warm. Reduce the cooking liquid to a good, well-flavoured stock and pour over the fruit and herbs so that they are just covered. Simmer gently until the fruit is soft. Thicken with the flour and butter cooked to a roux. Add the wine and serve the chicken in the sauce, accompanied by rice or another plain grain.

Boiled chicken may also be served in a thickened apple purée spiced with cinnamon.

Amich

CHICKEN OR TURKEY WITH ALMONDS AND APRICOTS
The Armenians have passed on to the Russians their enthusiasm for cooking meat and poultry with fruit, including this classic.

> 100 g (4 oz) rice
> 75 g (3 oz) butter
> salt and pepper
> 3 tablespoons dried apricots (soaked for a few hours or overnight)
> 3 tablespoons raisins (soaked for a few hours or overnight)
> 4 tablespoons blanched almonds or apricot or plum kernels
> a few hazelnuts
> 1 tablespoon fresh basil
> 3 cloves
> 1 teaspoon cinnamon
> 1 medium roasting chicken (double the amount of stuffing if using a small turkey)

Boil the rice until half-cooked, drain, fry lightly in a little of the butter, and remove from the pan to a bowl. Add a little more butter and season well. Fry the soaked dried fruit and the nuts in the remaining butter. Add the basil, cloves, and cinnamon, combine with the rice, and stuff the chicken with the mixture. Rub the chicken with butter, salt and pepper and roast for about 40 minutes per 500 g (1 lb) in a medium oven, adding about 6 tablespoons of water to the roasting pan. Baste occasionally with the liquid in the pan.

Turkey with apricots
A Moldavian dish.

> 500–750 g (1–1½ lb) turkey off the bone
> 2 tablespoons butter
> 2 large onions
> 6 tablespoons tomato juice or the equivalent in tomato purée diluted with water
> 1 teaspoon sugar
> ¼ teaspoon red pepper
> ½ teaspoon cinnamon
> ½ glass dry white wine
> 200 g (7 oz) fresh apricots
> 1 teaspoon wine vinegar

3 bay leaves
salt to taste
½ tablespoon flour
1 tablespoon each fresh chopped dill and parsley
½ a head of garlic

Chop the turkey into smallish pieces, brown them in butter and put in a heavy pan. Fry the chopped onion lightly, and add to the turkey with the tomato juice, sugar, red pepper, cinnamon and wine. Simmer for 30 minutes. Add the fresh apricots, vinegar, bay leaves and salt and cook for a further 12 minutes on a low heat. Make a roux with the flour and a little butter, dilute with a little of the liquid from the pan and add to the dish. Finish cooking for 2–3 minutes with the chopped fresh herbs and garlic. Leave to stand for another 5 minutes with a lid on before serving.

The same recipe may be followed for chicken and using plums instead of apricots.

Oven chicken

This recipe appeared in a women's magazine in 1914, just three years before the Revolution, and indicates the degree of French-influenced culinary sophistication which had become established in the middle-class kitchen. The Russian ingredients are still there – dill, *smetana*, mushrooms – but the finished dish has a smoothness and a finish that were learnt abroad.

1 large onion
500 g (1 lb) mushrooms
3 tablespoons butter
4 portions of chicken
salt and pepper
2 tablespoons flour
1 small (5 fl oz) carton sour cream
200 ml (⅓ pint) single cream, top of the milk or milk
2–3 tablespoons fresh dill, or 1 tablespoon or more dried, to taste
150 g (6 oz) flaky pastry

Slice the onion and the mushrooms finely. Melt a little butter in a saucepan and add the mushrooms, onions, chicken pieces and seasoning. Brown the chicken evenly, then sprinkle the contents of the pan with a teaspoon of flour and transfer to a baking dish in the oven to keep warm. Add the remaining butter to the pan, make a roux with the flour and gradually stir in the sour cream and the single cream or milk to make a fairly thick sauce. Add more milk as required. Stir in the dill, cook the sauce for a few minutes, then pour over the chicken. Cover the dish with a pastry top and bake in a medium oven for about 45 minutes.

Chicken tabaka

More of a method than a recipe in itself, Georgian chicken *tabaka* means boning a chicken down the middle so that it can be cooked flat under a heavy iron lid in a shallow pan. In the Soviet Union today these black cast iron pans with a ridged bottom may be bought very cheaply. You can manage without by using a heavy-bottomed frying pan and perhaps a handleless lid on which you can rest a heavy weight. My chicken *tabaka* lid weighs a good 5 kilograms (over 10 lb). The chicken is seasoned with red pepper and garlic several hours before cooking and is served traditionally with a vegetable and herb side-dish called *borani* (recipe below). Outside Georgia, however, it tends to be thought of as a dish in its own right and may be eaten just with fresh herbs and garlic. My favourite way is to serve it with a Georgian sauce, either tomato, walnut or garlic.

Remove the innards from the chicken and cut it lengthwise in half from the underside, removing the breast bone, so that it will lie flat. Beat it lightly with a meat mallet and lay it in an oiled heavy pan, folding the wings and the legs by making slits in the chicken to tuck the ends into. Rub with olive oil and season generously with salt and red pepper. You may insert thin slivers of garlic under the skin of the chicken or dust it with a little garlic powder if you like. The chicken may be cooked straight away, but is best left for a few hours or overnight in the refrigerator to allow the flavours to develop. Fry it in a little oil, butter or chicken fat under a weighted lid for about half an hour each side.

Borani

       500 g (1 lb) spinach
       salt
       3 tablespoons fresh chopped basil
       2 tablespoons fresh thyme
       2 tablespoons fresh coriander leaves
       3 large onions

butter
4 eggs
300 ml (½ pint) thin yoghurt or buttermilk
pinch of cinnamon
pinch of saffron or turmeric

Wash the spinach, and without shaking off the water put it in a pan. Add a pinch of salt and cook over a medium heat for no longer than 3 minutes. Drain, chop finely and mix with the fresh herbs and the chopped onion lightly fried in butter. Cook together for a minute in the buttered pan. Add the beaten eggs, mix well and cook for a further 2 minutes until the eggs set. For the *borani* and chicken make a dressing with the yoghurt by stirring in the cinnamon and the turmeric. Saffron if you have it should be infused in a little warm water first.

Borani may be varied by substituting aubergines or string beans for the spinach. All three variations are also served as vegetarian dishes (page 204).

Chicken *tabaka* may also be served with the Georgian tomato sauce given on page 132, or with one of the following:

Garo sauce

200 g (7 oz) shelled walnuts
3 tablespoons fresh coriander
4 cloves garlic
salt to taste
4 tablespoons wine vinegar
400 ml (⅔ pint) chicken stock
2 onions
2–3 egg yolks

Pound the walnuts, coriander, garlic and salt together. Add the vinegar and then the stock and stir to a smooth paste. Add the finely chopped onion and simmer for 10 minutes over a medium heat. When the liquid in the pan has cooled a little, beat the egg yolks, gradually introduce a little of the stock, and then add this mixture to the pan, stirring all the time. The eggs should not scramble. Pour over the chicken.

Garo sauce is also good with oven roasted turkey.

Garlic and vinegar sauce

> 2 heads of garlic
> salt
> 1 teaspoon fresh herbs (coriander, dill, parsley, basil,
>   tarragon)
> 2 chopped spring onions
> 4 tablespoons wine vinegar
> 4 tablespoons cold water

Pound the garlic in a mortar with salt. Add the herbs, chopped onion, vinegar and water, stirring to make a smooth mixture. Pour over the chicken.

Although it is mixing the cooking of one republic with another, the Moldavian garlic dressing *muzhdei*, given on page 121, is excellent with chicken.

Chicken chakhokhbili
A Georgian dish very popular with Russians for home entertaining.

> 1 chicken
> 2 tablespoons butter
> 3 large onions
> 450 g (1 lb) potatoes
> 750 g–1 kg (1½–2 lb) tomatoes, fresh or tinned
> white wine (optional)
> ½ teaspoon red pepper
> 1 teaspoon crushed coriander seeds
> 1 teaspoon *suneli* (see page 24)
> 1 teaspoon turmeric
> 1 tablespoon each parsley, thyme, coriander leaves, basil
> ½ tablespoon each mint and tarragon

Chop the chicken into about 10 pieces and put into a heated pan with a small quantity of butter. Cook covered for 5 minutes over a low heat, pour off and reserve the juices, then continue cooking uncovered for another 10 minutes. Add the chopped onion and the rest of the butter and cook for 5 minutes more. Boil the potatoes (I leave them unpeeled) and cut into 4 or 5 pieces each. Soften the tomatoes in a separate pan, skinning them first if you wish. Add first the tomatoes then the potatoes to the chicken. Add the reserved chicken juices, a little of the water used to cook the potatoes (or more extravagantly, white wine), the dry spices and the fresh herbs and cook for a final 5 minutes. Allow to stand off the heat without removing the lid for 5–10 minutes before serving.

Satsivi

COLD CHICKEN WITH WALNUT SAUCE

The essence of this cold dish is the walnut sauce. There are said to be some twenty legitimate varieties and they are unique of their kind in the world's cuisine. Georgia is almost the only country in the world where this rich, oily nut is used as an integral part of daily cooking and not just as a garnish for salads and cakes.

    1 chicken
    2 onions
    3 bay leaves
    $\frac{1}{2}$ tablespoon tarragon
    $\frac{1}{2}$ tablespoon thyme
    salt

Cook the chicken in enough water to cover it plus the onion and herbs for about half an hour, simmering it over a medium heat. Remove the chicken from the pan, rub with salt, and roast it breast down in a roasting pan in a medium oven with 2 tablespoons of the stock from boiling until it is done. Baste occasionally with the juices from the pan. Cut the chicken into about 10 pieces, pour over up to 600 ml (1 pint) of *satsivi* sauce (see below) and allow to cool. Serve lightly chilled.

    FOR THE SAUCE
    3 medium onions
    chicken fat
    $1\frac{1}{2}$–2 tablespoons flour
    400 ml ($\frac{2}{3}$ pint) chicken stock+a few tablespoons extra stock
    225 g (8 oz) shelled walnuts
    2–3 teaspoons minced garlic
    generous pinch red pepper
    1 teaspoon ground black pepper
    1 teaspoon ground coriander
    2 cloves
    $\frac{1}{2}$ teaspoon each cinnamon, turmeric, *suneli* (see page 24)
        and any fresh green herb

1 teaspoon wine vinegar
2 egg yolks (optional)

Fry the chopped onion in about 4 tablespoons of chicken fat until transparent. Stir in the flour, cook for a few minutes and gradually introduce the stock. Pound or grind the nuts and mix with the garlic, red and black pepper and coriander. Season to taste, dilute with a little extra stock and add to the onions. Cook for about 20 minutes. Add the cloves, cinnamon, turmeric, *suneli*, herbs and vinegar and heat gently for a further 5 minutes.

The quantity of nuts may be halved and 2 egg yolks added to thicken the sauce in the last 5 minutes of cooking.

OTHER CHICKEN RECIPES

Kurnik
See page 237.

Kharcho
See page 83.

Chorba
See page 86.

Cherry sauce for turkey

for 6 turkey portions:
500 g (1 lb) cherries
1 clove
¼ teaspoon cinnamon
¼ teaspoon powdered cardamom or 4 crushed seeds
pinch of mace
sugar to taste

Stone the cherries, reserving about 15 of the stones. Cook the cherries and spices over a gentle heat with a little water until you have a thick purée. Liquidize or rub through a sieve. Meanwhile crush the reserved cherry stones in a mortar, bring them to the boil in half a cup of water, strain and mix with the purée. Add sugar to taste and bring to the boil once before serving.

Liver stuffing for turkey
See stuffing for festive loin of pork (page 118).

Stuffings for roast goose

Roast goose was long the common man's festive dish, particularly in western Russia and the Baltics. Goose is so fat by today's standards that it needs no extra larding, but pork fat was traditionally used. Rub the goose inside and out with caraway and stuff it with peeled and quartered sour apples. Roast, and serve with baked onions and potatoes or grain.

Alternatively the stuffing may be sauerkraut, cooked with apples:

> 1–1½ kg (2–2½ lb) sauerkraut
> 100 g (4 oz) pork or bacon fat
> 3 onions
> 2 cooking apples
> 1 tablespoon caraway seeds
> salt
> 1 teaspoon ground allspice

Braise the sauerkraut in the fat for about 15 minutes, then add the chopped onions, sliced apples and caraway seeds. Rub the goose inside and out with salt and allspice and stuff with the sauerkraut mixture. Roast.

Stuffed goose neck

A favourite dish in both Russian and Jewish cooking, which may be served as a *zakuska* or a main course.

> 1 goose or chicken neck
> 1 goose liver or several chicken livers
> 100 g (4 oz) cooked chicken or goose
> 50 g (2 oz) stale breadcrumbs or cooked buckwheat
> 200 ml (⅓ pint) milk
> 1 large onion
> seasoning
> 2 eggs

Clean and bone the neck, remove the fat from the inside and put it through a mincer with all the ingredients except the milk and eggs. Stale bread may be soaked in some of the milk before mincing. Otherwise beat the milk and eggs together and add them to the minced mixture. Stuff the neck, not too tightly, and sew up the ends. Prick with a pin in several places and simmer in salted water for about an hour.

Alternatively cook the neck slowly in the oven for about 2 hours in a rich meaty stock or gravy. Serve sliced like a sausage, with a sauce made by thickening the stock and juices in the pan.

Roast duck
Most recipes for goose apply also to duck. Stuff a roasting bird with peeled, chopped apples, rubbing inside and out with salt and plenty of ground cumin, or fill the breast with a mixture of cooked mushrooms and buckwheat. Roast duck may also be served plain with various marinated salads, buckwheat and roast apples cooked separately.

Boiled duck with Savoy cabbage
Boil the duck in water with a carrot, an onion and a few bay leaves and peppercorns. Quarter a Savoy cabbage and plunge it into salted boiling water. Bring to the boil twice, then finish cooking in a thickened stock, made by lightly frying an onion in bacon fat, adding a little flour and then stock and nutmeg. Serve with the duck.

Leftover duck can be used in *shchi*, where it has a traditional place. Stock made from a duck's carcass is the traditional base for *Borshch Poltavsky*.

GAME

Russians hunt wild birds and larger game with an abiding enthusiasm. Before the Revolution great importance was attached to the appearance of roast game on the well-stocked dining table. The native hazel-grouse or hazel-hen (*ryabchik*), a smallish bird about the size of a pigeon, was unquestioned favourite. The novelist Vladimir Nabokov remembered it as the most prominent taste of his Russian childhood. In summer *ryabchik* was plentiful around St Petersburg,

The ryabchik *(hazel-hen), Russian's most favoured game bird, named after the vari-coloured plumage on its throat and breast. Illustration from S. T. Aksakov.*

where the Nabokov family estate lay. Though excellent, it could not have been called a recherché dish. Indeed, it seems to have been staple fare on Russian trains when it was still possible to dine in style on those vast journeys overland. The best *ryabchik* in the world is still generally thought to come from Russia, particularly from the regions of Vologda, Archangel and Kazan. Russians prize it for its delicate flavour and the tenderness of its flesh. As Aksakov noted:

> The white meat of the hazel hen, tender, healthy and although dry still excellent in taste, is well-known to everyone; its entrails and claws are slightly bitter, which makes it particularly revered by gastronomes.

Two other birds which used to be eagerly hunted and brought to the table were heathcock (*teterev*) and capercailye (*glukhar'*). Pheasant was sometimes found in western Russia or brought from the Caucasus. There were also favourite recipes for partridge and for a host of small birds, among them quail, snipe, waldstein and doubles, all of them considered great delicacies by nineteenth-century Russian gourmets. Songbirds, notably the thrush and the lark, were killed mainly to decorate larger roasts on the grand table.

Of four-footed game, hare was hunted more for pageantry and sport than for the quality of its flesh. Bear, elk, venison, chamois, reindeer and wild boar were far more highly esteemed. Two great nineteenth-century delicacies were bear ham and marinated bear's trotters. The latter were simmered in stock with spices, then cut lengthwise in half, grilled in egg and breadcrumbs and served with a sour-sweet sauce. The French gastronome Urbain Dubois, writing in the 1870s, recorded his view that this was a speciality hardly likely to appeal to Western palates, but one imagines it retains its crusty devotees in the heart of Russia where bear-hunting is still common. Bear and reindeer loin were also enjoyed smoked.

There will be Russians today who have special hunting rights and can take advantage of the recipes for game which are still published in State cookery books. Bear-hunting might even be claimed as the sport of Soviet political leaders. The ordinary shopper can sometimes find feathered game in season, in special shops called 'Gifts of Nature' which old Russia brought into being and which tradition has kept alive. Modern Russia is moreover so full of anomalies and unexpected throwbacks to grander days that one should not be surprised to see partridge on the menu of an otherwise poor Moscow restaurant and find it served exquisitely.

All game birds were usually roasted and served either in a sour cream sauce, or with sauerkraut, red cabbage or marinated salads. Beetroot was also popular as the base for a sauce, or as a cooked vegetable to accompany almost any game. The flavour and texture of the meat was usually enhanced by marinating it in an acid-based marinade, in *kvas*, or simply in water or milk.

Marinade for pheasant, capercailye, heathcock and any larger game (e.g. hare, venison)

    1 small carrot
    1 celery root

½ small parsnip root or 1 Hamburg parsley root
1 onion
6 bay leaves
12 allspice berries
6 cloves
seeds from 3 cardamom pods, crushed
200 ml (⅓ pint) cider vinegar
400 ml (⅔ pint) water
½ head of garlic

Chop the carrot, celery, parsnip and onion finely, mix with the bay leaves, allspice, cloves, cardamom, vinegar and water and bring to the boil. Add the finely chopped garlic to the hot marinade and if the game is old, pour the liquid over it while still hot. Young game is better treated if the marinade is allowed to cool first. Cold water with onion and garlic is a simple alternative. For heathcock one Russian chef suggested 3–4 days in an oil and vinegar marinade.

Marinade for partridge and hazel-hen and generally for smaller game

1 tablespoon dried mint
a bunch of fresh marjoram or 1 tablespoon dried marjoram
1 tablespoon juniper berries
5–6 cloves
6 allspice berries
1 onion
400 ml (⅔ pint) water
2–3 tablespoons lemon juice
2 teaspoons salt
½ head of garlic

Secure the herbs and spices in a muslin bag and put it with the finely chopped onion in a pan with the water. Bring to the boil, add the lemon juice, salt and chopped garlic, and cover. Allow to cool slowly, then chill in the refrigerator before adding the game. Alternatively, hazel-grouse and partridge may be soaked in milk before cooking.

Roast heathcock, roast partridge, roast hazel-hen
Marinate the birds for 24 hours before cooking. Wipe dry, rub inside and out with salt and crushed juniper berries, and brown quickly on all sides in bacon fat, oil or a mixture of oil and butter. Reduce the heat and continue cooking without a lid until done. The test is to be able to

insert a wooden toothpick with ease into the flesh. Partridge and hazel-hen will take a minimum of 30 minutes and I prefer to cook them quite a bit longer, but that is very much a matter of preference. For heathcock allow over an hour. The birds should be basted frequently with the pan juices. Towards the end of the cooking time a tablespoon of sour cream may be poured over each bird and allowed to become warm before serving. The birds may also be roasted in the oven or on a spit.

Hazel-hen in sour cream, partridge in sour cream

This is probably the most traditional Russian game recipe. The bird is cooked very slowly in sour cream after being browned lightly in butter. This method of cooking has the reputation of producing particularly tender and tasty dishes. Allow at least 1½ hours for the cooking. In Russia one used to be able to buy sour cream of different thicknesses depending on what use was to be made of it, and these recipes would surely have called for a thinner variety than is usually available in this country. For 2 birds add 1–1½ small (5 fl oz) cartons of sour cream and the same quantity again of thin stock, milk or water to the pan. If the sauce is too liquid after the birds are cooked, reduce it quickly over a high heat before serving.

Partridge baked with sauerkraut

Simmer some sauerkraut in a little bacon fat until soft. Fry the partridge lightly in butter until brown. Line a greased baking dish with sauerkraut, add the partridge in two halves, cover with more sauerkraut, and dot with butter. Bake in a medium oven for an hour or a slower oven for 1½ hours. This is an adaptation of the classic French *perdrix aux choux*.

Pigeon in the style of hazel-hen

This recipe was given to me by a Russian living abroad. She had the equivalent of a musician's talent to play by ear, and could recreate the tastes of her childhood by juggling with the only ingredients available to her in England and France. She swore she could transform the humble pigeon, never very popular in Russia, into a celebrated hazel-hen.

Marinate the pigeon as for hazel-hen (page 165), or in equal parts of vinegar and water, leaving it at least 24 hours, then set the bird to cook slowly in a pan of water spiced with 1 or 2 bay leaves, 2 cloves, some chopped onion and a few peppercorns until thoroughly tender. Use the matchstick test to be sure. Remove the birds, chop each in half and brown for a few minutes in the oven. Serve with sour cream sauce (page 135), or beetroot sauce (page 125 and below), with cooked red cabbage or sauerkraut and sauté potatoes.

Beetroot sauce to accompany game
This preparation, called a sauce, actually turns out to be more of a vegetable accompaniment unless you chop your beetroot into minute pieces. Vary the texture and the liquidity according to the requirements of the dish.

> 750 g (1½ lb) beetroot
> a little chopped onion (optional)
> 1 scant tablespoon butter
> ½ tablespoon flour
> 1 small (5 fl oz) carton sour cream or 200 ml (⅓ pint) stock
> salt and vinegar
> pinch sugar (optional)

Bake the beetroot till tender, peel, and chop finely (or use ready-cooked beetroot). Lightly fry the onion in the butter, stir in the flour and the beetroot then add the sour cream or stock, stirring all the time. Season with salt and about a tablespoon of vinegar and bring gently to the boil. A pinch of sugar may be added according to taste.

For heathcock and hare it is customary to make this sauce with stock rather than cream. Alternatively, the chopped cooked beetroot may be added to a finished béchamel (white) sauce which has been strongly flavoured with lemon juice.

Partridge or quail kebabs from Central Asia
Soak the birds in milk for 24 hours before cooking, then put them in salted water for 15 minutes. Remove the skins and rub the birds with butter, crushed caraway seed and black pepper. Coat them with flour and roast them on skewers, ideally over an open fire or on a spit. According to local Uzbek and Tadzhik recipes the ideal wood to burn on the fire is juniper, but most of us will have to make do without a fire at all. Rest the skewers on either side of a deep roasting pan, so that the birds are suspended in the oven and may be turned several times while cooking. Use the matchstick test to tell when they are tender.

Hare or rabbit in sour cream
In its own way this dish is a Russian classic, though hare was not highly regarded by nineteenth-century gourmets. Nabokov, with a typical mixture of affection for his Russian past and a streak of cruel snobbishness, recalled in his autobiography that it was a speciality of the village schoolmaster. It did not belong on the aristocratic table.

1 hare
marinade (page 164)
small pieces fat bacon (optional)
salt and black pepper
2 carrots
1 turnip
1 parsnip
1 large onion
1 stick celery
3 tablespoons oil or bacon fat
1–2 tablespoons flour
2 tablespoons butter
200 ml (⅓ pint) stock or water
2–3 small (5 fl oz) cartons sour cream

Skin, clean and joint the hare. Marinate it for 3–4 hours or overnight, using the marinade for larger game. Ideally the meat should be larded by making small incisions and filling them with small pieces of fat bacon. Then salt the hare, put it in a roasting pan with a macédoine of carrot, turnip, parsnip, onion and celery and a little oil or bacon fat, and brown in a hot oven or in a frying pan. Baste occasionally with the pan juices.

Make a roux with the flour and the butter, gradually add the stock or water, and cook for 3–4 minutes. Add the sour cream and the juices from the pan (skim according to taste), and add seasoning to taste. (Halve the quantities of sauce for coating rabbit or hare portions.)

Transfer the hare to a baking dish, pour over the sour cream sauce, cover and bake in a medium oven for 30–40 minutes. Serve with boiled potatoes.

Latvian hare or rabbit cheese

1 hare
a little bacon fat and stock
6 eggs
100 g (3½ oz) curd cheese, cream cheese or grated Cheddar
200 g (7 oz) mushrooms
200 g (7 oz) butter
a few tablespoons red wine and strong meat stock
1 tablespoon caraway seed
3 teaspoons dried marjoram } OR
2 tablespoons dried dill weed } grated nutmeg to taste

Roast the hare for about an hour in a medium oven, then joint it and braise it in a heavy pan with a little bacon fat and stock until it is perfectly tender. Strip the meat from the bones and put it through a mincer. Cook the eggs and cheese together into a kind of thick omelette then chop finely. Boil and mince the mushrooms. The butter may be softened but it should not melt. Mix the minced hare with the eggs, mushrooms and butter, add the wine, stock, herbs or nutmeg, and bake in a greased pâté dish in a slow oven for 1–1½ hours.

Serve cold in slices with vinaigrette. The 'cheese' may also be baked in a shortcrust pastry case in a loaf tin and served hot or cold. Halve the quantities if making the cheese with a 1 kg (2 lb) rabbit.

Georgian pheasant

Much of the pheasant eaten by the nineteenth-century Russian gentry was brought either fresh or frozen from the Caucasus, whence also this unusual recipe.

1 pheasant
30 walnuts
1½–2 lb grapes
3–4 oranges
1 glass of Malmsey or other fortified wine
1 glass strong green tea
40 g (1½ oz) butter
salt, pepper and nutmeg to taste

Truss the pheasant for cooking and place it in an oval casserole. Skin the walnuts by immersing them in boiling water and then in cold, and add them to the casserole along with the juice of the grapes and the orange juice. (Put the grapes through a liquidizer, then sieve to obtain the juice.) Add the Malmsey and green tea, the butter, salt, pepper and nutmeg. Cook the pheasant in this liquid, covered, in a medium hot oven for an hour until almost done. Strain off three-quarters of the cooking liquid and reduce it to a good sauce while the pheasant browns uncovered in the oven for a further 5 minutes or so. Carve, and serve surrounded by the nuts and a little sauce. Serve the rest of the sauce separately.

Jane Grigson suggests cooking guinea fowl the same way.

Left-over game

Game left-overs can be incorporated into *pirozhki* and served with a bouillon made from the bones, or rolled in *blini*. Cold partridge is the most important ingredient in the classic *salat Olivier* (page 51), or simply serve any cold game with cranberry sauce or marinated salads.

Little Russian wild boar

Cheat and make this unusual dish with any reasonably lean cut of pork, either as a joint or cut into chops.

> 1 kg (2 lb) pork
> ½ carrot
> ½ onion
> ½ stick celery
> butter or oil
> good brown stock
> 4 tablespoons red wine or cider
> 4 tablespoons cherry purée
> powdered cinnamon
> salt and pepper
> brown or black breadcrumbs (optional)
>
> FOR THE MARINADE
> 400 ml (⅔ pint) cider or wine vinegar*
> 4–5 bay leaves
> 20 peppercorns
> 20 crushed juniper berries
> a little thyme
> a few parsley stalks
> 2 onions, chopped finely

* Left-over red wine or draught, flat cider may be used.

Bring all the marinade ingredients to the boil, remove from the heat, and when cool pour over the meat and leave covered in the refrigerator for several days – 5 days are not too many. Economize on the amount of marinade needed by placing both the meat and the liquid inside a plastic bag in a bowl.

When the dish is required, remove the meat from the marinade, wipe, and braise in a heavy-bottomed pan in which you have sweated the finely diced carrot, onion and celery in butter or oil. Add 4 tablespoons of stock and the red wine or cider, put a lid on the pan and allow the pork to cook gently until it is tender. More stock may be added if needed. Do not cook this dish fiercely otherwise you will boil off all the wine.

The pork is served in a sauce of 3 parts stock to 1 part cherry purée with cinnamon, salt and pepper added to taste. The meat may be placed in a serving dish, sprinkled with brown or black breadcrumbs, masked with sauce and placed in the oven for a few minutes before bringing to the table. The vegetables used in braising may be added to the sauce as they are or puréed. Serve with rice and a plain green vegetable.

Vegetables, Vegetarian and Grain Dishes

GRAIN

It is a mark of the unmodernized state of Russian cooking that if you walk into any grocer's, city or country, or stroll through a market, you will find an assortment of unrefined grains that many Westerners cannot even name. The Russian national diet is inconceivable without the rye it needs to make bread and *kvas* and the buckwheat it needs for *kasha*. For hundreds of years these food plants, together with cabbage, constituted the greater part of the peasant diet. If in the past a bad crop meant a dearth of bread, today it means a shortage of animal foodstuffs and consequently a reduction in the already scant consumer meat supply. The Soviet grain harvest receives so much attention from economists because it is according to its prosperity that the country's well-being still stands or falls. Old loyalties to the soil are drawn upon to encourage support for the Marxist economy. Newspapers speak of buckwheat (though it is not strictly a grain) as a national food. Every year from April to October news of the harvest features as a main item in news bulletins, and field workers are depicted as heroes and heroines of the State.

Rye, wheat, barley and millet have been native to Russian soil from the earliest times. Buckwheat is a plant related to sorrel and rhubarb. It produces a nourishing endosperm which may be ground into flour or left in the form of groats. It was introduced to Russia over 1,000 years ago from northern India, Central Asia and the Middle East. Apart from its own qualities as food, it is enormously attractive to bees and encourages an excellent flavoured honey. Oats were introduced to Russia from Central Europe and were an established crop by the late Middle Ages. Rice came from the East in the fifteenth and sixteenth centuries and was later planted closer to home in Astrakhan and Saratov. Today it is being intensively cultivated by artificial irrigation in southern Russia near the Black Sea, in an area known as the Kuban. Probably because of its comparatively short cooking time and deceptive simplicity, it has become widely available in restaurants to the exclusion of the older, to my mind tastier, grains. In the nineteenth century the grain picture was completed with the arrival of sago and potato flour. Neither of these is a true grain, sago being extracted from the marrow of the palm tree and potato flour being just what it says, but they were sources of almost instant food bulk. Also, particularly in sweet cookery, they performed many of the functions previously fulfilled by fine wheat (semolina), fine (*smolensk*) buckwheat and fine barley. Cornmeal, cooked in the South for centuries, is largely a modern discovery for Russian home cooks.

KASHA

Thick kasha won't drive away the family.

Russian proverb

Apart from sweet puddings, cakes and bread, the various grains and pseudo-grains were traditionally used to make *kasha*. I am a great devotee of porridge made with oats for breakfast, but the English word is no good for translating *kasha*. It deters those who do not share my early morning tastes and suggests sticky mush, whereas *kasha* covers almost all ways of cooking all grains in water, milk, stock and cream to a variety of consistencies ranging from dry (like rice) to set (like Italian *polenta*) to a thick purée. *Kasha* can be baked in the oven with the addition of curd cheese, or onions and mushrooms, and herbs, or it can be cooked on top of the stove. Occasionally *kasha* is also used to mean a vegetable and cooked pulse or purely vegetable purée. The various forms of *kasha* give it a place at every meal of the day – sweet in the morning and before bed, savoury to accompany soup or fill pies or pad out the main meal of the day. Buckwheat flour with milk and sugar is a Russian baby food.

Buckwheat kasha

Buckwheat groats or kernels have a unique nutty taste when cooked. I find buckwheat good to eat when it has been cooked for 15–20 minutes. It is swollen and soft but not mushy. After that it may be left to stand for an hour or so with the lid on and then gently reheated before serving, but I find it quite acceptable to serve it almost straight away after cooking. Some people recommend browning the kernels first in a dry frying pan or mixing them with a beaten egg and drying them the same way before cooking in liquid.

Use the following proportions for a fairly dry *kasha*:

100 g (3½ oz) buckwheat
150 ml (¼ pint) water
¼–½ teaspoon salt

Wash the buckwheat carefully under running water. Bring the salted water to the boil, add the groats, remove any scum that comes to the surface and simmer gently until the buckwheat is cooked and the water absorbed. One Russian cook told me that it was strictly forbidden to add water after this point, but I have found it perfectly acceptable to use the same technique I use for risotto, which is to err on the dry side and to keep a close eye on the pot, stirring often and adding liquid just before the grain begins to stick to the bottom. Leave standing off the heat, covered, for a few minutes after cooking. Drain if necessary. The simplest and traditionally blessed way to serve this *kasha* is with plenty of good butter. As the saying goes: 'You can't spoil kasha with butter'.

The father of classical French cuisine, Urbain Dubois, did think, along with several other French chefs exposed to Russian ways, that he could improve it, however. To follow his advice, cook the buckwheat as above until it is thick, transfer to a baking dish with the remaining liquid, add the butter and nutmeg, cover, and put in a warm oven until all the liquid is absorbed. Add more butter and Parmesan cheese to taste. Leave to stand covered for another 5 minutes or so before serving. This *kasha* may be cooked wholly on top of the stove if you are in a hurry, but it must be kept on the dry side. This way, Dubois enthused in his *Cuisine de tous les pays*, 'il devient excellent'.

More homespun ways of finishing *kasha* are to add fried onions, chopped hard-boiled eggs and butter, fried chopped bacon and onions, or cooked mushrooms and sour cream. For this last recipe, dried or fresh mushrooms may be used and the stock they yield after simmering used to cook the buckwheat as far as it will stretch. Heat the cooked mushrooms in a pan with the sour cream and add them to the cooked buckwheat. The dish may be put in the oven to warm through for 5–10 minutes. The classic version of this is called *Dragomirovskaya kasha*, after General Dragomirov who helped defend Russia against Napoleon. Any of these *kashas* may be moistened to taste with a good meat or mushroom stock.

Buckwheat or barley krupenik

Krupa is the collective word for grains prepared for cooking. *Krupenik* is a simple, homely dish, and is probably best translated as simply 'bake'. It uses various combinations of milk, eggs, cottage or curd cheese and sour cream with a hint of sugar. I particularly like the following buckwheat bake with the cod and onions given on page 102.

> 200 g (7 oz) buckwheat groats
> 400 ml (⅔ pint) water or milk
> 200 g (7 oz) cottage or curd cheese
> ⅔ small (5 fl oz) carton sour cream
> 2 eggs
> 1–2 tablespoons sugar
> ½ teaspoon salt
> 2 tablespoons butter

Cook the buckwheat in water or milk as for *kasha* (above). When it is swollen and soft add the cheese, which should be well stirred and smooth, the sour cream, beaten eggs, sugar and salt. Mix well, pile into a buttered baking dish, dot with butter or a thin layer of sour cream, and bake in a hot oven for 30 minutes.

Barley should be cooked for the first 10 minutes or so in water, then drained and cooked in milk until thick. Either follow the recipe as for buckwheat, or simply add the cheese and butter, mix well, leave to stand for 5 minutes, and serve.

Barley kasha with thyme

This *kasha* may be eked out into an easy supper with boiled bacon or a cheese topping. Alternatively it may be substituted for buckwheat in the recipe above and baked with an extra egg into a *krupenik*.

> 150 g (5½ oz) large grain pearl barley
> 1 litre (1¾ pints) water
> ½ teaspoon salt
> 2 tablespoons dried peas, soaked in water overnight
> 1 onion
> 2 tablespoons butter
> 1–2 tablespoons fresh thyme or savory, or up to 1
>   tablespoon dried

Wash the barley under running water. Bring to the boil in the salted water, then simmer gently for about 15 minutes, skimming the surface as necessary. Cook the peas separately in water until soft. Drain the barley and add it to the peas with a chopped, lightly fried onion and a little of the cooking liquid from the peas. Cook gently until the barley is done to taste. It is good fairly firm, like rice. Add the butter and thyme, cook for a few minutes more, remove from the heat, and allow to stand covered for a further 5 minutes before serving. Vary the amount of liquid left in the pan according to whether you want to spoon it out of a bowl or eat it dry with a fork like rice.

Millet kasha

I find it a pity that the only use we seem to find in this country for millet is as bird seed. Not only is it more than fit for human consumption, it contains 10 per cent protein and 4 per cent fat as well as carbohydrates. It has a long history of preparation for the table. There are references to it in the Old Testament. The Romans called it *milium*. In Southern Russia and the Caucasus, where it is sometimes known as *proso*, it is cooked into a thick bland paste with water and flour and served with spicy chicken and tomato dishes and *satsivi* (pages 156–9). The Georgian preparation is called *gomi* and uses millet and water in the ratio of 1:4 with a thickening of 2 tablespoons of cornflour to each 200 g (7 oz) of millet. I find it best cooked in milk with a hint of sugar.

> 200 g (7 oz) millet
> 400 ml (⅔ pint) water
> 400 ml (⅔ pint) milk
> 2 tablespoons butter
> sugar and salt to taste

Wash the millet under running water, picking out any black grains, bring to the boil in plenty of water and skim several times until the surface is clear. Drain and return to the heat with half the milk and water given in the recipe. Simmer until done, adding more milk and water as needed. Add the butter, sugar and salt when cooked. Millet cooks to a fairly soft consistency like cornmeal, but it should not be runny unless you are making it for breakfast.

Cooked millet *kasha* may be baked into a *krupenik* which is very good with chicken by adding the following ingredients for every 200 g (7 oz) cooked millet:

1 tablespoon sugar
2 tablespoons butter
1 tablespoon sour cream
1 egg
¾ teaspoon salt

Mix together all the ingredients and pile into a buttered baking dish. Spread the surface with a mixture of beaten egg and sour cream and bake in a medium oven until brown on top.

Millet and pumpkin kasha
These two are proverbial partners. To make the pumpkin purée steam it in chunks or simmer in a little butter until soft, then liquidize or put through a food mill.

200 g (7 oz) millet, cooked to a *kasha* with milk as above
200 ml (⅓ pint) pumpkin purée
3 tablespoons butter
100 ml (⅛ pint) single cream
salt, black pepper and nutmeg to taste
1 teaspoon sugar

Combine the cooked millet and the pumpkin purée and heat through, stirring in the butter and cream. Season with salt, black pepper and nutmeg, also adding a teaspoon of sugar.

Cornmeal
To their native *kashas* Russians have this century introduced southern preparations of cornmeal, the most popular of which is *mamalyga*. Add fine cornmeal to boiling salted water in the proportions by volume of about three parts water to one of meal, stirring all the time to prevent it going lumpy. Cook slowly for 25–35 minutes, stirring often. The heat may be turned off for the last 10 minutes and the pan left to stand, tightly covered. The *mamalyga* should be very firm. Season, and eat with chopped fried onion, butter and grated cheese, or simply garlic and butter.

Mamalyga may also be cooked with milk instead of water, and grated cheese stirred into the pan. Serve with sour cream.

Mchadi
These are small baked Georgian cornmeal cakes, also eaten with cheese. Mix fine cornmeal with half its volume of water, form into balls, flatten and cook slowly in a dry preheated pan with a lid,

turning them once and finishing uncovered. Alternatively, bake *mchadi* in shallow *blini* pans or on a baking tray in a medium oven.

RICE

Fruit plov

This is cooked along the lines outlined for a standard lamb *plov* on page 147. In the Caucasus and Central Asia it is a wedding dish which is set alight with brandy. It is served with roast lamb or kebabs, but will stand on its own if you are a vegetarian with a sweet tooth. Combine it with plenty of chopped fresh herbs – my favourite, a purely invented accompaniment, is barely cooked spinach or sorrel, the tartness of which I find just right to offset the sweet fruit. *Gurinsky plov, plov Ararat, shirin plov, plov with pumpkin* are just four of the many versions of fruit *plov* I have come across. Providing you have raisins and almonds you can vary the other ingredients to suit yourself. The first time I made it, many years ago before I became interested in Russian food, I thought it would do for pudding and consequently cooked the rice to saturation point. It was a dreadful mistake.

350 g (12 oz) rice
100 g (3½ oz) butter
pinch of saffron or turmeric
200 g (7 oz) dried apricots (soaked for a few hours)
200 g (7 oz) raisins (soaked for a few hours)
100 g (3½ oz) almonds, or more to taste
AND
2–3 peaches
5–6 fresh damsons
OR
150 g (5½ oz) fresh apple or carrot, cut in matchsticks
150 g (5½ oz) quince
OR
500 g (1 lb) pumpkin
200 g (7 oz) fresh apple
OPTIONAL SYRUP
100 ml (⅛ pint) unsweetened grape juice or pomegranate
    juice
1 teaspoon cinnamon
2 cloves
sugar or honey to taste

Cook the rice with butter and saffron or turmeric according to any of the three methods given for *plov* (page 146). Braise the chopped dried and fresh fruit lightly in butter with the almonds, allowing longer for the dried fruit and the apple (if used) than for the soft fresh fruit, which needs barely a minute in the pan to be sealed and heated through. The pumpkin, if used, should also be braised in butter until soft. Remove from the heat, add the warmed juice, cinnamon and cloves, and serve either separately or mixed in with the rice. Mixing the fruit and rice is not considered correct by culinary authorities, but the dish looks much more appealing with the rice coated with the rich red juice.

Personally I cannot take any more sugar in one dish than is already present in the fruit, but there is nothing to stop you adding a couple of teaspoons of honey or sugar or even more if you have a really sweet tooth. Both this and the egg *plov* below may also be made with bulghur wheat.

Egg plov
A great Azerbaijani dish for vegetarians.

> 500 g (1 lb) rice
> 150 g (5 oz) butter
> pinch of saffron or turmeric
> 6–8 eggs
> 150 g (5 oz) dried cornelian cherries or dried apricots (soaked for a few hours or overnight)
> 3 tablespoons vegetable oil
> 500 g (1 lb) onions
> 250 g (8 oz) spring onions with green tops
> 1 tablespoon fresh mint (or ½ tablespoon dried)
> 1 tablespoon fresh thyme or tarragon (or ½ tablespoon dried)
> plenty of freshly ground black pepper
> a little salt

Cook the rice with the butter and saffron or turmeric according to any of the methods given for *plov* on page 146. Separate the eggs, leaving the yolks whole. Beat the egg whites. Cook the soaked dried fruit in a little water until very soft and purée it in a food mill or liquidizer. Melt a little butter and the vegetable oil in a heavy-bottomed shallow pan or frying pan, and add the two kinds of onion, chopped. Cook gently for about 8 minutes, add the fruit purée, cook for another 5 minutes and then over a very low heat fold in the beaten egg whites. At this point, depending on your pan, it may be easier to transfer the mixture to a well-buttered baking dish. The idea is to make as many hollows in the mixture as there are egg yolks, drop a yolk into each one, sprinkle over the chopped fresh herbs and pepper and a little salt, and stand on a low heat or in the oven for a few minutes until the eggs are set. The *plov* is then served by spreading the rice in a layer over a large serving plate and turning out, right side up, the egg, onion and fruit mixture all in one piece to sit on top of it. I can only see this working with a heavy frying pan or a baking dish. Burst egg yolks rather spoil the visual effect of an otherwise splendid dish.

VEGETABLES

POTATOES

Historically speaking, the potato is a controversial and provocative vegetable. Introduced to France from South America as an ornamental plant in the mid sixteenth century, and to England via North America a decade or so later, it did not come to Russia until its popularity in Europe had finally been established in the late eighteenth century, after years of suspicion that it caused disease. At the same time as the failure of the potato crop in Ireland caused the famine of 1845 and sparked mass emigration, Russian peasants were rioting in protest against the forced introduction of the potato in place of their native crops. It took a long time to acquire a veneer of respectability and ordinariness.

In the Russian diet the potato and its derivate, potato starch, never took the place of the native grains. The new vegetable had a German name, *kartofel'*, and crept only incidentally into the great soups. Not surprisingly, most of the recipes introduced in the nineteenth century were either French or from western Russia and the Baltics, areas which from a culinary point of view were often closer to German traditions. The Baltic influence is particularly apparent in the many Russian combinations of potatoes and cured fish.

Whatever tradition one attributes them to, new potatoes in their jackets dressed with a couple of spoonfuls of sour cream and a sprinkling of chopped fresh herbs (dill, parsley or chives) are wonderful. New or old boiled potatoes are also excellent dressed with butter, dill and chopped hard-boiled egg. This is the Polish sauce given for fish on page 101. Or coat them with seasoned buttermilk and herbs. Large old potatoes may be baked until they are half done, the middles scooped out and mixed with butter and cream or sour cream, salt and black pepper, and a pinch of sugar, then returned to the oven with their tops on to finish cooking. Any of the savoury butters given on pages 32–3 are also suitable for eating with plain boiled or baked potatoes.

Potatoes stuffed with smoked sprats and mushrooms in lemon sauce

> 6 large potatoes
> 75 g (3 oz) mushrooms
> a little stock

6 smoked Baltic sprats (brisling)
2 tablespoons flour
2 tablespoons butter
2 tablespoons sour cream
½–1 tablespoon lemon juice
salt and black pepper or nutmeg to taste
a little lemon peel

Clean but do not peel the potatoes. Bake or boil them until they are half done, then cut them lengthways to give a top and a large bottom that can be scooped out. Simmer the mushrooms in a little stock, chop them finely, reserving the stock, and combine with the scooped-out potato, mashed, and the finely chopped sprats. Stuff the potatoes with this mixture, put the tops on and finish cooking in a medium oven. Meanwhile make a roux with the flour and butter, dilute with the reserved mushroom stock, strained, and add the sour cream and lemon juice. Season to taste with salt, nutmeg or black pepper and lemon peel and serve hot, poured over the potatoes.

Potatoes stuffed with herring, mushroom and onion in sour cream sauce

6 large potatoes
½ large or 1 small salted herring
a little milk or water
1 medium onion, grated, with its juice
50–75 g (2–3 oz) mushrooms
vegetable stock
1 egg
¾–1 small (5 fl oz) carton sour cream
3 tablespoons butter
chopped fresh herbs
freshly ground black pepper
½ tablespoon flour

Follow the instructions in the previous recipe for preparing the potatoes. Soak the herring in milk or water until it is almost free of salt, then cut it up finely or pound to a paste in a mortar. Combine with the mashed potato insides, the onion, the mushrooms which have been simmered in vegetable stock, the beaten egg, 3 tablespoons of sour cream and half the butter. Add fresh herbs to taste and black pepper. Stuff the potatoes with this mixture, replace the tops and stand in a baking dish. Pour over a thin sour cream sauce, made by cooking the flour and remaining butter to a roux and diluting with 2 parts sour cream to 1 part vegetable stock. Bake in a medium oven until cooked.

Potatoes braised with bacon
This recipe calls for what the Germans and the Russians call *Speck*, that bacon which is sold in chunks rather than rashers and is nearly all fat, but you can to good effect substitute chopped bacon pieces, which many shops sell off cheaply. There is usually quite a lot of fat and because they are ends and scraps the pieces are often quite thick. Use smoky bacon if you can get it.

> 500 g (1 lb) potatoes
> 1 onion
> 100 g (3½ oz) fat bacon
> butter or lard as necessary
> 1 tablespoon parsley
> 1 tablespoon dill
> 1 bay leaf
> salt and pepper

Peel the potatoes and cut into cubes or thin slices. Chop the onion finely and cut the bacon and fat into small pieces. Fry the bacon lightly in a heavy pan until the fat melts, then add the potato (it should be dried with a tea towel before you add it to the pan) and the onion and brown them quickly. If the bacon does not give off enough fat to stop the potato sticking, add butter or lard. Remove the pan from the heat, add about 5 tablespoons of boiling water and the parsley, dill and bay leaf. Season. Put a lid on the pan and simmer gently until the potatoes are cooked and all the water absorbed. You may need to add more water during cooking. These potatoes are particularly good eaten with pickled cucumbers or with cabbage flavoured with caraway.

Potatoes braised with mushrooms

> 500 g (1 lb) potatoes
> 1 large onion
> 350 g (12 oz) fresh mushrooms
> 2 tablespoons butter
> ½ small (5 fl oz) carton sour cream
> salt and pepper

1 bay leaf
fresh parsley and dill

Peel and slice the potatoes thinly. Chop the onion and the mushrooms. Melt the butter in a pan and fry the mushrooms and onion until the onion is transparent and soft. Remove to a casserole and stir in the sour cream. Brown the potatoes in the pan and transfer them to the casserole. Add water until they are just covered. Season with salt, pepper, a bay leaf and a couple of sprigs of parsley and simmer, or bake, covered, until the potatoes are cooked. Remove the bay leaf and the parsley before serving and sprinkle with freshly chopped dill or parsley.

Potato purée with poppy seed

500 g (1 lb) potatoes
a little milk
2–3 tablespoons butter
salt to taste
2 tablespoons poppy seed

Boil the potatoes in their jackets, allow them to cool until you can handle them, then peel and mash with a little milk and the butter. Add salt to taste. Pour boiling water over the poppy seed and leave to stand for 5 minutes. Drain and repeat the process. Drain again and pound in a mortar. Add to the purée and either serve straight away or put in a buttered casserole to brown in the oven.

VARIATION
A Ukrainian version adds a white bean purée, raw onion, lovage and sugar:

120 g (4 oz) haricot beans, soaked overnight and cooked in water until soft
potato and poppy seed purée as above
2 onions, grated with juice or finely chopped
2 teaspoons sugar
1 tablespoon each fresh parsley and lovage
freshly ground black pepper

Purée the beans while they are still hot with as much of the cooking liquid as is needed to give a smooth consistency, and add hot to the potatoes and poppy seed as prepared above. Stir in the raw onion, the sugar sprinkled on the surface of the purée, the chopped herbs and the black pepper.

Gul'bishnik

POTATO PURÉE BAKED WITH CURD CHEESE AND HERBS
A Belorussian speciality.

500 g (1 lb) potatoes
2–3 tablespoons curd cheese
2–3 tablespoons sour cream
1 onion
1 tablespoon dill or ½ teaspoon caraway seed
½ teaspoon salt
black pepper

Boil the potatoes in their jackets, allow to cool a little, then peel and mash with a little milk and butter. Add the cheese and the sour cream mixed together, beating them in with a wooden spoon. Grate the onion and add it with its juice along with the herbs, salt and black pepper. Pile into a buttered baking dish and finish in a hot oven.

Pampushki
These are made like Jewish *latkes*, combining raw grated potato with cooked potato purée, and usually with a filling of chopped meat or cottage cheese. There are many variations. They are also good unfilled and in all cases served with warmed sour cream and grated onion.

600 g (20 oz) raw potato
150 g (5 oz) cooked mashed potato
salt
filling: (a) cooked minced beef and onion
        (b) cottage or curd cheese beaten with 1 egg per 250 g
            (8 oz), chives or other fresh herbs
sour cream and grated onion to taste

Grate the raw potato and squeeze out as much of the liquid as possible in muslin or a clean tea towel. Combine it with the mashed potato and add salt. Form into little cakes and in the middle place a teaspoon of filling. Close up the cake to enclose the filling and form into the shape of an egg. Cook the *pampushki* in boiling salted water for 20 minutes. Remove carefully with a draining spoon and serve coated with warmed sour cream and onion.

Olad'i

POTATO PANCAKES

500 g (1 lb) potatoes
2–3 teaspoons dried yeast
150 ml (¼ pint) warm water
100 g (3½ oz) flour
1 egg
salt and pepper
fresh or dried herbs to taste
butter for frying

Either grate all the potato raw and squeeze out the juice as in the previous recipe, or boil two of them and combine them, mashed, with the rest of the grated raw potato. Dissolve the yeast in the warm water, stir into the flour, add the potato mixture with the beaten egg, and season, adding any fresh or dried herbs to taste. Leave the mixture in a warm place to rise. Cook in butter as for *blini* (page 223), preferably in a small, heavy-bottomed frying pan over a high heat, turning once. Serve very hot, with sour cream or more butter.

Potato and dried pea purée with bacon

350 g (12 oz) dried peas (soaked overnight)
5 medium potatoes
150 g (5 oz) streaky bacon
½ litre (scant 1 pint) milk or cream
salt and pepper

Cook the soaked peas in unsalted water until soft. Add the potatoes, cut in smallish pieces, and the chopped bacon and cook until the potato is soft and the water all absorbed. Add the milk or cream, season to taste and beat to a purée. Serve with sausages.

BEETROOT

Beetroot is the vegetable most readily associated with Russian cooking, thanks to the fame of *borshch*. Outside soup it is served hot and dressed with cream or oil and fresh herbs, baked into a casserole with pork or made into an excellent sauce for game. In every case it bears almost no relation to the acrid crimson spheres or, worse still, slices, that come bottled and submerged in malt vinegar. Russian cookery values beetroot for its deep Bordeaux colour, its sweetness and the richness of its natural juice. Young beets are doubly valuable in the kitchen, as their leaves are a useful addition to soup. Good specimens will be a deep crimson when cut. The fewer white trunk rings the better.

Hot grated beetroot (1)

This recipe comes from a Russian friend living in England.

'A vegetable I'm sure is Russian because I acquired it from my mother and I have never known anyone else serve it is beetroot, cooked, peeled, shredded and then heated up with a little butter, lemon juice and pepper. We used to have it with *kotlety* or with brain fritters and it was quite delicious.'

Hot grated beetroot (2)

> 1 kg (2 lb) beets
> 1 large cooking apple or 2 small
> ½–¾ small (5 fl oz) carton sour cream
> salt, sugar and vinegar or lemon juice to taste
> ½ tablespoon butter
> ½ tablespoon flour
> chopped fresh parsley or dill

Grate the raw peeled beetroot coarsely, put it in anything but an aluminium pan with a little water, and simmer gently for 15–20 minutes before adding the peeled and grated apple and the sour cream. Cover the pan and leave to simmer gently for 20–25 minutes or until the beetroot is cooked. Add a little water if the liquid in the pan evaporates too fast. You should have a generous quantity of sauce without the dish being too watery. Add salt, sugar (1 teaspoon to start off) and vinegar or lemon juice to taste. Make a roux with the butter and flour, dilute with a couple of spoonfuls of the sauce and add to the pan. Heat through gently, stirring, and serve strewn with chopped parsley or dill. This is an excellent vegetable to serve with boiled bacon, beef or tongue. For vegetarians it would go well with *blini* filled with chopped hard-boiled egg, with buckwheat *kasha* or a vegetable *pirog*.

Baked beets with onion and sour cream

Follow the recipe for beetroot to eat with game, given on page 167, leaving the beetroot in cubes rather than reducing it to a purée.

Lenten beetroot
This recipe comes from one of Russia's earliest cookery books, published in 1828, when honey rather than sugar was the common sweetener and quantities were both vast and vague.

> 1 kg (2 lb) beets
> about 300 g (10 oz) Dutch cabbage
> 1–2 onions
> oil or butter
> salt, pepper and sugar or honey to taste
> water or *kvas*

Grate or shred the beetroot and the cabbage coarsely and chop the onions. Melt a little oil or butter in a heavy pan, add the onion, beetroot and cabbage and cook for several minutes, stirring until all the vegetables are well coated. Season lightly, add a teaspoon of sugar or honey and about half the volume of the vegetables in water or *kvas*. Simmer gently, covered, until the beetroot and cabbage are thoroughly cooked and the water evaporated. Dress with oil or butter and black pepper. No butter was allowed during Lent so the original recipe allowed no choice. Poppy seed oil was often used, otherwise hemp seed or unrefined sunflower oil.

Beetroot po zavolzhsky
This is a unique vegetarian beetroot casserole which I suspect also had its origins in Lenten cooking but is unthinkable, once you have tasted it, without the sour cream. With a grain it could be a light meal in itself, or it could be served in small quantities as a starter, either on its own with black bread or in small pastry cases, with plenty of sour cream and fresh chives or spring onions to garnish it.

> butter
> 1–2 medium onions
> 1 kg (2 lb) beetroot
> 250 g (8 oz) carrots
> 5–6 dried or 150 g (5 oz) fresh mushrooms
> 1 teaspoon salt
> 2–3 bay leaves
> freshly ground black pepper
> ½–1 teaspoon dried mint
> 1 lemon
> 10 cloves garlic or to taste
> ½ teaspoon red pepper
> 1 small (5 fl oz) carton sour cream

Melt a little butter in a heavy pan and add the chopped onions, followed by the beetroot and carrot, peeled and cut in cubes. Stir until all the vegetables are coated. Add the mushrooms, quartered, or whole if they are very small, and about half the volume of the vegetables in water. Bring to the boil, season with salt, add the bay leaves, and simmer, covered, until the vegetables are soft. The water should almost have evaporated. Add the black pepper, mint, grated lemon rind and half the garlic and cook gently for a further 5 minutes. Turn off the heat, add the lemon juice, and allow the pan to stand covered for at least 5 minutes. Meanwhile crush the remaining garlic and add it with the red pepper to the sour cream. Serve the vegetables hot, dressed with the cream. If the mixture is used to fill pastry cases they should be lightly baked first, the filling added and the tartlets returned to a medium oven for a further 10 minutes. Serve with the same sour cream dressing.

CARROTS

The Russians also rate the carrot as a sweet vegetable, which it undoubtedly is at its best, and the most characteristic recipes tend to enhance the natural sugar content with added sugar, dried fruit or apples. In the peasant diet it was and still is often used to fill pies or to make cutlets. The following or similar preparations will all be found in traditional Jewish cookery from Eastern Europe, which makes maximum use of the sweet carrot by baking it into a cake.

Carrot and apple vzvar

A Russian Jewish friend prepared this sweetish, buttery mixture for me one evening for supper. We ate it after eggs, with sweet white bread and butter, accompanied by glass after glass of steaming tea made the Russian way, fairly weak and without milk. It was a frugal meal but unexpectedly tasty, unusual and satisfying. Think of it as a good, homely standby, useful for serving with chicken, pork, tongue, veal or sausages, or indeed after a dish of fried eggs.

> 500 g (1 lb) carrots
> 1 medium cooking apple
> butter
> salt, black pepper and sugar to taste

Peel the carrots and slice lengthwise. Cut the apple into similar sized pieces. Melt a little butter in a heavy saucepan or casserole with a lid.

Add the carrots and the apples, stir until they are well coated, and add a couple of tablespoons of water to the pan. Cover and leave to cook gently for at least an hour, adding a little butter and water if it gets too dry. The carrots when they are cooked should be very soft and the apples mushy. Stir them with a wooden spoon a couple of times to mix them together and add salt, black pepper and sugar to taste.

Stewed carrots with dried fruit

> 500 g (1 lb) carrots
> 1 tablespoon butter
> 1 teaspoon flour
> 125 g (4 oz) dried fruit (raisins, sultanas, apricots, prunes),
> soaked for a few hours
> black pepper
> 1–2 tablespoons sour cream

Peel the carrots and slice lengthwise. Melt the butter in a pan, stir the carrots until they are well coated, sprinkle with flour and cook for a couple of minutes over a low heat. Add half their volume of water and the dried fruit and simmer gently, covered, until the carrots and fruit are soft. Season with black pepper, and stir in the sour cream to make a light sauce with the juice in the pan. Heat through and serve.

CABBAGE

> No fire without fir and birch,
> no food without horseradish and cabbage
> *Russian saying*

Beetroot is the Ukrainian national vegetable. The honour in Russia falls to the humble cabbage, which becomes astonishingly versatile in the Russian kitchen, ready to appear in all guises in all seasons, in salads, soups, pies, vegetarian bakes and cutlets. It can accompany meat and fish, but often in poorer circumstances it is meant as a replacement for them. It is invariably cooked long and slowly, but the result is never that soggy, tasteless heap anyone with half an interest in good food has taken time to damn.

Cabbage and apples, stewed

> 1 medium white cabbage, about 800 g (1½–1¾ lb)
> 2 tablespoons butter
> 1 tablespoon flour
> 3–4 eating apples or 2 large cooking apples
> 2 tablespoons caraway seed
> salt, sugar and vinegar to taste
> 1 small (5 fl oz) carton sour cream
> fresh herbs to taste
> chopped tomato to garnish (optional)

Chop the cabbage finely. Melt the butter in a tall pan, add the cabbage, and stir until it is all coated. Sprinkle with flour and cook for a couple of minutes, stirring. Add about a quarter of the cabbage volume in boiling water and bring to the boil again on the stove. Add the grated or finely chopped apple and the caraway seed, and simmer, covered, for 10 minutes or longer. Add salt and sugar to taste and a dash of vinegar and stir in the sour cream. Heat through and serve sprinkled with fresh dill and chopped raw tomato.

Cabbage and apple, baked

> 1 medium cabbage
> 4 tablespoons butter
> 2 tablespoons flour
> 200–300 ml (⅓–½ pint) water
> 4–6 eating apples or 3 cooking apples
> 2 eggs
> ¾ small (5 fl oz) carton sour cream
> salt and pepper
> 1 tablespoon toasted breadcrumbs

Chop the cabbage finely. Melt the butter in a pan or casserole, add the cabbage and stir until coated. Add the flour, cook for a few minutes then add the water. Set to cook gently, covered, for about 20 minutes, stirring from time to time, then add the grated apple. Beat together the eggs and sour cream, season, and add to the mixture in the pan. Turn into a buttered baking dish strewn with breadcrumbs, dot with butter and bake in a medium oven until the cabbage is brown on top.

Lithuanian cabbage

> 400 g (12 oz) bacon pieces or streaky bacon in a chunk
> lard or butter (optional)
> 2 onions
> 800 g (1½–1¾ lb) cabbage
> 300 ml (good ½ pint) bacon or other meat stock
> 2 cooking apples (optional)
> black pepper

Melt the bacon, chopped in small cubes, in a pan either on its own or with a little extra lard or butter if liked. Add the chopped onion and brown lightly, then add the finely chopped cabbage and the stock. Season, then simmer, covered, for about 40 minutes. The cabbage should be fairly soft and a brownish colour. Peeled, finely chopped apples may be added about 10 minutes before the end of cooking. Sprinkle with plenty of freshly ground black pepper and serve with sausages.

Cabbage baked with cream and cheese

> 1 medium cabbage
> 1 litre (1¾ pints) milk
> salt and pepper
> 200 ml (⅓ pint) single cream
> 4–5 tablespoons toasted breadcrumbs
> grated Edam cheese or Parmesan for topping

Chop the cabbage finely and set to cook gently in the milk, seasoned with salt and pepper, until it is soft. Strain off the milk* and put the cabbage in a buttered baking dish. Mix in the cream, sprinkle with breadcrumbs and cheese and bake until the top is nicely browned. Serve as a vegetarian main dish with boiled potatoes and baked tomatoes or with garlic bread, or in small quantities with boiled bacon.

---

* The milk left over may be used to make soup by adding a couple of table-spoons of rice, herbs, an onion, 2–3 carrots and a bay leaf. Cook until the rice is soft and either liquidize or serve it as it is. Potatoes may replace the rice and caraway seed may be used to flavour the soup. Add butter to taste.

Baked solyanka or Moscow solyanka in a pan
This dish, which is served alone as a light meal, shares its name and some of its ingredients with one of the classic Russian soups. Versions exist with and without meat (for a vegetarian version see the next recipe).

> 1 onion
> 100 g (3½ oz) butter
> 750 g (1½ lb) cabbage or sauerkraut
> ½ tablespoon flour
> 750 g (1½ lb) coarse pork sausage or garlic sausage in chunks
> 2 pickled cucumbers
> 10 olives
> 1 tablespoon capers
> a few marinated mushrooms
> meat stock

Chop the onion and fry it in the butter until transparent. Blanch the cabbage in boiling water, chop it and add it to the pan. Sauerkraut, if used, should be squeezed free of most of its liquid first. Stir to coat the cabbage with butter, sprinkle with the flour and leave to cook gently, covered, for 1–1½ hours. Transfer to a buttered baking dish, arranging the cabbage, sausage and sliced cucumbers in layers, ending with a layer of cabbage. Decorate with sliced olives, capers and marinated mushrooms. Pour over a good meat stock and bake in a medium oven until the top begins to brown.

Vegetarian solyanka

> 750 g (1½ lb) cabbage
> 2 carrots
> 1 parsley root or parsnip
> 50 g (2 oz) butter
> 2 onions
> ½ tablespoon flour
> 2 tablespoons tomato purée
> 1 pickled cucumber
> 2 eggs
> ½ tablespoon sugar
> 1 tablespoon vinegar
> salt and pepper
> 1 tablespoon grated cheese or toasted breadcrumbs

1 tablespoon capers
1 tablespoon marinated berries (see page 310) (sweet pickle
is a good substitute)
vegetable stock

Chop the cabbage and cook in a little water until tender or to taste. Peel and chop the carrots, parsley root and onions and fry them lightly in the butter. Add the flour, cook for a couple of minutes, then add the tomato purée and the finely chopped cucumber. Mix this with the drained cabbage and add the beaten eggs, sugar, vinegar and salt and pepper to taste. Arrange in a buttered baking dish. Sprinkle the top of the *solyanka* with cheese or toasted breadcrumbs and the capers and berries (or pickle). Pour over vegetable stock and dot with butter. Bake in a medium oven until the dish is hot and the top bubbling.

Sauerkraut vzvar
The basic Russian way of cooking sauerkraut is with oil or bacon fat and sugar or honey, producing a rich sweet and sour mixture which is an excellent accompaniment to pork, goose, bacon or sausages. There are many variations – version 3 below, with sour cream and mushrooms, is an excellent vegetarian one. For a home-made sauerkraut recipe, see page 311.

(1) 800 g (1¾ lb) sauerkraut
     50 g (2 oz) butter
     2 onions
     2 tablespoons vinegar
     2 tablespoons honey
     plenty of black pepper
     salt to taste

Drain the sauerkraut well, squeezing out most of the liquid, and fry it lightly in the butter with the chopped onion until it is soft. This will take about 20 minutes with a lid on the pan. Heat together the vinegar, which should be good quality wine or cider vinegar but not too strong (3°), and the honey and pour over the cabbage. Simmer gently for 15–20 minutes. Season with plenty of black pepper and salt to taste. The butter may be replaced with bacon or goose fat.

(2) 800 g (1¾ lb) sauerkraut
     50 g (2 oz) butter, vegetable oil, lard or bacon fat
     2 tablespoons sugar

     1 teaspoon dry mustard
     cranberries (substitute blackcurrants or redcurrants) to taste
     a few marinated plums or cherries, marinated grapes
       (optional)
     1 cooking apple, peeled and chopped

Cook the sauerkraut in the fat as in the previous recipe until soft, then add all the remaining ingredients and return to a low heat for about 30 minutes. Alternatively leave in a slow oven to cook for several hours, adding a little water if the mixture becomes too dry. Sauerkraut is like *shchi* in that it benefits greatly from being left overnight to stand before it is eaten. It is perfectly feasible to use tinned berries, including their juice, but in that case halve the quantity of sugar. Half a small tin of berries is sufficient for this quantity of sauerkraut. The marinated fruits are an excellent addition if you have them.

  (3) 150 g (5 oz) fresh mushrooms or 6 dried mushrooms
       400 ml (⅔ pint) water
       2 tablespoons butter
       800 g (1¾ lb) sauerkraut
       1 tablespoon flour
       1 tablespoon sugar
       1 small (5 fl oz) carton sour cream

Bring the mushrooms to the boil in the water and simmer for 15 minutes. Drain, reserving the liquid, and chop the mushrooms. Melt the butter in a pan and add the sauerkraut, squeezed dry. Stir well over a low heat, sprinkle in the flour and cook for a few minutes before adding the mushroom stock. Cover and simmer gently for half an hour, then add the mushrooms, sugar and sour cream. Return to a low heat and cook covered until very tender, or bake covered for 2 hours in a slow oven.

  (4) 400 g (12 oz) boiling bacon or pork belly
       800 g (1¾ lb) sauerkraut
       90 g (3 oz) pearl barley
       1–2 onions
       oil or butter
       1 teaspoon sugar
       salt and pepper

Chop the meat into chunks and place in a heavy, preferably cast iron, casserole. Cover with the sauerkraut, squeezed dry, sprinkle over the dry barley without mixing in and pour over boiling water to a height just above the contents of the pan. Leave to bake in a medium oven for about 2 hours until all the water has been absorbed. Before serving, chop the onion and fry lightly in oil or butter, sprinkle with sugar and add to the sauerkraut. Season with salt and pepper.

OTHER ROOT VEGETABLES AND VEGETABLE MIXTURES

Russian cooking makes use of turnips and swedes in combination with sour cream and breadcrumbs just as it does almost any other food, but the nicest way to cook these roots is simply to bake them whole in a medium oven and eat them with good unsalted butter. Do not salt them until they are cooked. Put a little butter and a few tablespoons of water in the bottom of the casserole to stop them sticking and serve this juice with the vegetables. Onions, turnips, swedes, potatoes, kohlrabi and carrots may also be baked together in one pot, cut into large pieces. The same vegetables with the addition of cabbage may also be parboiled separately and finished together in a white sauce.

Traditional Russian cooking features what I think must be a unique combination of cooked pink radish and honey. The habit of eating radish hot, braised like turnip, has been known in other Western cuisines, for example in the French provinces in the last century, but for the original inspiration one probably has to look east, to China and Japan, where the common radish is thought to have come from. Use small pink radishes whole, or larger ones cut into two or three pieces, and braise in butter, covered, over a low heat, until they are tender. Add a little honey during the cooking according to taste, and season with salt before serving.

Onion vzvar

STEWED SWEET ONIONS

> 900 g (2 lb) onions
> 2–3 tablespoons vinegar
> 2 tablespoons butter or vegetable oil
> 1–2 tablespoons honey or brown sugar
> salt and plenty of freshly ground black pepper

Chop the onions finely, sprinkle with the vinegar and leave to stand for 10 minutes. Melt the butter or oil in a pan, add the onion and cook very gently, covered, until very soft. Do not allow the onion to brown.

Add the honey or sugar, salt and pepper. The mixture should be fairly thick. If it is not, reduce it over a medium heat. Serve with roast lamb, goose, turkey, sausages, or boiled tongue.

Marrow vzvar

I think of this as a poor man's *ratatouille*. It is a tasty, but by no stretch of the imagination elegant, combination in more or less any proportion of fresh cabbage, marrow and onion. The vegetables are cooked slowly until they are almost a pulp. Begin by braising the onion in butter, add the other vegetables and leave to cook gently with a lid on for about 45 minutes. The marrow will give off plenty of liquid. Add 1 or 2 tablespoons of tomato purée during the cooking, and season with salt and pepper before serving.

Braised pumpkin or marrow with yoghurt and garlic

Pumpkin is eaten a great deal in Armenia, puréed, stuffed, baked with grain or simply braised in butter and served with a well-flavoured sauce, which I think is the nicest way.

> 500 g (1 lb) pumpkin
> salt
> 1½ tablespoons flour
> 50 g (2 oz) butter
> ½ head of garlic
> 1 small (5 fl oz) carton plain yoghurt
> red (cayenne) pepper

Slice the pumpkin into thin pieces, sprinkle with salt and leave to stand for 5 minutes. Drain, coat with flour and fry in butter. Pound the garlic, mix with the yoghurt, and serve with the pumpkin, sprinkled with red pepper.

Baked pumpkin with apple

> 500 g (1 lb) pumpkin
> 1 tablespoon butter
> milk
> 2 apples
> 90 g (3 oz) semolina
> 2 eggs
> 2 teaspoons sugar
> salt to taste
> 1 small (5 fl oz) carton sour cream

Peel and grate the pumpkin and put in a pan with the butter and a little milk. Cover and simmer until the pumpkin is tender, adding the grated apple about half-way through. Cook the semolina in milk and mix with the apple and pumpkin mixture. Allow to cool slightly before adding the egg yolks, sugar, and salt. Add the beaten egg whites, mix well and transfer the mixture to a buttered baking dish. Dot with butter and bake in a medium oven for 35–40 minutes. Serve with sour cream. This is yet another dish which is excellent with sausages.

Red pepper gulash
A modern recipe which takes advantage of the sweet red peppers to be found in northern markets in summer.

> 2 medium onions
> 500 g (1 lb) sweet red peppers
> 60–80 g (3 oz) butter
> 1 teaspoon flour
> salt and cayenne pepper to taste
> about 8 tablespoons meat stock
> 1 small (5 fl oz) carton single or sour cream
> 1 teaspoon tomato purée

Chop the onions and the peppers and fry lightly in the butter until both are well coated. Sprinkle with the flour, salt and cayenne pepper and pour over the meat stock. Cover and simmer for 15 minutes. Add the cream and the tomato purée and continue simmering gently for another 5 minutes. Serve this delicious combination with plain rice as a light vegetarian meal.

Hot fresh or salted cucumber

> 2 large straight cucumbers or 6–8 pickled or fresh ridge
>   cucumbers
> salt
> 50 g (2 oz) butter
> 1 onion
> 1 tablespoon flour
> meat or vegetable stock
> 1 small (5 fl oz) carton sour cream

Peel the cucumbers and cut into fingers about 5 cm (2 inches) long. If using fresh cucumber, sprinkle with salt and leave for 30 minutes, drain and dry with a cloth. Melt the butter in a pan, add the finely chopped onion and the cucumber. Cook with a lid on until tender, then add the flour, cook for a couple of minutes and pour over a scant cup of meat or vegetable stock and the sour cream. The dish may be finished off in the oven or served straight from the pan. Excellent with lamb or veal.

Lentil purée

> 200 g (7 oz) lentils, preferably green or brown (soaked overnight)
> 1 small carrot
> 1 small onion
> 1 small leek
> stock
> 2–3 tablespoons butter
> 3 tablespoons sherry (optional)
> 75 g (3 oz) ham
> salt to taste

Put the soaked lentils in a casserole with the peeled carrot, onion and leek, left whole. Cover with stock, bring to the boil, and bake covered in the oven until the lentils are cooked. Remove the vegetables and purée the lentils. Stir in the butter, sherry or more stock, the pieces of cooked ham chopped small and salt to taste, and heat through before serving.

Vegetarian stuffed marrow

> 1 marrow weighing about 1 kg (2 lb)
> about 4 tablespoons butter
> 100 g (3½ oz) rice (uncooked weight)
> 1 large onion
> 400 g (12 oz) fresh mushrooms
> 2 eggs
> salt and pepper
> toasted breadcrumbs
> 1 teaspoon flour
> ½ tablespoon tomato purée
> 1 small (5 fl oz) carton sour cream
> chopped fresh parsley and dill

Peel the marrow, slice it into rounds about 5 cm (2 inches) thick and scoop out a hollow in each of these pieces to a depth of about 4 cm (1½ inches). Fry lightly in a little butter with the bottoms uppermost in a covered pan for about 8 minutes. Meanwhile prepare the stuffing: cook and drain the rice, sauté the onion and mushrooms in butter, and mix with the rice and beaten eggs. Season the stuffing well and fill the marrow cups. Sprinkle with toasted breadcrumbs and dot with butter. Bake in a medium oven until the marrow is soft and starts to brown. To make the sauce, melt a little butter in a pan, sprinkle in the flour, cook for a few minutes, then add the tomato purée and the sour cream. Pour over the cooked marrow cups, return to the oven for 10 minutes, and serve sprinkled with parsley and dill.

Vegetable stuffed peppers
Excellent hot or cold, either as a starter or with rice or pasta as a vegetarian main dish.

> 8 medium sweet green peppers
> 500 g (1 lb) carrots
> 500 g (1 lb) onions
> 250 g (½ lb) celery
> up to 450 ml (¾ pint) sunflower oil
> salt and freshly ground black pepper
> good bunch parsley
> 500 g (1 lb) tomatoes
> 4 bay leaves
> 1 clove of garlic
> 4 tablespoons finely chopped greenery such as parsley,
>   chives or any other fresh herb to garnish

Pour boiling water over the peppers and leave covered until they are cold. Cut off the tops and remove the seeds. Peel and chop the carrots, chop the onion and celery, and sauté in a little of the oil until tender and golden. Add salt, plenty of pepper and parsley to taste. Stuff the peppers with the vegetable mixture, and put them tops upwards into a saucepan. Surround with the chopped tomatoes, the rest of the oil and the bay leaves. Cook on a low flame without a lid. The tomatoes and the oil should form a rich sauce. No harm will come if a little water is added to stop the mixture sticking to the pan. When the tomatoes and oil have blended to make a thick juice, remove the pan from the heat, add the finely chopped garlic and a little chopped greenery, allow to cool and serve strewn with more greenery. Alternatively serve hot. The oil makes it a very filling dish.

Other stuffed vegetables

For how to prepare vegetables for stuffing see page 142. Cabbage leaves, aubergines and marrows may all be stuffed with the filling given for green peppers (page 201) and served in a rich tomato or tomato and sour cream sauce (pages 132, 141). During Lent Russians also used to stuff vegetables with mixtures of cooked buckwheat and mushrooms. Here are three more vegetarian stuffings, the first two for aubergines, the third for vine leaves, which come from Armenia.

(1) Stuffing for 500 g (1 lb) aubergines

> 50 g (2 oz) dried beans (chick peas, haricot beans, red
>   beans), soaked overnight
> 2–3 onions
> 40 g (1½ oz) butter
> 2–3 tablespoons tomato purée
> salt and black pepper

Cook the soaked beans in water until tender. Chop the onions and fry lightly in the butter until transparent. Add to the pan the tomato purée, the drained beans, salt and black pepper, mix well and fill the prepared aubergines.

Serve with yoghurt mixed with pounded garlic and seasoned with red pepper.

(2) A second stuffing for 500 g (1 lb) aubergines

> 2 hard-boiled eggs, chopped
> 75 g (3 oz) grated cheese
> salt and pepper
> 40 g (1½ oz) butter

Mix together the eggs and cheese, season and fill the prepared aubergine halves, dot the surface with butter and bake covered for about 30 minutes in a medium oven or until the aubergines are tender. The cover from the baking dish may be removed to brown the tops during the last 5–10 minutes.

Serve with yoghurt mixed with pounded garlic and seasoned with red pepper.

(3) To stuff vine leaves for 4 people

> 100 g (3½ oz) dried beans (soaked overnight)
> 2–3 tablespoons rice
> 2 small onions
> 5 tablespoons vegetable (sunflower) oil
> 4 fresh plums
> 40 g (1½ oz) raisins (soaked overnight)
> 1 tablespoon coriander leaves
> ½ tablespoon fresh thyme
> ½ tablespoon fresh parsley
> 1 teaspoon fresh mint
> 1 teaspoon fresh basil
> plenty of black pepper
> 40 g (1½ oz) dried apricots (soaked overnight)

Cook the soaked beans and the rice separately. Chop the onions and lightly fry in 1 tablespoon of the oil. Chop the plums into small pieces and mix with the beans, rice, onions and other ingredients except the apricots, mixing well. Stuff the vine leaves with the mixture and place in a casserole with the apricots on top. Add water until it just reaches the top of the leaves, then add the remaining vegetable oil, cover the casserole and cook over a low heat or in a slow oven until they are cooked, about 1–1½ hours. Serve alone or with a tomato sauce (page 132).

AUBERGINES

These imports from the South have been popular in Russia for over a century, as long as Russians have enjoyed Caucasian cooking. They can be stuffed and baked as above, made into poor man's caviare (page 43) or cooked (baked or steamed) and served with Garo sauce (page 157), garlic and vinegar sauce (page 158) or any tomato sauce (page 132). They may be sliced, braised in butter or oil, or steamed and served with garlic-flavoured yoghurt. Aubergines also mix well with other vegetables, and many varieties of such mixtures are canned for instant use.

Armenian aubergine stew

> 250 g (8 oz) aubergines
> salt
> 250 g (8 oz) potatoes

2 onions
2 small sweet red peppers
2 tomatoes
100 g (3½ oz) green beans
a handful of assorted fresh herbs
½ head of garlic or to taste
¼ teaspoon red pepper
black pepper to taste
50 g (2 oz) sunflower or olive oil

Slice the aubergines crossways, salt lightly and leave to stand for 15 minutes, then squeeze out the juice. Slice all the other vegetables and chop the herbs and garlic finely. Arrange in layers, starting with the aubergines, in a buttered casserole, sprinkling each layer with red and black pepper, salt and herbs, pour over the oil and cook covered over a low heat until all the vegetables are tender. The dish may be baked in the oven or simmered very gently on top of the stove. In the latter case 4 or 5 tablespoons of water may be added to prevent it sticking or frying.

Aubergine borani

5 aubergines
salt
3 onions
4 tablespoons oil or butter
1 tablespoon each coriander leaves, basil, mint
1 teaspoon cinnamon
1 teaspoon salt

Slice the aubergines, sprinkle with salt, leave for 15 minutes, then squeeze out the juice. Slice the onions in rings and fry lightly with the aubergines in the oil or butter, adding the herbs, cinnamon and salt to taste. Serve with chicken (see page 156) or as you wish.

Green bean borani

400 g (12 oz) green beans
2 onions
4 tablespoons vegetable oil
1 tablespoon each basil, coriander, dill
1 teaspoon cinnamon
1–1½ small (5 fl oz) cartons yoghurt

Bring the beans quickly to the boil in salted water, drain, cut into 2 or 3 pieces, fry lightly with the chopped onion in the oil and mix with the chopped herbs and the cinnamon. Allow to cook for 2 more minutes, remove the pan from the heat, and stir in the warmed yoghurt. Serve straight from the pan, or with plain roast chicken.

See also spinach *borani* (page 156), which may be prepared as a vegetarian dish with or without the addition of 250 g (8 oz) of chopped spring onion.

Moldavian vegetarian musaka

A colourful, light dish which has nothing in common with the rich Greek combination of mince and cheese custard, or the anglicized mince, potatoes and grated cheese *musaka* which is a glorified cottage pie.

> 2 medium aubergines
> 4 tomatoes
> 3 large onions
> 1 marrow weighing about 1 kg (2 lb)
> ¼ Savoy cabbage
> 3 bay leaves
> 1 tablespoon each parsley and dill or oregano and dill
> black pepper
> 1 head of garlic or to taste
> 2 tablespoons sunflower or olive oil
> up to 2 small (5 fl oz) cartons of sour cream
> potatoes (optional)

Slice all the vegetables except the cabbage, which should be cut in strips. Arrange in layers in a buttered casserole, starting with the aubergines, sprinkling each layer with a little of the herbs, pepper, finely minced garlic and oil. End with a layer of marrow and pour over the remaining oil. Bake, covered, in a medium oven for 1 hour, adding the sour cream in the last 15 minutes of baking and removing the lid so that the top may brown. Thin slices of potato could also be added to this *musaka* to make it a complete dish.

Mushrooms

Among the various objects men are wont to chase the humble pursuit of picking mushrooms too has its place. Although it cannot be compared to the more lively forms of hunting for the obvious reason that these are concerned with living creatures . . . there is an element of the unknown, of the accidental, there is success or failure, and all these things together arouse the hunting instinct in man and constitute its particular interest.

S. T. AKSAKOV, *Remarks and Observations of a Mushroom Hunter*

La Russie fournit une grande variété de champignons; en automne les marchés en regorgent, et j'ai vu vendre des espèces dont la physionomie n'avait rien de fort rassurant, mais les Russes les mangent sans crainte, et il faut croire que c'est aussi sans danger . . .

URBAIN DUBOIS, *Cuisine de tous les pays*

By August every year a huge signboard identifying a score of the commoner varieties of mushroom has gone up in Moscow's Central Market, midnight mushroom trains are departing regularly from the railway stations, and the newspapers are carrying reports of giant discoveries in this or that province. The Russian pursuit of mushrooms, which the nineteenth-century writer Sergei Aksakov called 'the third hunt', cannot be described merely as a pastime. It is love, recreation, closeness to nature, passionate science and national heritage. Men, women and children go mushroom-picking for food, for profit, for the sheer pleasure of being in the forest and for the delight of an unusual find or a rich crop. The season is bounded by the last April snow and the first flurries of winter in October, although connoisseurs know of frost mushrooms, and a spell of warmer moist weather in December can cause a freak crop to shoot up in the forests. Dawn is the best time to hunt. The mushrooms are fresh and the competition thinner on the ground, hence the special night trains which take devoted city-dwellers deep into the countryside with their baskets and flasks. Schoolchildren learn in class how to recognize the over forty edible varieties of mushroom native to Central Russia and which to leave alone. The same wisdom is passed down from generation to generation and repeated in magazines and books. The state now sets up 'mushroom points' at the edges of forests and near rivers, where mushroomers can hand over their spoils for cash or enjoy a working holiday at the centre, helping to wash the fungi in the river and dry them in the ashes of a huge Russian stove. A few years ago, during a good season when the weather had been mild and wet, there were over 150 of these points around Moscow alone. The record for a single mushroom find stood at 10 kilograms (21 pounds) and 1.7 metres (over 5 feet) in diameter.

Mushroom lore brings the forests alive. These strange and wonderful growths have names which locate them in a fungous elfin kingdom of old men with ear trumpets, little women with long-stemmed umbrellas, men wearing hoods in the rain, Caesar's favourites, little foxes, little pigs, little hawks and cows and goats with beards, those that live under the birch tree and those that prefer to live under the pine tree. Always lurking under some tree or other is the devil.

Russian cooking makes greater and more varied use of mushrooms than any other cuisine in the world. Fresh ones are eaten raw, dressed with herbs, cooked into soups and pies, or baked with cream. Others are dried on strings for use during the winter in soups, or powdered to flavour *kasha*. Every year the price of dried mushrooms is a cause for national concern. A popular winter delicacy is pickled or salted mushrooms, which are eaten as a snack and washed down with vodka. In country districts mushrooms are still a substitute for meat.

The prize of the third hunt after large and small game is the *white mushroom* (the Boletus family, French *cèpe*), followed by the *ryzhik* (saffron milk cap, chanterelle) and the *smorchok* (morel). All three are to be found in the British Isles but are not nearly as common as the field mushroom or *champignon*. This is an agaric for which the best Russian cookery has little time, although it can be adapted to produce second-best results. In *Speak, Memory*, Vladimir Nabokov, recalling his mother picking mushrooms around their St Petersburg estate, made the comparison with typical snobbishness:

One of her greatest pleasures in summer was the very Russian sport of *hodit' po griby* (looking for mushrooms). Fried in butter and thickened with sour cream, her delicious finds appeared regularly on the dinner table. Not that the gustatory moment mattered much. Her main delight was in the quest, and this quest had its rules. Thus, no agarics were taken; all she picked were species belonging to the edible section of the genus Boletus (tawny *edulis*, brown *scaber*, red *aurantiacus*, and a few close allies), called 'tube mushrooms' by some and coldly defined by mycologists as 'terrestrial, fleshy, putrescent, centrally stipitate fungi.' Their compact pilei – tight-fitting in infant plants, robust and appetizingly domed in ripe ones – have a smooth (not lamellate) under-surface and a neat strong stem. In classical simplicity of form, boletes differ considerably from the 'true mushroom,' with its preposterous gills and effete stipal ring. It is, however, to the latter, to the lowly and ugly agarics, that nations with timorous taste buds limit their knowledge and appetite, so that to the Anglo-American lay mind the aristocratic boletes are, at best, reformed toadstools.

Rainy weather would bring out these beautiful plants in profusion under the firs, birches and aspens in our park, especially in its older part, east of the carriage road that divided the park in two. Its shady recesses would then harbor that special boletic reek which makes a Russian's nostrils dilate – a dark, dank, satisfying blend of damp moss, rich earth, rotting leaves. But one had to poke and peer for a goodish while among the wet underwood before something really nice, such as a family of bonneted baby *edulis* or the marbled variety of *scaber*, could be discovered and carefully teased out of the soil.

On overcast afternoons, all alone in the drizzle, my mother, carrying a basket (stained blue on the inside by somebody's whortleberries), would set out on a long collecting tour. Towards dinnertime, she could be seen emerging from the nebulous depths of a park alley, her small figure cloaked and hooded in greenish-brown wool, on which countless droplets of moisture made a kind of mist all around her. As she came nearer from under the dripping trees and caught sight of me, her face would show an odd, cheerless expression, which might have spelled poor luck, but which I knew was the tense, jealously contained beatitude of the successful hunter. Just before reaching me, with an abrupt, drooping movement of the arm and shoulder and a 'Pouf!' of magnified exhaustion, she would let her basket sag, in order to stress its weight, its fabulous fullness.

Near a white garden bench, on a round garden table of iron, she would lay out her boletes in concentric circles to count and sort them. Old ones, with spongy dingy flesh, would be eliminated, leaving the young and the crisp. For a moment, before they were bundled away by a servant to a place she knew nothing about, to a doom that did not interest her, she would stand there admiring them, in a glow of quiet contentment. As often happened at the end of a rainy day, the sun might cast a lurid gleam just before setting, and there, on the damp round table, her mushrooms would lie, very colorful, some bearing traces of extraneous vegetation – a grass blade sticking to a viscid fawn cap, or moss still clothing the bulbous base of a dark-stippled stem. And a tiny looper caterpillar would be there, too, measuring, like a child's finger and thumb, the rim of the table, and every now and then stretching upward to grope, in vain, for the shrub from which it had been dislodged.

Fried mushrooms

A mixture of 'noble' mushrooms (any of the Boletus family) and other well-flavoured lower-born varieties such as *russula* and chanterelles is wonderful just fried gently in butter or sunflower oil with a little onion for 10–15 minutes. Another method is to coat them in flour before frying. Finish in the pan with sour cream, dill and parsley. Mushrooms cooked in sour cream this way are excellent with plain rice or buckwheat. Some cooks recommend starting the mushrooms off in a dry pan with a lid on it over the heat and adding the oil or butter and onion only when they have exuded their juice. But if you are limited to champignons whose juice is not so great a delicacy, you may feel there is no need for this extra measure. A third method of frying mushrooms is to blanch them quickly in boiling water, dry them, dip them in flour, and then in egg and breadcrumbs. Fry them in butter and serve pyramid shape on a plate, sprinkled with parsley and accompanied by wedges of lemon.

Baked mushrooms

ZHULIEN

Chop the mushrooms, coat them in flour and fry in butter. After 10 minutes add sour cream and seasoning to taste, heating gently until the mushrooms are surrounded by a thick, rich sauce. Transfer to individual oven-proof dishes and bake in a medium hot oven until the tops brown. Serve in small quantities as a first or second course at dinner or as part of a light lunch. Baked mushrooms sit very happily between smoked salmon and a good ·dressed salad. In Russian restaurants they are a favourite second course after *zakuski*, and especially after caviare. *Zhulien* comes served in little silver pots with long handles like miniature Turkish coffee pots, and with a tiny spoon to scoop out the rich contents. This wonderful mixture may also be used to fill shortcrust pastry tartlets.

Mushroom caviare

RAW MUSHROOMS DRESSED WITH OIL AND HERBS

I first enjoyed this in a country restaurant outside Moscow which specialized in traditional cooking. Fresh mushrooms are chopped coarsely, sprinkled with a little salt, black pepper, pressed garlic and the juice of an onion, pressed down with a plate and a weight on top of it, and left to marinate for several hours. Add oil, lemon juice and fresh herbs to taste before serving. Fresh tarragon is the best complement, but use only a tiny amount.

Salted mushrooms

To have mushrooms in winter which could be like fresh mushrooms, in stews, soups and cold dishes like the one given above, Russians devised several ways of preserving them. One method was to wedge them tightly in layers in a large barrel, placing blackcurrant leaves on the bottom and sprinkling each layer with a little coarse salt, chopped onion, pepper and sometimes garlic and herbs. The mushrooms would give off a lot of juice in the presence of the salt and were preserved in it. Each variety was salted separately. When they were needed for cooking they were soaked in water to remove the salt, dried and used like fresh mushrooms. Some Russian housewives carry on the same process today, but using glass jars rather than barrels. They hand round these mushrooms with suitably flavoured chilled vodka. The fungi are very salty eaten this way, rather slimy and altogether an acquired taste. For me the only experience that comes near to eating them is swallowing oysters.

Another old way of preserving mushrooms was to fry them in butter or oil without seasoning them and keep them, covered with clarified butter, in a jar which was then kept cool in the cellar or in the snow. This way the mushrooms were preserved whole and without any additional flavour. The great advantage was that they could be used in pies or simply fried again.

Marinated mushrooms

For latterday cooks the marinade is certainly the easiest preserving method to imitate well. The result is an excellent snack to hand round with drinks before dinner. Choose a time for preserving when mushrooms are fairly cheap, usually in late summer and early autumn, but do not sacrifice quality and size to get a bargain: the economy will mean failure. Choose small, firm button mushrooms. Clean them, wipe dry, bring to the boil in salted water, and simmer for 5–10 minutes. Strain, and when cold put in jars. The mushrooms shrink quite considerably during this initial process and at least 300 g (10 oz) of fresh mushrooms can be packed into a standard 450 g (1 lb) jam jar. In a pan bring to the boil a mixture of equal parts of water and good wine or cider vinegar, seasoned with a little salt, a few peppercorns, a bay leaf, a clove and a few dill seeds. Allow to cool before pouring over the mushrooms. Cover the top with olive or sunflower oil, and screw on the lid. Leave for at least 3 weeks before eating.

Dried mushrooms

This is traditionally done in a Russian stove in the wood ashes or on rods above them, or by stringing up the mushrooms like giant necklaces around the stove, which gives them a woody flavour. When they are cooked in boiling water, they yield a rich stock and all the fragrance of the Russian forest in early autumn. Sadly, many town cooks have to resort nowadays to drying mushrooms in their ovens, which means an inevitable loss of flavour and aroma. Others find time to build bonfires at the edge of the forest in late evening, especially if they are on holiday and hunting at the same time. That way the scent of the woods is safely brought home for rediscovery in mid-winter. There can be no comparable romance attached to mushroom hunting and drying in Britain, but when mushrooms are cheap it is useful to dry them for soup stock. If you can stand the extravagance, turn the oven on as low as possible, put the cleaned and dried mushrooms on a baking tray inside, and leave them for at least 24 hours with the oven door open. It is a long expensive process and not, I think, sufficiently rewarding given its cost. A more economical method is to thread the mushrooms on a thick thread by passing a needle through them and to hang them up over a hot radiator. But this effectively removes all the romance of 'the third hunt'. . .

Soloukhin, the Soviet nature writer, should have the last word on mushrooms:

> While you are sorting out the mushrooms you recall each one, where you found it, how you first saw it, how it was growing beneath this bush or that tree. Once again you experience the pleasure of each discovery, particularly if they were rare and fortunate discoveries. Once again all the images of the mushroom forest drift through your mind, all the secluded wooded spots, where you are no longer, but where the dark firs still lour and the crimson-touched aspens speak their language in a low breath.

VALENTIN SOLOUKHIN, *'Tret'ya okhota'*

The Boletus edulis *or white mushroom, considered the pick of the hunt. Illustration from Aksakov.*

Hot Zakuski and Supper Dishes

Hot *zakuski* are meat, fish, vegetable dishes and pies whose hallmark is that they can be prepared quickly and alone, without further garnishing. In pre-Revolutionary Russia they would very often be served, several different dishes together, at supper or at lunch, whenever *obed*, the main meal of the day, was not taken. Supper was the time for *réchauffés*, cunning combinations of leftovers, quick one-saucepan dishes, things on toast, inventions with eggs, slightly sweet curd cheese dishes which could be eaten morning, noon or night and were always popular with children, and pasta with a sweet or savoury filling. I have also included here the classic Russian pies, and pancakes, which strictly speaking are part of an *obed* but in practice, especially Western practice, are likely to be thought of almost as meals in themselves.

When the preparation of food speeds up and the emphasis is on convenience, national distinctions and traditional cooking methods tend to disappear and only odd features and combinations of ingredients turn up in their place. Combinations of minced cooked meat and potatoes, cooked grain bound with egg, seasoned and fried, mixtures of cooked vegetables in a cheese sauce, leftover fish or chicken baked with eggs and milk and bread, the same leftovers rolled inside pancakes and masked in tomato sauce, omelettes and eggs on toast: which country or cuisine would claim any of these as a typical or special dish? If Russian supper-time cooking has a distinctive feature, it is the readiness to prepare whole dishes that are slightly sweet, like curd cheese fritters (*syrniki*) or apple or jam omelettes, and to combine meat and fish without demur. Stale bread is invariably stale black rye bread, which has a very pronounced taste of its own. Dill and sour cream are unchanging.

FISH

Herring and sausage on black bread toast

> 1 large salted herring, kipper or bloater
> milk or weak tea for soaking
> 3 hard-boiled eggs
> 2 teaspoons mustard powder
> 1 tablespoon olive oil
> 2 teaspoons fresh dill
> 4 thick pieces of black bread
> butter
> 3 cold cooked sausages (English pork, frankfurters or
>   saveloys)
> sour cream to taste

Fillet and soak the herring in milk or weak tea until most of the salt has been removed. Chop it finely and mix with the chopped hard-boiled egg and the mustard powder mixed with the oil and the chopped dill. Toast the bread well on one side and very lightly on the other. Butter the second side generously and spread it with a thick layer of herring mixture. Cut the sausages lengthways in thin strips and lay them over the filling. Dot with butter and put briefly under the grill to heat through. Serve with a dollop of sour cream to each portion.

White fish and sardine bake

> butter
> 500 g (1 lb) any white fish fillets
> 1 small can sardines
> 2 large slices bread
> 2–3 eggs
> 400 ml ($\frac{2}{3}$ pint) milk or buttermilk
> salt, pepper, nutmeg
> juice of 1 onion or 1 onion very finely chopped
> chopped fresh parsley

Butter a large baking dish, line it with a layer of fish fillets and spread it with the mashed sardines. Cut the bread in quarters or smaller pieces and fry in butter. Cover the fish with a layer of fried bread and sardines, then add another layer of fish. Alternate the layers, ending with a layer of bread and sardines. Beat the eggs and milk together, season well with salt, pepper and nutmeg, add the onion or onion juice and pour over the mixture in the dish. Sprinkle with parsley and bake in a medium oven for 20 minutes or until the eggs are set. Serve either alone, followed by a plain salad, or with fresh peas, baked tomatoes, or carrots and boiled potatoes if you want a really filling meal. The Russian way would also be to eat the fish bake with a little extra buttermilk or sour cream, or I think ideally a mixture of the two.

Though it is naturally better with fresh fish, this is a great way of using up any leftover white fish, or salted fish, which is worth keeping in stock for emergencies. The dish has no pretensions to elegance but it is extremely nourishing and an ideal opportunity to make use of cheaper fish like coley.

Supper forshmak

The *forshmak* given on page 107 is a relatively light dish, and is the one to choose if you want a hot starter to a full meal, served in small quantities and preferably individually baked in pancake-size shallow pans or ramekins. The homelier version uses up scraps of cooked meat and stale bread or cooked potatoes along with the salted herring that used to hold body and soul together in winter months.

> 1 medium salted herring (or 3–4 sardines, drained of their oil)
> milk or weak tea for soaking
> 250 g (8 oz) boiled or roast meat or poultry
> 2–3 cooked potatoes
> 1 onion
> butter
> 1 tablespoon flour
> 2–3 eggs
> 2–3 tablespoons sour cream
> black pepper
> grated cheese

Soak the herring in milk or weak tea to remove the salt, then chop it into pieces and put through a mincer or food mill together with the meat and potatoes. Stir into this mixture the onion, fried in butter, the flour, egg yolks, sour cream and butter to taste, and the stiffly beaten whites. Season with plenty of black pepper and put into a greased baking dish. Sprinkle the top with grated cheese and bake in a medium oven for 30 minutes. Serve with sour cream sauce, either plain or flavoured with tomato purée (page 141).

Fried smelts or sprats
This makes a very quick starter or part of a supper. Clean the fish through the gills, leaving the heads on. Wipe them, coat well in flour, and fry with some chopped green onion in a mixture of butter and vegetable oil. Add a splash of vinegar to the pan when the fish are cooked, which will not take more than a few minutes. Serve with black bread.

EGGS

Omelettes are instant good food. Russians make them with eggs and milk and eat them with melted butter. Chopped raw spring onion is a good addition, or fry thin slices of apple in the pan before adding the omelette mixture. For an Armenian style omelette (*skrob*) add grated *brynza* (or feta) cheese or fried onions, aubergines, tomatoes, garlic and fresh herbs to taste, and season the omelette with red pepper.

Drachena
This traditional Ukrainian dish is a near relative of the omelette. It is thickened with flour, enriched with cream or butter, sometimes slightly sweetened with sugar, and baked. It may be eaten savoury with butter or sour cream, or sweet with honey. Though tradition demands black rye flour mixed with wheat or buckwheat, for my taste ordinary wheat flour with buckwheat flour in the proportions 2:1, or all wholemeal flour, are better.

> 5 eggs
> 1 tablespoon caster sugar
> 3 tablespoons flour
> 100 ml (about 6 tablespoons) cream or milk
> 30 g (1¼ oz) melted butter
> salt
> melted butter and chopped fresh herbs for serving

Mix the egg yolks with the sugar and slowly add the sifted flour, stirring to make a smooth mixture. Add the cream gradually and the butter. Season with salt, and add the beaten egg whites. Turn the mixture into a well buttered soufflé dish and bake in a medium oven for 25 minutes. Serve with melted butter and freshly chopped herbs. Mint and parsley together are excellent.

Drachena may also be cooked like an omelette, without separating the eggs. The following is a lighter, richer version.

3 tablespoons flour
1 small (5 fl oz) carton single cream
1 small (5 fl oz) carton sour cream
4 eggs
50 g (2 oz) butter
chopped fresh parsley
salt, pepper and a pinch of sugar

Mix the flour to a smooth paste with the single cream, mix in turn with the sour cream and beat into the eggs. Add the melted butter, the parsley and seasoning and a pinch of sugar and cook in an omelette pan with butter.

Hard-boiled eggs in cream
Hard-boiled eggs, though you are unlikely to have any left over if you are cooking Russian food, may be sliced lengthways, covered with sour cream, seasoned with salt and pepper and put in a hot oven for 10 minutes. Eat them with black bread and seasoned with fresh dill.

Baked eggs

½ teaspoon butter
½ teaspoon flour
6 tablespoons chicken or vegetable stock
½ small (5 fl oz) carton sour cream
5 slices French bread about 2 cm (1 inch) thick
5 eggs
salt and pepper
fresh parsley, dill or other fresh herb

Melt the butter, sprinkle over the flour, cook for a minute and then add the warmed stock. When this has thickened add the sour cream. Keep this sauce hot. Hollow out the centres of the bread slices so that they form thick-walled rings, and fry them on both sides in butter. Butter a shallow baking dish, pour into it the hot sour cream sauce, and then set the bread rings in the sauce. Into each ring break an egg, season with salt and pepper, and put in a very hot oven until the whites are cooked. The yolks should still be runny when you serve the eggs straight from the dish, strewn with chopped parsley, dill or any fresh herb to taste.

CHEESE

The cold *zakuski* cheeses given on pages 44–5 convert to a light supper when served with hot starches. The Georgians eat cheese with millet *kasha* (page 177). The Belorussians serve *mokanka* (page 45) hot with boiled potatoes. Both curd cheese and brine cheese also cook well in their own right.

Syrniki/Tvorozhniki

CURD CHEESE FRITTERS
These have always been my favourite breakfast in Russia, together with Russian cheesecake (page 272). They may be served sweet with sugar or jam, or semi-savoury with nutmeg and melted butter. Adults invariably prefer the latter, and certainly that is the way to make supper-time *syrniki*. Curd cheese mixed with eggs and flour and fried is popular throughout central Russia and Central Asia.

> 250 g (8 oz) curd cheese
> 3–4 tablespoons flour
> ½ beaten egg
> 1 tablespoon caster sugar
> few drops vanilla essence, or use vanilla sugar instead of
>   caster sugar
> nutmeg and salt to taste
> 1 tablespoon butter
> melted butter, sour cream or jam for serving

Beat the cheese until very smooth and sprinkle over it half the sifted flour. Work in along with the egg, sugar, vanilla, and seasonings. Form into small balls or rissoles on a floured board and fry in butter on both sides until brown. Serve with melted butter, sour cream or jam. In savoury *syrniki* finely chopped fresh herbs may be included in the mixture.

Khachapuri

These are a wonderful Georgian preparation, midway between a pie and a fritter, filled to the brim with cheese. Eat them hot, when they are at their best. I have seen them served as a first course at dinner, leaving everyone too full to enjoy the rest of the meal. They are enough on their own for a light lunch or supper, followed by a green salad. There are many recipes for the dough, which may be flour and milk raised with yeast, or sour milk and flour and egg like a scone dough. The latter provides a change from standard Russian baking and is quicker and richer. The filling would normally be a Georgian cheese like *brynza* preserved in brine, which is soaked to remove most of the salt before it is used. Feta cheese may be used in the same way, but any of the crumbly English cheeses (white Lancashire, white Cheshire, etc.) are excellent and easier to come by. What is more, not being brine cheeses they do not need the preliminary soaking before they can be used.

FOR THE DOUGH
200 ml (⅓ pint) sour milk, thin yoghurt or whey
2 eggs
¼ teaspoon salt
plain flour to make a soft but not sticky dough

FOR THE FILLING
500 g (1 lb) cheese
1 egg
25–50 g (1–2 oz) butter
melted butter and beaten egg to glaze

Mix together the sour milk, beaten eggs and salt and add the sifted flour until you have a smooth elastic dough. Turn out on to a floured board, divide in four and roll out each quarter about half a finger thick. Cut rounds 6–8 cm (about 3 inches) in diameter out of two of the quarters, and rounds slightly smaller out of the other two. Make the filling by crumbling the cheese and mashing or pounding it smooth with the egg and butter. I find a large wooden pestle ideal for the job. Put a good spoonful in the middle of the larger dough circles until you have used up all the cheese. Slightly flatten them and cover each with a smaller circle of pastry. Pinch the edges together. (For richer *khachapuri* you may add extra butter to the dough as it is being rolled out. Each quarter may be dotted with butter, folded in four, rolled out again and then cut into rounds. Use a good 100 g (3½ oz) of butter for pastry made in the proportions given above.) The pies are then fried in a heavy-bottomed pan in butter or butter and oil, top side down, over a moderate heat, with a lid or plate covering the pan. After 6–8 minutes, when the underside is brown, turn the pie over, brush on top with melted butter and beaten egg, and continue cooking without a lid for about 5 minutes or until the underside is done. Serve very hot. *Khachapuri* are also sometimes baked open or as one large pie in the oven.

Fried brine cheese

Cut slices of brine cheese (or feta) about 2 fingers thick, roll them in flour and fry in hot butter, sprinkling each piece with more flour in the pan. The cheese should be cooked, covered, for 3–5 minutes. Serve it with fresh herbs and *mchadi*, the Georgian cornbread given on page 178.

PANCAKES

Blini, traditional Russian buckwheat pancakes, have been eaten for centuries by rich and poor Russians without distinction during *Maslenitsa*, the week of supposed semi-fasting before Lent. But in trying to come up with a good recipe I have come to agree almost entirely with what Elizabeth David calls her personal and heretical view. Buckwheat flour alone produces a tasty enough *blin*, but it is far more of a crumpet than a pancake. It is robust and strongly flavoured, and you deserve a prize if you can get it to roll up around its filling without cracking. The ideal texture to aim for is crumbly and light, but if you achieve it the only way to proceed is to put the filling on top as one would put something on toast. It is a curious thing, but for reasons of taste and texture buckwheat pancakes are not such good complements for their traditional caviare filling as one is led to suppose.

The solution to these problems in Soviet Russia has been simple. No restaurant which I have eaten in there has ever used buckwheat flour or even yeast to make its *blini*. They serve black and red caviare with *crêpes*. Nor have I seen buckwheat flour on sale in the shops. What has appeared in its place, sadly, is instant pancake flour mixture, which contains baking powder, seasoning, and dried egg and milk. One needs only to add water. The result is unimpressive.

Collectors of Russian recipes in the West have generally suggested keeping to the yeast formula but using a mixture of buckwheat and white flour, or even all white flour, to make a lighter pancake. Such pancakes still bear a marked resemblance to the crumpet in my view.

My own compromise with tradition has been to use buckwheat and white flour together but to renounce the yeast. What emerges is a pancake which is thin and pliable but far tastier and I think more distinguished than a *crêpe*. It goes well with caviare or smoked salmon, and I have discovered it does have genuine Russian parentage in what Mrs Molokhovets called the *Gurev* pancake.

Although buckwheat made Russian pancakes famous, those made

with true grains such as millet and barley used also to be very popular. They belong to the ordinary table and there is no question of lightening them or delicately rolling them around caviare. Experiment with savoury fillings like chopped hard-boiled egg or spring onions, or sweet fillings like honey or jam.

In a full Russian *obed*, *blini* are served after the cold *zakuski*. They may be followed by consommé, then pies, and then the main meat course. For all this you would need a gargantuan appetite and I suggest in the normal course of things serving *blini* either as a starter, say two per person, or as a light lunch, preceding them with soup and finishing with a salad or fruit.

A traditional recipe for blini

> 300 ml (½ pint) water and another 100 ml (⅛ pint) milk or
>   water
> 2 teaspoons dried yeast
> sugar to taste
> 350 g (12 oz) buckwheat flour
> ½ teaspoon salt
> 1 egg
> whipped cream to taste (optional)
> butter or butter and oil

Warm the water and milk slightly and dissolve the yeast and sugar. When the mixture begins to foam and bubble slightly add it to half the flour, stirring with a wooden spoon to keep it smooth. Leave to rise for 1–2 hours in a warm place, covered with a tea towel or inside a plastic bag. Add the salt, the egg yolk and the rest of the flour, beating well. Leave to rise again for another 1–2 hours. Just before cooking fold in the stiffly beaten egg white and a spoonful of whipped cream for extra lightness and crumbliness. The mixture before cooking may be quite thick.

For cooking use a small, heavy-bottomed frying pan and heat it gently for a few minutes before you are ready to start. Use butter or butter and oil, and reckon, especially the first time, to throw away the first few pancakes until you get the heat and the amount of fat and batter just right. 'The first pancake turns out a mess' is an old and true Russian saying. Cook for about 4 minutes each side, turning with a spatula. *Blini* do not toss. A 10-cm (4–5 inch) pan will need about 2 tablespoons of mixture, depending on its thickness, for each pancake. Re-oil the pan after each one is cooked. If you have a set of *blini* pans they may also be slipped into a hot oven to cook, which was the original method. The mixture makes about 12 *blini*, which are probably best eaten with chopped hard-boiled eggs and sour cream and/or melted butter. Like English crumpets, they are also excellent just with butter and may be kept warm in the oven. Chopped herring and sour cream is another traditional accompaniment.

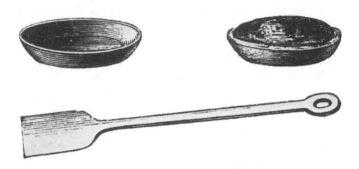

Russian cast-iron blini *pans and a ladle for spooning in the mixture. The pans often fitted into a six-pan holder which could go in a hot oven or on top of the stove.*

Blini with white and buckwheat flour mixed

Mixing wheat and buckwheat flour to make *blini* may not be a habit stretching back to medieval Russia but it has certainly been around as long as refined wheat flour and the influence of French ideas on Russian cooking.

> 2 teaspoons dried yeast
> pinch of sugar
> 100 ml (⅔ pint) milk or water and milk
> 350 g (12 oz) white flour
> ½ tablespoon butter
> 100 g (3½ oz) buckwheat flour
> 1 egg
> ½ teaspoon salt

Dissolve the yeast and sugar in three-quarters of the warmed milk or water and milk. When the mixture starts to bubble, stir it into the white flour, together with the melted butter. Leave to rise for 1–2 hours. Beat well, add the buckwheat flour, the egg yolk, the salt and the rest of the liquid, warmed. Leave to rise again. Fold in the beaten egg white just before using. Cook and serve as in the previous recipe. This recipe may also be followed using all white flour.

Lenten pancakes without eggs

Ingredients for these are as in the previous recipe, but omitting the egg and butter.

Dissolve the yeast in a little of the milk and mix it with the buckwheat flour and half the white flour to make a thick dough. Cover and leave in a warm place to rise, if possible overnight. Next morning add the rest of the flour, the salt and the sugar, and half an hour before baking dilute the mixture with warm milk to the texture of thick cream.

Gurevskie blini

RUSSIAN PANCAKES WITHOUT YEAST

These are the pancakes I recommend serving with caviare or smoked salmon. They can be made with white flour or wheatmeal flour alone, but are tastier and equally light made with a little buckwheat flour as well. Unlike other traditional recipes they can be assembled in minutes.

> 1 teaspoon baking powder
> 350 g (12 oz) white flour
> 100 g (3½ oz) buckwheat flour
> salt
> 2 eggs
> Sour or fresh milk
> 4 tablespoons melted butter

Sift together the baking powder, the flours and a pinch of salt and add the egg yolks one at a time, stirring with a wooden spoon. Gradually add the warmed milk and butter until the mixture has the texture of heavy cream. Beat the egg whites stiffly and add just before cooking. Serve straight from the pan with any of the following:

> Finely chopped herring and lemon
> Any smoked fish in thin slices, with lemon and butter
> Sour cream
> Lumpfish caviare and sour cream or lemon and butter
> Very finely chopped onion, cooked beetroot and cucumber
>   in French dressing with plenty of sugar.

♦ Various ingredients such as chopped hard-boiled eggs, chopped onion and drained cottage cheese may be incorporated into the *blini* mixture as soon as it has been poured into the pan.

♦♦ If all the mixture is not needed, or if it is made in advance, it will keep very well in the refrigerator, provided it is given the chance to warm up and rise before it is cooked.

♦♦♦ An excellent way to use up pancake mixture when you have had enough of pancakes is to incorporate it into your next home-made loaf. Buckwheat mixtures are particularly good as they add a distinctive nutty flavour and a good light brown colour. Buckwheat itself has no gluten, but combined with a greater proportion of strong wheatmeal flour it makes an excellent loaf of no particular origin. The Lithuanians once baked unleavened buckwheat bread, but I have not come across any recipes for combining it with wheat flour to make a leavened loaf.

♦♦♦♦ A more traditional way of using up cooked *blini* made wholly or mainly of wheat flour is to make a *blini* pie (*blinchatyi pirog*) or *karavai*. The pancakes are piled up on top of each other with a filling of minced meat and onions, chicken livers and onions, mushrooms and cream, or cottage or curd cheese and chopped onion and herbs, masked with a good tomato or mushroom sauce, and put in the oven to heat through.

Millet, barley and semolina pancakes

The word *blin* (a single pancake) comes from *mlin*, meaning, like the French word *gruau*, something ground. Try substituting barley flour in place of the buckwheat in the yeast recipes above, using milk to make the batter, or follow the two recipes below which incorporate cooked millet (millet *kasha*) and semolina respectively; they will make about 24 fairly thick 15-cm (6-inch) *blini* rather like crumpets.

    (1) 300 g (11 oz) millet (uncooked weight)
        400 ml (⅔ pint) milk
        3–4 tablespoons melted butter
        300 g (11 oz) buckwheat flour or buckwheat and white flour
           mixed in equal proportions
        3 teaspoons dried yeast
        2 eggs
        1–2 tablespoons sugar
        1–2 teaspoons salt
        melted butter and sour cream for serving

Cook the millet as on page 197. It should be fairly liquid. Bring a quarter of the milk to the boil with 1 tablespoon of butter, and stir it into half the flour. When it cools to room temperature add the yeast, dissolved in a little warm water, and leave the mixture to rise in a warm place. Add the cooked millet, the rest of the flour, the egg yolks, sugar, and salt, and finally the rest of the milk, warmed. Stir well to give a smooth mixture and leave to rise again twice. Just before cooking in small frying pans fold in the beaten egg whites. Serve with melted butter and sour cream.

(2) 300 g (11 oz) semolina (uncooked weight)
milk for cooking semolina
3 tablespoons melted butter
300 g (11 oz) white flour
400 ml (⅔ pint) milk
3 egg yolks
1–2 teaspoons salt
butter and sugar for serving

Cook the semolina in as much milk as is needed to make ordinary pudding consistency, and add the butter while it is still hot. Add the flour, the 400 ml (⅔ pint) milk from the recipe, and a few tablespoons of water. Stir until smooth and add the egg yolks and the salt. Cook as for ordinary unleavened pancakes, and serve with butter and sugar.

PASTA

Few people, I think, would credit the Russians with a tradition in pasta. For most of us its home is Italy. But whereas the Italian tradition came via Ancient Greece from Oriental cuisine, Russia took the habit directly from the East during the thirteenth- to fifteenth-century Mongol occupation. And while Italian pasta dishes were adapted almost 2,000 years ago to make use of ingredients plentiful in the Mediterranean, like tomatoes and olive oil, Russian preparations retained an Oriental quality until spaghetti and tomato sauce invaded as a quick twentieth-century food. The outstanding dish was and still is *pel'meni*, a version of what the Italians call *ravioli* and the Chinese *wraplings* or *chiao-tzu*, in which noodle paste is formed into pouches containing usually a meat filling. Variations on this theme are to be found today throughout the Soviet Union, all of Oriental derivation, but with many different names. The Ukrainians call them *vareniki* (meaning things that are boiled in water). In Armenia they are called

manty. Like the Chinese and the Japanese, Russians often eat their classic pasta dish in quick street cafés called *pel'menye,* to be found in big cities like Moscow and Leningrad.
A second borrowing from the East is noodles. These are invariably eaten in soup. In the past they were made of buckwheat flour, which gave the Russians a unique culinary link with the Japanese, but the habit has all but died out today. Packaged, Italian-style durum wheat pasta in all shapes and sizes is to be found now in every grocer's store.

Pel'meni

Under the Mongol yoke *pel'meni* became established in Siberia and the Urals, from where the number of recipes and varieties is infinite. Traditionally a mixture of beef, pork and elk is used, and it is said that whole villages in Siberia still turn out one afternoon before the onset of winter to make a vast batch of *pel'meni.* The women make the dough and chop the meat, the men do the folding. For their exacting work the latter enjoy a glass of vodka every hundredth *pel'men'.* The traditional form is ear-shaped but they come in all shapes from squares to triangles. The villagers have an immediate feast after their work, with which ice-cold vodka is obligatory. The rest of the *pel'meni* are deep frozen in goatskin bags in the snow. *Pel'meni*-eating contests take place periodically.

It is a mark of their popularity that *pel'meni* can now be bought ready-made in Russian supermarkets. Not without cause are they sometimes celebrated as an ideal dish for bachelors by those who feel the latter are generically unable to cook. Just throw them into boiling salted water, wait until they rise to the surface, remove with a straining spoon and serve with sour cream, butter and lemon juice, or oil and vinegar and seasoning. They are extraordinarily tasty and filling.

FOR THE DOUGH
300 g (11 oz) white flour
salt
1 egg
4–5 tablespoons water

Sift the flour with a pinch of salt. Beat the egg and mix in, and add the water to make a smooth fairly stiff paste. Roll out on a floured board and cut out in small rounds about 5 cm (2 inches) in diameter. Place a generous spoonful of filling (see below) on each round and fold over, pinching the edges together. The dough should be kept as cool as possible and ice-cold water should be used to make it to ensure the best results. The filling should be as dry as you can make it. *Pel'meni* may be made in advance and kept in the refrigerator for several hours or overnight, but unless they are totally dry you run the awful risk of them sticking together and becoming impossible to separate. Brushing them lightly with oil will help.

FOR THE FILLINGS

For pel'meni: well-seasoned raw minced meat, preferably a mixture of beef and pork, with a little minced onion added.

For Azerbaijani dyushpara: finely minced lamb, seasoned with garlic, onion, mint, basil, pepper and, ideally, dried barberries. Almost half the filling should consist of herbs, and it should have a slight sour taste.

For Turkmenian manty: raw fish fillet, chopped finely, seasoned with onion, black pepper, red pepper, salt, cardamom, fresh dill and parsley and a few crushed fennel seeds, bound with raw beaten egg.

For Ukrainian vareniki: curd cheese, seasoned with salt and sugar to taste. For every 500 g of cheese add 1–2 tablespoons sour cream and 1–2 beaten eggs.

For Russian nalisniki: chopped, cooked and well-drained spinach, seasoned with nutmeg and mixed with a little thick cream.

All these pasta pouches are cooked in boiling salted water and eaten with any of the dressings suggested above. The Armenians in addition like a dressing of yoghurt and garlic. Alternatively the *pel'meni*, *manty*, *dyushpara* and *vareniki* may be served in an appropriate clear broth of beef, chicken, fish or vegetables.

Yet a third way is to shallow or deep-fry the pouches after brushing them with beaten egg. Cooked this way they become *chebureki*, a Central Asian speciality.

Boiled *pel'meni* and *vareniki* may also be finished in the oven by pouring sour cream over them in a baking dish and sprinkling them with fresh herbs. This is a particularly good way to treat *nalisniki*.

PIES

Pies (*pirogi*) have been staples of high and low Russian tables for as long as Russian cooking has existed. They have evolved almost completely free of foreign influence. The word *pirog* comes, some experts think, from an old word *pir*, meaning feast. Until fairly recent times pies were festive food, and no name-day party or wedding feast was complete without one, usually of grand proportions and possibly wrapping up a whole fish. 'Houses make a fine street, pies make a fine table' runs the saying. At a full *obed* they would be served between the fish and the roast meat or game, but being great fillers they were often for the poorer classes a meal in themselves. The pastry literally wrapped up the usual midday meal – bread, cabbage, *kasha*, mushrooms – and made it ideal portable fare.

Despite a frail body, Nikolai Gogol's travelling collector of souls had an insatiable appetite for pies. It took the best inns to match it in *Dead Souls*. Only one of his hosts defeated him with the lip-smacking imagination that left this recipe to posterity.

'Make a four-cornered fish pie,' he was saying, smacking his lips and sucking in his breath. 'In one corner put a sturgeon's cheeks and dried spinal cord, in another put buckwheat porridge, little mushrooms, onions, soft roes and brains and something else – well – you know, something nice ... And see that the crust on one side is well browned and a little less done on the other. And make sure the under part is baked to a turn, so that it's all soaked in juice, so well done that the whole of it, you see, is – I don't want it to crumble but melt in the mouth like snow, so that one shouldn't even feel it ... feel it melting.'

NIKOLAI GOGOL, *Dead Souls*

The best-looking pies I have ever seen in Russia were sold at Pskov railway station, one of those delightful long, low, Russian nineteenth-century buildings painted a pale green and trimmed in white, like a piece of Wedgwood or an iced cake, separating the street from the railway line. The *bufet* had just taken delivery of a fresh wooden tray of large pies which gleamed golden brown under their egg polish and were warm to the touch. It was a terrible disappointment then to break one open and find inside nothing but unseasoned rice awash in starch. Literally the tradition of grand cooking for travellers had gone hollow. Today Russians make their own pies or manage sadly without. I never found a restaurant that served them.

The hallmark of classic Russian pies, apart from the raised pastry, is that they contain not one or two but many ingredients, some to give flavour, some to ensure succulence, others to provide texture. Some are lined with pancakes, many contain chopped egg, mushroom and cooked rice or buckwheat. Everyday pies would often be mainly rice or buckwheat with vegetables, or just cabbage. However, the one special, uniquely Russian, ingredient was *vyaziga*, dried sturgeon's spinal cord, which was bought powdered or in fine leaves like old-fashioned gelatine and had to be soaked for several hours in water and simmered for another 3 or 4 hours until it was ready for use.

Generally it was added to fish pies to improve their flavour. It was not considered a staple ingredient in its own right, though it might be the only flavouring added to cooked grain in a smaller pie. There is no real substitute, although the flavour of fish pies may be enhanced with anchovy essence.

Like Russian bread and cakes, traditional pastry was made with rye flour until the end of the fourteenth century, and only slowly did it become first a mixture of wheat and rye and then a wholly wheat dough made with the most refined flour available. The medieval versions must have been extremely solid and on the sour side. I would certainly not recommend imitating them for anything other than authenticity, though a handful of rye flour in any of the pastry mixtures given here could not go amiss in a savoury pie.

Doughs can be leavened or unleavened. The usual raising agent is yeast, but baking soda, yoghurt, sour cream and beer were all used in nineteenth-century recipes.

The actual baking process is simple, though some writers in love with the idea of the old Russian stove will insist that the temperature inside the oven must fall gradually as the pie is baking. This means putting the pie in a hot oven, turning it down to medium as soon as the pastry begins to brown, and then after another 10 minutes or so, depending on the size of the pie and the type of filling, down to low. I take a more relaxed approach, the only two rules being to start off with a hot oven (about 400–450°F, gas 6–7) and to keep an eye on what is happening inside. Only fish is used raw as an ingredient. Serve the pies straight from the oven either alone with melted butter, or with a bouillon appropriate to their filling. As for yesterday's pie, if like me you have a mania for not throwing food away, gently reheat it in a warm oven for 5–10 minutes and serve with plenty of hot bouillon spooned over it.

Pastry
Here is an excellent shortcrust pastry recipe from Mrs Molokhovets:

> 250 g (½ lb) butter or margarine
> 2 egg yolks + 1 whole egg
> 4 tablespoons rum, vodka or cold water
> 500 g (1 lb) flour
> pinch of salt

Cream the butter, add the yolks, whole egg and rum, and slowly work in the flour which has been sifted with the salt. Allow to stand for a few minutes in a cool place before using. I have found that in emergencies this pastry keeps very well for a day or so in the refrigerator, and is also eminently suitable for freezing. It rolls out beautifully and has a rich, buttery taste and a light texture. If you feel it is too rich or too expensive, cut down on the eggs and butter and use a little more water. Or follow one of the following recipes for pastry during Lent, which use no eggs and only vegetable oil. Apart from being modest they are also remarkably quick to assemble. The flour, oil and water formula has become my regular standby in a rush.

> (1) 6 tablespoons oil (sunflower, poppy-seed, arachide, walnut)
> 10 tablespoons cold water
> 500 g (1 lb) flour
> pinch of salt

Mix the oil and water thoroughly and gradually add the sifted flour and salt. Brush the finished pie with a mixture of oil and water before baking.

> (2) 500 g (1 lb) flour
> 2 teaspoons cream of tartar
> $\frac{1}{4}$ teaspoon baking soda
> $\frac{1}{2}$ teaspoon salt
> 2 tablespoons vegetable oil
> 150–200 ml ($\frac{1}{4}$–$\frac{1}{3}$ pint) warm water

Sift together the flour, cream of tartar, baking soda and salt, and proceed as in the previous recipe.

Raised dough

> 2–3 teaspoons dried yeast
> pinch of sugar
> 5 tablespoons warm water
> 60 g (2$\frac{1}{2}$ oz) butter
> 500 g (1 lb) flour
> pinch of salt
> 8 tablespoons milk
> 2 eggs

Dissolve the yeast and a pinch of sugar in the warm water. Sprinkle in a teaspoon of flour and leave for 15 minutes in a warm place. Pour into a bowl, mix in the softened butter, sifted flour and salt, the milk and the beaten eggs, and knead into a smooth dough. Leave to rise until it has doubled in volume. Knead again and roll out. Dough left over after making a pie can be formed into *bulochki* (page 258).

Kulebyaka

The best-known Russiàn pie abroad, thanks to its popularity with nineteenth-century French chefs, is *kulebyaka*. It sounds less attractive than it is when translated as fish pie. *Kulebyaka* consists of alternate layers of fish, cooked grain, and sometimes hard-boiled eggs, flavoured with dill, parsley, and onion, caught up in a raised pastry case. Made originally with salmon, pikeperch or sterlet, it was one of the first authentic Russian dishes to catch the French gastronomic eye and so find a place in the classical repertoire. Plumerey included it in his edition of *L'Art de la cuisine française au XIXe siècle* (1833–44). Carême also noted a 'salmon pie in the Russian manner' which he saw being made by a Russian cook at the house of the Russian ambassador to Paris. The recipe he gave seemed, however, to be already rather French. Rice replaced *kasha*, *foie gras* was slipped generously between the layers of fish and egg, and the whole was flavoured with nutmeg and *fines herbes*. It also swam in butter. Both Carême and Plumerey suggested a tablespoon or two of concentrated veal stock (*sauce espagnole*) for extra succulence. The sauce, which the Russian cook did not add, 'will give more taste and will render this strange ragoût more delicate', wrote Carême.

The traditional Russian way of eating *kulebyaka* – alongside a bowl of fish consommé or *ukha* (page 70) – solved the problem in its own way.

Here is a classic version:

FOR THE DOUGH
2 teaspoons dried yeast
6 tablespoons milk
350 g (12 oz) flour
60 g (2 oz) butter
1 egg yolk
½ teaspoon salt

FOR THE FILLING
350 g (¾ lb) pikeperch
90 g (3 oz) butter
1 onion
chopped fresh dill
1 egg
100 g (3½ oz) buckwheat (uncooked weight)
150 ml (¼ pint) water
salt
100 g (¼ lb) salmon
200 g (½ lb) sturgeon

Dissolve the yeast in the warm milk and when the mixture is spongy add to half the flour. Mix well and allow to rise. Add the rest of the ingredients, knead and allow to rise again. This is a modest *brioche* dough, for which you may substitute a richer one if you have a particular favourite.

To assemble the filling, fillet the pikeperch, cut it up into smallish pieces, and fry them lightly in 30 g (1 oz) of the butter with the chopped onion and dill to taste. Pound all these ingredients together when just cooked to form a stuffing. Break the egg into the buckwheat in a dry frying pan and mix until all the grains are covered. Heat gently until dry. Bring the water to the boil with the remaining butter and a little salt and add the buckwheat, stirring all the time. Cook for 10 minutes and add to the fish mixture. Slice the salmon and sturgeon finely.

Roll out the dough into a long rectangle. Place in the middle of it a layer of the fish and buckwheat mixture, followed by slices of salmon and sturgeon. Alternate, ending with a layer of mixture. Close the pie by bringing up the two sides and forming a tallish shape. Leave to rise for half an hour in a warm place. Brush with egg and bake for 35–40 minutes in a hot oven. Prick the pastry with a needle, which should come out clean if it is done. Cover the pie with damp paper if it shows signs of darkening too much during cooking. It is also a good idea to turn it round once. After you take the pie from the oven, cover it with a clean cloth to prevent the pastry from hardening. Serve with *ukha* (page 70).

Plumerey suggested using turbot instead of sturgeon/sterlet/pikeperch, since none of these fish were available in nineteenth-century Paris. Eel has also been successfully substituted for sturgeon. Other possibilities include, shark, dogfish, monkfish or huss, used in conjunction with a good firm white fish like char (whitefish), halibut, skate, Dover sole or brill to replace the salmon and pikeperch. One economical adaptation I came across, given by a Russian émigré living in the United States, used flounder (or any of the flat fish) to make the pounded mixture and slices of whiting to make up the other layers. It used semolina instead of buckwheat, and cooked it first in a fish stock enriched with butter.

Here is another adaptation of *kulebyaka*.

> shortcrust pastry made with 350 g (12 oz) flour
> 60 g (2½ oz) semolina
> fish stock for cooking semolina
> 125 g (4 oz) butter
> pancakes made with 180 g (6 oz) flour, 200 ml (scant ⅓ pint)
>   milk, 1 egg, a pinch each of salt and sugar and oil or
>   butter for frying
> ½ small can anchovies or sardines
> 5 hard-boiled eggs
> 1 onion
> 150 g (5 oz) mushrooms
> a little stock and lemon juice or cream
> 700 g (1½ lb) good white fish
> chopped fresh parsley and dill
> salt and pepper
> beaten egg to glaze

Roll out the pastry into a rectangle about ½ cm (¼ inch) thick. Cook the semolina in fish stock and enrich with 90 g (3 oz) of butter. Arrange the pie ingredients in layers – first the pancakes which may be cut so that the entire surface of the pastry is covered, then the semolina, then half the pounded anchovies or sardines well spread out, then half the sliced eggs. Next add the onion lightly fried in the remaining butter, all the mushrooms which should be quartered and cooked in a little stock and lemon juice or cream beforehand, all the fish, the remainder of the eggs and anchovies or sardines and the remaining semolina. Sprinkle in the parsley and dill, salt and black pepper as you go. Fold the pie carefully into the middle to make a tallish shape and seal carefuly at both ends and along the centre seam. Glazing the pie with a beaten egg will help to do this and give it a wonderful shine when it is cooked. Prick the pie with a fork in several places and bake it, central seam downwards, in a very hot oven to start with until it is brown, then reduce the heat to medium – about 40 minutes in all. Serve with a clear fish stock or *ukha*.

Urbain Dubois's Moldavian coulibiac

Follow either of the procedures given above for *kulebyaka*, using either a raised or a shortcrust pastry, but omitting the pancakes in the second version. Fill the pie with layers of cooked rice seasoned well with fresh or dried herbs to taste, salt and black pepper and butter, slices of poached brains (see page 135), minced veal kidney and thinly sliced hard-boiled eggs. Serve with a brown sauce enriched with madeira.

A mushroom pirog

For this use shortcrust or raised pastry made with about 350 g (12 oz) flour. Prepare a filling as follows.

> 500 g (1 lb) fresh mushrooms
> salt and pepper
> fresh dill
> chopped spring onion
> 60 g (2½ oz) butter
> 4–5 tablespoons sour cream

Chop the mushrooms, sprinkle with salt, pepper, dill and spring onion, and cook first in a dry pan until they give off their juice and then with the addition of the butter and sour cream. The mushrooms need only remain on the heat for about 5 minutes in all. Roll the pastry into two rounds, one slightly smaller than the other, to fit a shallow pie dish. Allow the mushrooms to cool, test for seasoning, and spread over the lower round of pastry. Cover with the other half of the pastry, sealing the edges well. Prick with a fork in several places, brush with egg and bake in a hot oven, gradually reduced to medium, for no longer than half an hour. This pie has a wonderful rich taste and is very easy to prepare. It is less good heated up.

A cabbage pie

For this use a raised pastry made with about 350 g (12 oz) flour, and a filling of fresh cabbage prepared in the following way.

> 1 small Dutch cabbage
> salt
> 2 tablespoons butter

2 onions
1–2 teaspoons dried sage
2–3 teaspoons lemon balm
½–1 teaspoon dried marjoram
plenty of freshly ground black pepper
salt to taste
2 hard-boiled eggs

Shred the cabbage, sprinkle with salt, and leave under a weight for a few hours. Drain off the juice and any superfluous salt. Blanch in boiling water for about 5 minutes, drain, transfer to a pan with the butter and onion and cook with a lid on for 10–15 minutes. Add the herbs and seasonings, mix with the chopped hard-boiled eggs, and arrange on a rectangle of pastry. Fold up into a *kulebyaka* shape, brush with beaten egg, prick the surface and bake with the central seam downwards in a medium to hot oven for about 40 minutes. Serve with melted butter and perhaps a vegetable or chicken consommé.

Kurnik

RUSSIAN CHICKEN PIE
This is the second most famous Russian pie. Use a raised dough made with 500 g (1 lb) flour, adding up to 250 g (8 oz) butter in place of the standard quantity.

FOR THE FILLING:
1 roasting or boiling chicken
1 bay leaf
1 onion
1 carrot
a few peppercorns
200 g (7 oz) buckwheat groats (uncooked weight)
1 beaten egg
120 g (4 oz) butter
5 hard-boiled eggs
fresh or dried dill weed
salt and pepper
up to ⅓ litre (½ pint) chicken stock
chopped mushrooms (optional)

Boil the chicken in a little water with the bay leaf, onion, carrot and peppercorns. When it is tender, remove the flesh from the bones and chop into smallish pieces. Meanwhile mix the dry buckwheat with half the beaten egg and dry it over a medium heat in a heavy-bottomed pan. Bring to the boil ⅓ litre (about ½ pint) of water to which you have added the butter, add the buckwheat, cook for 5 minutes and then leave to stand covered or in a warm oven until it begins to go dry. Mix in the finely chopped hard-boiled eggs, dill and seasoning. Line a pie dish with pastry. Spread with a layer of buckwheat, then the chicken, then the remaining buckwheat mixture. Cover the pie with a pastry top, leaving a hole in the centre through which you should pour a good, well-flavoured chicken stock before putting the pie in the oven. Cover the hole with a small round of pastry. Glaze the pie with the rest of the beaten egg and bake for 35–40 minutes in a hot oven. Serve hot with more chicken stock.

You may include chopped mushrooms fried in butter in the stuffing if you wish.

Stuffed onions in pastry

> 4 large onions plus up to another 200 g (7 oz) onion any size
> 120 g (4 oz) butter
> 1 small (5 fl oz) carton single or sour cream
> 75 g (3 oz) chicken, preferably uncooked
> 2 eggs
> 2 sardines
> a handful of fresh breadcrumbs or 4 tablespoons cooked rice
> salt and pepper
> rich shortcrust pastry made with 180 g (6 oz) flour, 1 egg and
>   90 g (3 oz) butter or margarine
> 1 egg white
> 2 tablespoons melted butter
> white sauce for serving (see recipe)

Wipe the 4 large onions but do not peel them. Plunge them into boiling water and allow to simmer for 1–2 minutes, remove, and cool. Peel off the outside layer and hollow out the insides, leaving a strong wall outside. Chop the other onions finely together with the scooped-out middles and cook them very gently in half the butter with a lid on the pan until they are very soft. They should not brown. Stir in the cream. Pound the chicken in a mortar and mix with the beaten eggs, the finely chopped sardines, the breadcrumbs soaked in milk and squeezed out (or the rice), the remaining butter, the onion and cream mixture and the seasoning. Fill the onions with this mixture. Roll out the pastry thinly and divide it into 4 squares each large enough to enclose an onion. Put an onion in the middle of each square, and bring the corners up to meet at the top. Press securely together at the top and sides so that the onion is completely enclosed. Brush with beaten egg white and allow to dry in the air. Place in a baking dish with a couple of tablespoons of melted butter and bake in a medium oven for 30 minutes. Serve with plenty of white sauce (you can use the butter in the baking dish to make the roux), made with milk or cream and flavoured with lemon juice to taste and plenty of black pepper.

Feasts and Fasts

Faith, poverty and poor local yields have accustomed most Russians to a frugal daily diet. Political systems have made little difference to that necessity. But there have always been feast days to bring large quantities of better food on to the family table occasionally. It is an eating pattern true of the humbler classes all over Western Europe in the nineteenth century, but in Russia things have not yet changed substantially. Russian food still belongs to the Victorian world which gave us our heavy, rich Christmas dinner to relieve the leanness of a Bob Cratchit diet.

There is a sense in which this violent swinging from feasting to voluntary or involuntary fasting suits the volatile Russian character. Now and again its routine moroseness will burst into wild gaiety. Despite the northern latitudes of most of Russia and the tyranny of the winter there often seems something Mediterranean about the Russian people, as they stroll ritually up and down the town or city boulevards on summer evenings and congregate in the inner court-yards and gardens of their apartment blocks, gossiping and watching the world go by. Though their harsh climate and daily grind undermine it, they are sociable, excitable, festive people.

Namedays or saints' days, more recently birthdays, Christmas, Easter and New Year are all celebrated. The Soviet calendar has added Revolution Day (7 November), International Women's Day (8 March), International Workers' Day (1 May) and a host of lesser holidays. Enthusiasts following the pre-revolutionary and the new calendars see in two New Years within the space of 10 days. Like everyone, the Russians like to eat, drink and be merry, but drinking is particularly important. They imbibe alcohol for merriment and bodily warmth, and the national character includes a strong need for both.

The main festive meal is organized round joints of roast meat, poultry and game. Sucking pig was the great favourite in the past, but today its cost is prohibitive and the roast is more likely to be turkey or red meat. At all meals there are *zakuski*, soup, pies and cakes, a *baba* or a *krendel'* with vodka and champagne, and probably chocolate truffles to finish.

A Russian loves to be able to offer hospitality to his neighbour, and quite often he will invite strangers to eat with him too. The traditional word for being hospitable is 'one who gives bread and salt'. Bread and salt are the symbolic offering of welcome and also a token of respect from host to guest. The guest is welcome to share even if the house has no more to offer than bread and salt. Bread and salt was also once part of the marriage ceremony, and has retained its symbolic value over many centuries. It was usual to offer bread and salt on a white cloth, and later on specially painted and inscribed bread and salt plates.

A Russian host is excessively generous at the table but he will not be happy unless his guests eat and drink to capacity, as many Westerners over the centuries have found out to their cost. He will devote hours of his time to entertaining his guests, and will probably want to give them presents as well as the best meal he can command. An eighteenth-century memoirist left the following typical picture of an occasion when three families were invited by a local landowner of sufficient means to 'come and live things up in the good old way':

> At lunch and supper were produced an endless number of glasses, vodka glasses, wine glasses and tumblers, and they were often passed round from hand to hand at other times too; all this made our dear guests very merry when they got up from the table and they stayed and celebrated with us for three days or more. In the morning we usually had a festive breakfast, then lunch and after that dessert; later on there would be drinks and *zakuski*, after that tea, and then supper. Everyone slept on the floor in a heap. In the morning when we woke up again we sat down to a meal and spent the rest of the time as we had done the day before.
>
> ANDREI BOLOTOV, *Zhizn' i prikluycheniya*

The writer noted that at Christmas there would be at least six families in the house, and in addition to feasting there would be dancing and singing. The food on such occasions would have been simple, bulky and plentiful. *Kvas* and fermented honey drinks as well as a variety of vodkas would have been consumed in abundance. There would have been pies, perhaps a roast, cakes and certainly *kasha*, which was considered a festive dish until the nineteenth century. According to one old book of superstitions, it was customary at name-day parties to break a *kasha* pie over the head of the person whose celebration it was before the festive meal began. This was thought to be a token of good luck. It was also considered unlucky if nothing was broken during the meal, whence perhaps the habit of deliberately breaking glasses which has become legendary outside Russia. The country's last Tsar, Nikolas II, imported the world's finest Baccarat crystal to follow it.

General festive fare of the kind already described was prepared for Christmas. Before the Revolution some families used to serve a compote of cooked dried fruit (*uzvar*) and a rice pudding with almond milk and raisins (*kutya*) on Christmas Eve to mark the end of a pre-Christmas fast, but there was no special Christmas meal as such.

The Orthodox Church keeps 12 feast days and 4 fasts. It celebrates the Resurrection as its greatest festival, not the birth of Christ. Consequently Easter, the 40-day Fast leading up to it, and the Carnival Week that was meant to prepare for the Fast, were much more important on the culinary calendar.

Before the Revolution a French chef wrote that Russian families of every standing observed the rules of Lent and Easter so strictly that no foreign chef could get by without a knowledge of the special dishes he would be required to prepare. Others have claimed that the intelligentsia and the aristocracy were not so obedient. But the influence of the Church on the daily table was still strong enough for them to need to dissent.

Carnival Week, or, to give it its Russian name, Butter Week (*Maslenitsa*), the Great Fast (*Velikii Post*) and Easter (*Paskha*) are inseparable from the long and devastatingly bleak Russian winter when the short days are so grey and the sky so low and laden it can seem as if life is dwindling away. *Maslenitsa* was originally a week of preparation for a dietary regime which would bring a similar austerity to the table. But almost inevitably, by proscribing meat but allowing fish and oil, it became a feast. By the sixteenth century it was a regular Rabelaisian *bouffe*. Men vied with each other to eat the most pancakes (*blini*), which they filled with caviare or smoked fish, rolled in butter and ordered by the 'elbow'. Rich merchants were reputed regularly to die of overeating at this time of year.

During the seven days of *Maslenitsa* travelling players would perform in the streets. Slides would be made on the ice and there would be skating, horse-drawn sleigh parties and, for the rich, winter picnics from hampers full of pies, wines and sweets. Though today Carnival Week evokes little more than the occasional fancy-dress parade, in the last century *Maslenitsa* had the atmosphere of a funfair on ice. Then, everyone, rich men and peasants alike, would drink vodka and eat *blini*. In the evenings the wealthy would also go to Carnival balls. The novelist Leo Tolstoy, a moralist and a puritan, conceived a particular disgust for such social merrymaking, and some of his greatest attacks on the leisured classes came by way of his pen portraits of *Maslenitsa*.

The carnival was essentially pagan with Christian overtones. Like the French *mardi gras* ('fat Tuesday') it celebrated the fatness of the fatted calf, a symbol of wealth and prosperity of the land. Both the Slavic and European festivals had their roots in ancient rites to mark the end of winter. In the north of Russia these were apparently still practised last century, and would include burning a straw effigy of the old season and marching it in procession to its grave with much dancing and singing. Pancakes would be baked for the dead with the entreaty 'send us life'. This habit spread in Russia from the last Saturday to the whole week of *Maslenitsa*. After *Maslenitsa* came the Great Fast. At its strictest (the first and the fourth week) it meant no meat, fish, or dairy products whatsoever. In the remaining weeks fish and vegetable oils were allowed to supplement a diet of preserved vegetables, pickles, pulses, grain, berries and water.

The best cooks in any country have never allowed themselves to be defeated by the meagreness of their ingredients, and Russians were no exception. It was considered important to keep usual meal times and courses and to give the appearance of a good spread. Soviet cookery books no longer feature Lenten recipes, but some of the classic vegetarian devices that derive from it, like using dried mushrooms to make a rich soup stock, baking cakes and pastry without eggs, and putting fish in every kind of soup and hot pot, became part and parcel of traditional cooking.

The last day of the Great Fast fell on Good Friday and was marked by total abstinence from food. In the kitchen it was also the day when elaborate preparations for the Easter table were reaching their height. The day before, Maundy Thursday, Holy Thursday salt (*chetvergovaya sol'*) would be made. Salt would be mixed in large quantities with egg white, wrapped in muslin and put for 24 hours in a hot oven. The result would be a little block of calcinated salt which was crumbled, sieved and used to fill the Easter salt-cellars.

The family would have been painting bowls of hard-boiled eggs for several days. Many different coloured dyes were used, together with paper transfers which left patterns and pictures on the eggs. The cyrillic letters XB would be painted on afterwards, standing for 'Christ is risen'. The eggs might also bear the initials of the person for whom they were intended, a gesture of affection which inspired the magnificent jewelled and enamel eggs produced by Karl Fabergé for Alexander III, Nikolas II and their families.

By Good Friday several pounds of *tvorog* (curd cheese) would have been sitting for at least 24 hours under a wooden press to extract from it the last drops of whey. *Paskha* would be made by combining the *tvorog* with cream, butter, dried fruit and nuts and packing it into a traditional wooden mould (*pasochnitsa*). Before Saturday evening there were also the traditional butter lambs to make and the *kulich* (see page 262) to bake. The lambs were made from fresh butter pressed into a mould roughly the shape of a lamb. Muslin would be pressed over the surface to give it a woolly appearance, two raisins impressed for eyes, a parsley collar added round its neck and a small green branch placed in its mouth. *Kulich* baking was a long process that demanded patience and good luck. It would be allowed to rise several times in the making. In the oven a 1½ kg (3 lb) cake was expected to rise to a height of about 26 cm (12 inches). But every family had its sorry tale of the time the *kulich* was 'killed' by an infelicitous appearance in the kitchen or someone innocently opening the oven door.

The finished Easter table, a spread of *zakuski* on a grand scale, provided virtually all the food a family and its guests would eat during Easter Week. This is what a French chef in the employ of a government minister in the middle of the nineteenth century learned to provide for the occasion:

> 2 *paskha* (about 2 kg (4 lb) each)
> 2 bowls of coloured eggs
> 2 *kulich*
> 2 butter lambs
> 2 joints of ham
> 2 stuffed lambs
> 2 sides of wild boar
> 2 stuffed sucking pigs
> 2 roast game birds or joints of poultry
> 2 sides of veal
> 2 *babas*
> 2 batches of *plyetski*
> 10 salt-cellars of Holy Thursday salt

In some households consommés and a few hot dishes would also be served. Every Easter table would sport many different kinds of iced vodka, wine and champagne. Cakes would vary from house to house but there would always be *kulich*. Mrs Molokhovets also suggested that no Easter table was complete without the cooked head of a wild boar, which would appear decorated and garnished among the meat dishes.

On Saturday night the table was laid. Every dish, including the Holy Thursday salt, had to be blessed. Many families would take their Easter food with them to church, where it would receive the blessing as part of the service. This practice is still common among Russian believers today, although it is usually limited to *kulich* and eggs. Sometimes the priest would visit local families in the evening, give his benediction and initiate the Easter celebration there and then with a glass of vodka. According to some sources it was not unknown for priests therefore to be very merry on Easter night. Various customs were followed on Easter morning. In some households only the men went out to neighbours to deliver Easter greetings. The women stayed at home to offer the food. In others Easter Day was a time when it was customary for everyone to hand out coloured eggs to friends and to pay festive visits. Among the wealthy it was also the custom to exchange small enamelled, gold, jewelled or crystal eggs with intricate designs. These were hung year by year on to a long chain, and over the Easter holiday women would wear these chains looped around their necks. Another habit which was widespread among the peasantry and is still widely practised was to visit family tombs and to leave an Easter meal of *kulich* and eggs on the grave of the dead person.

For the devout, the start of the Easter Feast came at the end of the midnight service when the priest repeated three times the salutation 'Christ is risen' and the congregation responded with 'Verily He is risen'. They returned home to a table that must have looked splendid wherever there was sufficient wealth to afford it in all its rich abundance. The *paskha*, turned out of its wooden form, would have the imprint of the Orthodox cross on one of its faces and on another the symbolic letters X B. Other attributes of the Passion, such as a ladder, nails or a sponge, might be depicted on the other two faces, the designs being embroidered with fruit and nuts on the surface of the cheese. The towering *kulich* would be crowned with white icing and decorated with paper flowers and perhaps crosses of gold paper. The table itself would be adorned with bouquets of fresh flowers. The sucking pigs would be golden brown where they had been basted with sour cream, and would crouch on the table whole with a soused apple or a paper rose in their mouths and perhaps a collar of greenery. The eggs, arranged pyramid shape in baskets, would occupy the places of honour. Eating was not formal. It was done standing up as for *zakuski*, and some food was taken every time a guest arrived. But it was usual to begin with salads and gradually to work one's way through the other savoury dishes, ending with *paskha* and *kulich*.

The Butter Week fair.

Although wealth was necessary to enjoy a rich table, Easter was always a festival celebrated by rich and poor alike, and everyone had the bare minimum of *paskha* and *kulich* to offer. It was a time of great superficial equality, when peasants and their master would exchange the traditional three kisses on the cheek and the salutation 'Christ is risen'. Those words would ring out everywhere for the duration of Holy Week, but most strikingly hour after hour, day after day in church. While I was preparing this book I happened by accident on a service in a small church outside Moscow several days after Easter. The inside was richly decorated in gold and silver and the letters X B were illuminated in red many times over. The congregation, who always stand or kneel (there are no pews in an Orthodox church), consisted mainly of old women in woollen stockings, dark clothes and headscarves who came and went as their time allowed. Over and over the Easter greeting was repeated in song. By chance both Easter and the coming of spring were late that year, but it was impossible not to notice the sudden, almost overnight appearance of buds on the trees and the smell of the warming earth outside. It was a celebration of the end of hardship.

Bread, Biscuits and Cakes

Crushed coriander's heavy odour
from black bread on the table...

CRAIG RAINE, *Old Woman at the Breakfast Table*

It has been claimed that Russians, unlike the rest of us, could live by bread alone, so nourishing and good are the scores of different loaves on sale in bakers' shops every day. The Russian staff of life is produced in vast quantities – 2,300 tons a day for Moscow alone in 1979. It is rarely pre-wrapped, never sliced and the darker loaves are full of roughage. Because of consumer demand freshness is virtually guaranteed. On every baker's shelf there is a special spoon with which customers test to see if a loaf has lost its springiness and is too old to buy. Kilo (2 lb) loaves are halved, quartered, even cut in eighths so that everyone can buy the quantity he needs daily. Hardly ever is even an odd eighth left lying after four o'clock in the afternoon. Thanks to the continuing state subsidy, good bread is also remarkably cheap.

White bread comes sweet or sour, soft or crusty, long, thin, round and tall, with and without poppy seeds. The blackest bread, *borodinsky*, made of rye and wheat, is indeed black, with a wonderful sweetness and moistness when it is absolutely fresh. It comes glazed and studded with coriander seeds. After it come a host of brown rye and rye and wheat loaves of differing degrees of coarseness and sourness. One of my favourites at the refined end of the scale was called *Riga* bread. Made with rye and wheat flours and flavoured with malt, it was light, slightly sweet, and very easy to eat too much of. A close relative of *Riga* bread was flavoured with the traditional Eastern European bread flavouring, caraway. For the specialist there are also diet breads, including what used to be called *Graham bread* (the American name for wholemeal, taken over by the Russians in the last century), and so-called *white bread* which is a low-calorie gluten loaf.

Dietary laws apart, Russians swear that black bread will not make one fat, I presume because it has too much bulk to be eaten in quantity. Towards the South the tradition in solid leavened rye breads peters out, and in its place come Middle Eastern flat breads and soft leavened white breads. The Russian tradition in bread is said to be at its strongest in the Ukraine, the country's proverbial breadbasket.

Whereas the brown heavy breads are unquestionably Russian and are eaten throughout the country daily, white bread still has a faint air of foreignness about it. The more rural the area, the less likelihood of finding it on sale. In the last century the difference was marked. White bread came from one bakery with a name adapted from the French, *bulochnaya*, while rye and other sour dough bread was baked on premises taking their name from the traditional Russian cooking range, *pekarnya*.

I have come across hardly a recipe anywhere which can equal what is produced today in Russian bakeries. In Russia itself no one needs to make his own bread, and there are no bread flours on sale nor recipes published in modern cookery books. Older books provide basic recipes for loaves made wholly of rye with a sour dough starter (a piece of dough left over from the last session of bread-making, or scrapings from around the dough trough). But they still do not yield anything as good as a *borodinsky* loaf and are invariably heavier. For me Russian bread-making remains after many experiments something of a mystery. I have not met an experienced bread-maker yet who would not admit that dough made wholly with rye flour is unworkable, lacking the gluten needed to give it elasticity and make it rise. How is the problem overcome? Then there is the question of colour. Just how does a *borodinsky* come to be so black when it contains wheat flour and doesn't taste unduly of molasses? In the past, Russian peasants used a rye flour that was much darker than that available in our shops today, so perhaps part of the answer lies there. But the real conclusion is that close imitation is impossible.

With the bread recipes I have brought together here I have tried to create good hearty breads of a similar type. I have seen many attempts to colour rye bread black with molasses, burnt rye crumbs, cocoa and the kind of instant 'coffee' that contains a high percentage of roasted chicory or barley. Molasses adds flavour and colour if you like its taste, but go easy to start with if you decide to experiment. Toasted crumbs work well and have a slight lightening effect in some recipes, such as Anna Thomas's excellent black bread, quoted below. But from coffee or cocoa I have drawn no advantage.

The dividing line between traditional bread and biscuits and cakes is hard to draw. The same must be said of much traditional yeast bakery in Britain and Europe. Russian Easter bread/cake, *kulich*, may contain so small a quantity of sugar that it can double as bread throughout Easter week. On the other hand it may resemble a raised fruit cake and contain a good measure of sugar and dried fruit. Outside the Easter context I have sometimes seen it called simply a *bulka* or white loaf. White rolls and buns made with *brioche* dough of varying richness are known as little loaves of this kind or *bulochki*. They always contain a little sugar, but their role on the table ranges from being a semi-sweet accompaniment to afternoon tea, like a scone, to a light bread at dinner, served in the form of tiny rolls glazed with egg.

The most ancient Russian cake, the *pryanik* or spice cake, is impossible to categorize according to modern ideas. It was originally made with rye flour, unleavened, and contained no eggs and often no milk or water. What bound the flour was honey, and the only other ingredients were spices. The result was like a sweet, dense pumpernickel. To the Russian way of thinking, the German unleavened rye bread was in fact a variety of *pryanik*.

From there it is only a short jump to what we now think of as a biscuit. For Russian cooks these were made from any sweet or savoury dough, baked and dried. If *bulochki* are left to dry in a warm oven which has been switched off, or in the sun, they turn out to be rusks rather than scones. Many of the smaller cakes were recommended for drying out in this way. They were soft by modern biscuit standards but hard going as cake.

With the exception of *kulich*, *baba* and fresh *bulochki*, modern Russian cooking, and certainly the Soviet food industry, have tended to shy away from the old recipes or adapt them. Light sponges and gâteaux, crisp short biscuits and unleavened, richly fatted cake mixtures and pastry from the West have replaced them. In Moscow I visited the city's busiest cake production line, which was turning out box after box of heavily iced and decorated sponges which could have been delivered to a children's party anywhere. Not one variety of cake was made with a yeast dough. Mannered, sugary reproductions of flora and fauna were obligatory on every 'quality' product.

Rye bread and the grains mentioned in Chapter 6 are in fact the great surviving exceptions to a national passion for refined foods. The Russians are still riding the first wave of enthusiasm for convenience foods. Ideology keeps alive the memory of a time in the last century when refined foods were a luxury and only the rich could buy sweet-meats, cream and chocolate. The elaborately iced cakes I saw coming off the line, although everyone can afford them now, are still regarded as a festive treat.

The day before a national holiday, such as 1 May, huge queues form outside Moscow cake shops, and buses and trams are full of people clutching white cake boxes. It pays to know the right bakery, or better still the baker himself. I knew a Russian who could procure the most wonderful rum *baba* from the back door of a large hotel in the city, though it was not cheap.

Elsewhere in the Soviet Union, ways with cake and attitudes to it are vastly different. In the Baltics coffee and cake are part of everyday living, as they are in Germany and Austria and Poland. In the South the traditions of baking are Middle Eastern, and rely on heavy flaky pastry, honey and nuts more than on the eggs and cream of the North.

WHITE BREAD

Since much white bread was traditionally considered in the same category as a yeast cake, many of the recipes are fairly rich, containing 1–4 eggs per 500 g (1 lb) flour, and at least 2 tablespoons of sugar. Tea bread spices such as cardamom, cinnamon, nutmeg and saffron may be added to any of them, according to taste. In the Ukraine, where the bulk of Russian grain is grown, white breads were given many different names according to their sweetness, shape and crust, such as *kalach, korzh, polyanitsya, korovai*. Savoury breads were flavoured either with aromatic seeds such as poppy, caraway or sesame seed, or with aromatic oil. Sesame seed oil, poppy seed oil, unrefined sun-flower oil, walnut oil, olive oil are all worth trying.

A daily white bread

 ¾ teaspoon dried yeast
 8–9 tablespoons milk
 2–3 tablespoons water
 500 g (1 lb) strong white or wholemeal flour
 ½ teaspoon salt
 2 tablespoons sugar
 2–3 tablespoons oil or butter or other fat
 1 egg (optional)

Dissolve the yeast in the warm milk and water, and when it foams add to the flour sifted with the salt and sugar. Add the oil or butter, the egg yolk and the beaten egg white and mix all the ingredients together to make a smooth dough. Knead for 10 minutes and leave to rise in a warm place. Knead again, pack into a greased loaf tin or form into loaves or rolls any shape you please, and leave to rise a second time. Brush with egg before baking in a hot oven for 40 minutes.

A rich white bread

BULKA

> ¾ teaspoon dried yeast
> 5–6 tablespoons milk
> 500 g (1 lb) flour
> ½ teaspoon salt
> 3–4 eggs
> 1½ tablespoons sugar
> 2½ tablespoons oil or butter

Dissolve the yeast in the milk, add to the flour, salt, beaten egg yolks, sugar and oil. Fold in the stiffly beaten whites and make a smooth dough. Knead and bake as in the previous recipe.

RYE BREAD AND WHOLEMEAL BREAD

It hardly seems necessary to point out that bread-making in the last century was a continuous process rather than a therapeutic exercise on a wet afternoon, but in the Russian kitchen the regularity of the craft made an important difference. It meant that fresh yeast almost never needed to be used. There was always a sour dough starter on hand, in the form of a piece of dough left over from the last session which could be scraped together from the sides of the dough trough. This *zakvaska* or leavening agent did all the work that was necessary to raise the new batch of loaves, and helped impart to them a characteristic sour-sweet taste which even with my own sour dough I have never been able to imitate successfully. What also must have secured a unique flavour was the length of the bread-making. Mrs Molokhovets advised between 3 and 6 days for her basic sour-sweet breads, all the time in a warm place and with twice daily kneading. To the darkest rye breads only water would be added, but some of the lighter wheaten varieties were recommended to be made with buttermilk, whey or yoghurt, in the proportion 4 parts flour to 1 part liquid. The flour had to be very dry. Towards the end of the kneading and rising process the dough would be formed into loaves and put aside for a last time to prove. A test of whether the wheatmeal loaves were ready was to immerse them in water 'the temperature of rivers in summer'. When they rose to the surface they were ready for baking.

The oven was heated until a few grains of flour would begin to turn brown immediately they were sprinkled on the oven floor. If the flour burnt, or did not brown at all, the oven was not ready for the bread. Baking, once the loaves were properly accommodated, took about 45 minutes for a 450 g (1 lb) loaf. It was advised to remove wheatmeal bread when it was nearly done, pour a jug of boiling water over it, and replace it in the oven for a final 5–10 minutes. The only water treatment recommended for rye was to brush it with cold water before it went in the oven. The bread was to be allowed to cool on a wire rack in a warm place with plenty of air circulating. It was not to be put in a cool pantry until completely cool itself. Caraway seed was often added to wheat and rye loaves. Among more curious past additions to bread were also the powders from dried berries, particularly barberries, dried pomegranate rind and dried orange and lemon rind. Their role seems to have been primarily aromatic, as was, I presume, the piece of oak bark about the size of the palm of one's hand which Mrs Molokhovets immersed for a day or so in a 20 lb batch of rye bread dough. Treacle, with which one may also consider molasses and honey and golden syrup, was another important secondary ingredient.

The recipes here are all nineteenth-century domestic prescriptions but with the quantities greatly reduced and the techniques simplified. I have also quoted Anna Thomas's excellent recipe for black bread from *The Vegetarian Epicure*, as it is the closest I have come in several years of searching to a dark rye loaf that rises well, is full of taste and does not involve the addition of curious ingredients to achieve its wonderful dark colour.

Sour-sweet bread

> 400 ml (⅔ pint) boiling water
> 900 g (28 oz) flour
> 3 teaspoons dried yeast dissolved in 8 tablespoons warm
>   water
> 2 tablespoons molasses, golden syrup, honey or malt extract
> 1 teaspoon caraway seed (optional)
> 1 tablespoon dried ground pomegranate rind (optional)

Pour the boiling water over the flour in a large mixing bowl. Dissolve the yeast in the warm water and wait till it begins to foam. Add to the warm flour and water with the remaining ingredients. Mix, knead well and leave to rise. When the dough has doubled in volume knead again, form into loaves and leave to rise again. Smooth the loaves over with wet hands and put in a very hot oven to bake, reducing the temperature gradually.

It was this loaf incidentally that was originally flavoured with oak bark. It may be made with wholewheat flour or a mixture of wheat and rye. Pure rye is also suggested, but I find it unworkable. Half rye, half wheatmeal has a wonderful taste but is also tough going. Three parts wheatmeal to one part rye makes an excellent bread. You may leave out the caraway seed if you dislike it, and substitute a teaspoon of mixed spice for the dried pomegranate rind, or omit that too. Some sweetening is desirable but it may be varied according to taste. I find molasses overwhelming except in small quantities and prefer to make up the necessary quantity of sweetening with honey or malt extract. Golden syrup is another possibility but rather cloying.

Sour-sweet teabread

> 200 ml ($\frac{1}{3}$ pint) boiling water
> 450 g (1 lb) wheatmeal flour or rye and wheatmeal mixed 1:3
> 2 teaspoons dried yeast dissolved in 4 tablespoons warm
>   water or warm sour milk
> 50–60 g (about 2 oz) prunes (previously soaked)
> 40 g (1½ oz) chopped or flaked almonds
> 150 g (5 oz) honey, treacle or golden syrup
> 1 teaspoon caraway seed (optional)

Pour the boiling water over the flour, mix, and leave in a warm place, overnight if possible. Add the dissolved yeast, knead well and leave to rise again. Add the stoned and chopped prunes, the almonds, treacle and caraway seeds, form into loaves and leave to rise for a final time. Smooth with wet hands and bake in a very hot oven for about 40 minutes, reducing the temperature gradually.

Rye, wheat and oatmeal bread

> 450 ml (1 pint) boiling water
> 180 g (5 oz) oats or oatmeal
> ½ tablespoon dried yeast
> 450 g (1 lb) wheatmeal flour or wheatmeal and strong white mixed
> 225 g (8 oz) rye flour
> 1 teaspoon salt

The addition of oats or oatmeal to bread makes for wonderful toast. The original recipe suggests immediately making this dough into rusks by drying it in slices in the oven, but while it is fresh it makes excellent bread. Pour the boiling water, less a few tablespoonfuls, over the oats and allow to stand for an hour or overnight. Add the yeast, dissolved in warm water, the flours and the salt to the cooled mixture. Blend well and knead until you have a smooth, unsticky dough. You may have to add more wheat flour until you get the right mixture. Leave to rise, form into loaves and leave to rise again. Smooth the loaves with wet hands and bake in a fairly hot oven (425°F) for about 50 minutes, gradually reducing the heat. Cool on a wire rack.

To convert the bread into rusks the Russian way slice it thickly, brush on both sides with beer, and sprinkle one side with a little salt and caraway seed. Toast in a medium oven, caraway side up, until crisp.

Anna Thomas's Black Bread (Peasant Bread)

> 450 ml (¾ pint) hot water
> 4 tablespoons dark molasses
> 200 g (6 oz) fine, dark breadcrumbs toasted (or 4 oz crumbs and 2 oz wheat germ)
> 2 teaspoons dry yeast
> 150 ml (¼ pint) lukewarm water
> 1 teaspoon sugar
> ½ teaspoon ground ginger
> 300 g (12 oz) rye flour
> 2 teaspoons salt
> 3 tablespoons melted butter
> 200 g (6 oz) white flour
>
> GLAZE
> beaten egg yolk

Pour the hot water into a large mixing bowl and dissolve the molasses in it. Add the breadcrumbs and mix. Dissolve the yeast in the lukewarm water, adding the sugar and ginger. Stir the yeast mixture and let it stand for about 15 minutes. When the breadcrumbs are cooled to lukewarm and the yeast is spongy, mix them together and stir in the rye flour.

To this very dry mixture add the salt and melted butter. Spread the white flour on a large board, and put the dark mixture on it. Turn the bowl over it and leave it covered this way for about 15 minutes. Knead it vigorously for at least 10 minutes, using as much of the white flour as necessary to keep the dough from sticking. When it is smooth and stiff, put it in a greased bowl, turn it over once, cover with a towel and let rise in a warm place until double in bulk, about 1½ hours. Turn out on to a very lightly floured board and shape into one large loaf, either quite long or round but, in any case, as high as you can make it: it will spread out as it rises again. Place it on a buttered baking sheet, cover, and let rise again for about 30 minutes. It should nearly double in bulk. Before baking, brush the loaf with beaten egg yolk. Bake for about 40–45 minutes at 400°F, gas 6.

A bran loaf
> 200 ml (⅓ pint) milk+a few tablespoons
> 75 g (scant 3 oz) bran
> 3 teaspoons dried yeast
> 4 tablespoons warm water
> about 500 g (18 oz) strong white bread flour
> 4 tablespoons melted butter or vegetable oil
> 1 teaspoon salt
> 1 teaspoon sugar
> oil and beaten egg for glazing

Bring the 200 ml (⅓ pint) milk almost to boiling and pour over the bran in a bowl. Mix well and allow to cool to warm before adding the yeast dissolved in the warm water. Add the white flour and the butter or oil, mix well, and add the salt, the sugar and a little more warm milk as necessary to make a firm dough. Knead well until smooth and unsticky and leave to rise in a warm place until almost double in size. Form into round loaves on a baking sheet and glaze with oil, or pack into rectangular tins. Leave to rise, glaze with beaten egg, and bake in a hot oven for 40 minutes or until cooked. The bran makes this heavier than an ordinary white loaf, but adds colour, taste and fibre, all well worth having.

Rye bulochki

SWEET OR SAVOURY RYE SCONES

These are somewhere between bread and scones, and very much easier to handle than rye bread because of the eggs and oil.

2 teaspoons dried yeast
4 tablespoons warm water
300 g (11 oz) rye and wheat flour equally mixed, or all rye flour
60 g (2 oz) butter or 4 tablespoons vegetable oil
1 tablespoon sugar
2 eggs

FOR SWEET SCONES

2 more tablespoons sugar or to taste
60 g (2 oz) raisins
cinnamon and lemon or orange peel to taste
icing sugar (optional)

Dissolve the yeast in the warm water and when it foams add to the flour, together with the butter or oil, sugar and beaten eggs. The extra sugar, fruit, and spices for sweet scones should also be added at this point. Form into a firm dough and knead for 10 minutes. Leave to rise until double in size, knead again, form into little balls and place on a greased baking tray, leaving sufficient space between them to allow the *bulochki* to expand without touching. Leave to rise again while the oven is heating up. Bake in a medium oven (400°F, gas 5) for 30–40 minutes or until lightly browned and you are able to insert a cocktail stick and it comes out clean. The sweet scones may be dusted with icing sugar.

Bulochki with caraway

2 teaspoons dried yeast
2 tablespoons warm milk
350 g (¾ lb) flour, either strong white or wheatmeal or a mixture of the two
75 g (3 oz) butter
1 tablespoon caster sugar
¼ teaspoon salt
beaten egg for glazing
2 tablespoons caraway seed

Dissolve the yeast in the warm milk. When it foams add to the flour with the softened butter, sugar and salt, and mix well. (The butter is best rubbed into the dry flour first.) Knead the dough for 10 minutes and leave to rise. Form into small rolls, place on a greased baking sheet, brush with beaten egg and sprinkle with caraway seeds. Allow to rise again and bake in a medium oven as in the previous recipe.

Bubliki

These are little rings of choux pastry baked hard which are on sale in all Russian bakeries and make excellent snacks. They are usually sprinkled with poppy seeds and are considered a Ukrainian speciality.

> 275 ml ($\frac{1}{2}$ pint) water
> pinch salt
> 180 g (6 oz) butter
> 1 tablespoon sugar
> 250 g (9 oz) flour
> 6 eggs
> poppy seeds

Heat together the water, salt, butter and sugar. Add all the flour at once and blend in quickly, trying to avoid letting it stick to the sides of the pan. Cook for 2 minutes, remove from the heat and allow to cool to hand hot. Add the egg yolks one at a time, then the beaten whites. With a spoon or a piping bag make rings with the paste on a greased baking sheet. Sprinkle with poppy seeds and bake in a hot oven until brown.

RUM BABA

Soviet historians claim the *baba* for western Russia, that is for the ancient principalities of Pskov and Novgorod and the modern republics of Belorussia and the Ukraine. *Larousse* is almost in agreement, attributing it to a Polish king, Stanislas Lesczinski, who found a new way of eating a tall raised cake originating in Lemberg (Lvov). A French pastry cook is said to have come across it when the Polish court was in exile in France. The difference is only a question of political geography. In the nineteenth century large areas of Poland were part of the Russian empire. Lemberg was Polish and Austrian and eventually, this century, Russian. All these countries enjoyed a tradition of yeast baking in the seventeenth and eighteenth centuries, with a penchant for tall near-cylindrical forms. Of the Russian raised cakes, the *bulka*, the *kulich* and the *krendel'*, the *baba* is the richest and the lightest, containing the highest proportion of eggs to flour. It is designed more often than not to be served warm. I think King Stanislas had the best idea when he transformed the Lemberg cake by sprinkling it with rum and setting it alight like a Christmas pudding before he ate a slice. It has otherwise been flavoured with spices, nuts and dried fruit or coated in a lemony syrup. If you don't like rum or have none, try brandy or kirsch or any distinctly flavoured eau-de-vie.

Nineteenth-century cooks called for a copper *baba* mould 40 cm (21 inches) high, in which the *baba* could rise three-quarters of the way up. Only the best eggs, yeast and flour would do, and prospective cooks were told to reckon with 7 hours total preparation time. This allowed for the dough to rise 3 times before baking and for its author to beat it for a good hour. The oven had to be very hot, and the *baba* was to be baked if it was a very tall one for 1½ hours. In the rising and the cooking it demanded the most exacting precautions: 'While the babas are rising in a warm place and when they are in the oven be careful to see that they do not come in contact with cold air or a draught and that no doors bang shut; during this time best of all do not allow anyone in the kitchen.' The next test was getting them out in one piece, although disaster might already have struck in the form of a hollow cake if you allowed it to rise too high third time round. The best way was to leave the *baba* in the mould standing just as it did for baking until it was just warm. Then it had to be laid on its side very gently on a pillow and slowly turned until the *baba* was loosened. The rum syrup was poured over it still on its side but on a plate, until all the liquid soaked into the cake. It took an upright position when almost cool and ready to serve.

> 5 tablespoons milk
> 2 teaspoons dried yeast
> 225 g (8 oz) flour
> ½ teaspoon salt
> 6 eggs
> 2 tablespoons caster sugar or more to taste
> 125 g (4 oz) butter
> grated lemon rind to taste

FOR THE SYRUP
6 tablespoons caster sugar cooked to a syrup in 250 ml
    (½ pint) water
6 tablespoons rum (or like King Stanislas, just use rum)

Warm the milk slightly and dissolve the yeast. When the mixture begins to foam add it tò the flour, sifted with the salt. Follow with the beaten eggs and sugar mixed together, the softened butter and the lemon rind. Mix well and beat for as long as you have time and patience with a wooden spoon, or use some mechanical help. Put on one side, covered, in a warm place, until the mixture has doubled in volume, then beat again for a few minutes, pour into a well-buttered tall mould and leave to rise again. The mould should be big enough for the mixture to fill not more than half of it before the final rising. It will reach up to three-quarters of the way up before baking. Transfer very carefully to the oven, which should be very hot, and bake for 30 minutes. Remove carefully from the mould when cool. Add the rum to the sugar syrup. Pour the syrup over several times so that the *baba* absorbs as much as possible, and serve with cream. Ideally use a tall, copper mould specially made for a *baba*, or a charlotte or *brioche* mould. The same mould will also serve for *kulich*. The *baba* may also be split in half horizontally and filled with whipped cream flavoured with rum.

Babka or baba without yeast

This nineteenth-century offshoot of the *baba* has all the merits of modern baking. It is quick, easy and untemperamental. Bake in a deep tin. In essence the result is a soufflé. The *babka* may be flavoured with lemon, almonds, chocolate or spices, or made plain and served with a fruit or wine syrup, a sweet sauce or thin cream. Here are two possibilities, the first, more traditional, made with either rye or white breadcrumbs, the second with almonds and flour.

Babka with breadcrumbs and spices

10 eggs
6 tablespoons dried rye breadcrumbs, finely milled, or a
    mixture of brown and rye breadcrumbs, or brown and
    white
a little sherry, wine or brandy
pinch salt
1½ teaspoons cinnamon

3 cloves, crushed to a powder
½ teaspoon powdered star anise
180 g (7 oz) caster sugar

Separate the eggs and beat the whites stiffly. Soak the milled bread-crumbs, which you can get perfectly smooth if you put dry through a coffee grinder, in a little sherry, wine or brandy, together with the spices. Beat the egg yolks with the sugar, add the soaked crumbs, salt and spices, fold in the whites and pour into a well-buttered tall mould or cake tin or soufflé dish with a collar. Bake in a medium oven for 45 minutes. Serve hot as suggested above. It will serve 6 people.

◆Made with dark crumbs which are richly flavoured, soaked in brandy, this *babka* would make a wonderful light replacement for our traditional pudding at Christmas.

Babka with almonds

150 g (5 oz) sweet almonds
40 g (1½ oz) bitter almonds
10 eggs
130 g (4½ oz) sugar

Blanch the two kinds of almonds, dry them, and pound very finely with 1 egg white. Beat the rest of the whites, and the yolks and sugar separately. Combine the sugar and yolks with the almonds, fold in the beaten whites, and bake in a buttered mould in a medium oven for 45 minutes.

To make this *babka* a little more economically use 8 eggs and add 3–4 tablespoons sifted white flour to the mixture. Bake in a slightly hotter oven, and do not remove from the mould until the *babka* has cooled slightly.

KRENDEL' AND KULICH

Krendel' and *kulich* are ancient festive cakes. They use the same rich yeast dough, to which nuts, spices and dried fruit may be added, but the *krendel'* is wound into a figure of eight whereas *kulich* is baked in a tall mould like a *baba*. The first is common at name-day parties and other celebrations. *Kulich* appears only at Easter, when it is the pride of the table. In some families it replaces bread for the entire Holy Week. Here is a recipe for a classical *kulich* dough, which would normally be made in at least double the proportion I have given here.

3 teaspoons dried yeast
250 ml (½ pint) milk
500 g (1 lb) flour
¼ teaspoon salt
150 g (5 oz) butter
100 g (3½ oz) sugar or up to 180 g (7 oz) according to taste
3 eggs
1–2 tablespoons each chopped almonds and raisins
¼ teaspoon ground cardamom or slightly more cinnamon,
   star anise or lemon peel

Dissolve the yeast in the slightly warmed milk and add to the sifted flour and salt to make a dry dough. Cover and leave in a warm place to rise. Cream together the butter, sugar and eggs, add the almonds, raisins and spices, and add to the dough when it has doubled in size. Beat well and allow to rise again. The mixture should be fairly thick.

To bake a *kulich* you will need a tall cylindrical tin or, failing that, a deep round tin which allows plenty of room for the dough to rise. Butter it well and pour in the mixture. It should reach not more than half-way up. Leave to rise again to the top of the tin. Brush the top with beaten egg very carefully and bake in a pre-heated medium oven for about an hour. All the precautions advised for *baba* baking (page 260) apply here. No draughts, no disturbances, and don't let the cake rise too high in the final proving. *Kulich* should be lightly browned on top when done, and a toothpick inserted into it should come out clean. Cover the top with tin foil if it begins to darken too much during baking. Cool on a wire rack.

To bake a *krendel'* after the second rising of the dough, roll it into a long tube on a floured board and form into one large or several smaller figures of eight or bow shapes. Brush with melted butter and water, sprinkle with sugar, and bake on a floured tray in a medium oven for 30–40 minutes. The top of a large *krendel'* may be decorated with whole nuts (walnuts) and glacé cherries before baking. Very often the smaller cakes used to be left in the oven after it was turned off and allowed to dry hard like rusks.

PASKHA

A cylindrical *kulich* is sliced from the top in rounds with the first slice preserved as a lid. It is traditionally eaten with *paskha*, an enriched mixture of curd cheese, spices, nuts, dried fruit and sugar. The word *paskha* means Easter, and the blend of dairy fats celebrates the end of Lenten prohibitions, though I have seen Soviet claims that the serving of a rich sweet cheese mixture like this has no religious connection, and only appeared on the tables of peasants once a year because they could not otherwise afford the ingredients. The polemics aside, no one would dispute the popularity of *paskha* among Russians from a purely gastronomic point of view. On the question of cost I count myself in with the peasantry. For a *paskha* to go with a 500 g (1 lb) *kulich* you will need:

> 600 g (1¼ lb) curd cheese or curd and cream cheese in equal proportions
> 150 g (5 oz) butter
> 2 egg yolks
> 150 g (5 oz) caster sugar or more to taste
> 2 tablespoons each chopped almonds and raisins
> 2 teaspoons lemon peel
> 3 drops vanilla essence

Paskha may be made up from raw ingredients and kept under a press for 24 hours, or it may be cooked very slowly for an hour in a *bain-marie* first. As far as I am concerned the longer method produces no noticeable difference in quality, so I have stuck to the simple way. The cheese should be dry and smooth before you start. One way of getting rid of excess whey is to put it in a fine sieve suspended over a bowl with a plate over it and a heavy weight pressing down on the plate. Leave overnight in a cool, airy place before combining with the other ingredients. The butter should be softened so that it will blend in with a wooden spoon. The traditional *paskha* mould was a pyramid-shaped wooden form with the imprint of the Orthodox cross on one of its faces and usually other decorations as well. (See pages 243–7 for more on Russian Easter.) The form was lined with muslin and the mixture packed inside. It was kept under the weight for at least 24 hours before it was unmoulded. Whatever device one uses as a substitute should have small holes through which any excess moisture can escape. Russian friends in England have suggested a plastic flower pot (clean, of course) lined with muslin or tin foil with a few holes poked through it from the bottom of the pot. Actually in my experience there is very little surplus moisture to escape at this stage and a deep jelly mould, greased with butter, does perfectly well. Pack the *paskha* in tightly, put a weight on top and refrigerate for a few

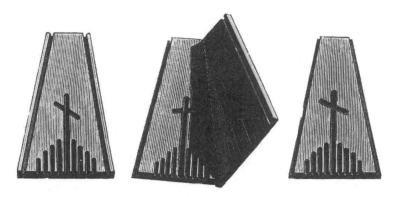

A traditional wooden pasochnitsa (paskha *mould), seen from inside.*

When the paskha *is turned out, the imprint of the cross is left on the surface of the cheese.*

hours. Unmould on to a serving plate (some Russians insist it should be a pretty one). The sides may be decorated with slivers of almonds, glacé cherries and angelica, or left plain.

♦Pistachio nuts or walnuts are good additions to *paskha*, either as well as almonds or in their place. Bitter almonds may be mixed 1:4 with sweet almonds. Home-made peel may be worked in instead of the raisins.

♦♦When the *paskha* runs out, try *kulich* English afternoon-tea style with cream and jam, or even curd or cream cheese and jam. It turns out to be a surprisingly similar treat.

PRYANIK

Spice cakes are among the most ancient recipes in European cooking. Russian historians claim that the *pryanik* (from the word *pryanost'*, meaning spice) dates back at least to the ninth century, when it was a simple combination of rye flour, honey and berry juice. Spices were added and the preparation took its modern name in medieval Russia. It remained in much the same form from then until the end of the nineteenth century, that is to say dense, unleavened, very sweet and highly spiced. It was usually cut into what we would think of as biscuit-sized pieces, and resembled a sweet pumpernickel. The combination of sweetness, stickiness and extreme density has not endeared the *pryanik* to modern palates. Modern Russian recipes have transformed it with the help of eggs and/or milk and sometimes baking powder into something light and foreign, somewhere between a tea bread and a sponge cake. The break with tradition has been almost complete. Honey is still used occasionally as a sweetener but in most cases sugar has taken its place. Treacle and sweet syrups have completely disappeared. Only the range of spices has remained constant and alluring: cardamom, cinnamon, cloves, pomegranate and lemon peel, allspice, nutmeg, star anise, mint, ginger, coriander and occasionally vanilla. Only galgan(t) and mastic, two oriental spices widely used in cooking and medicine in the Middle Ages, have dropped out. Combinations of these spices, with different measures and types of flour and with various sweetening agents, gave rise to over 40 different kinds of *pryanik*, many of them topped with white icing. Dried berries were also popular additions.

I am convinced that some adaptation is needed if *pryanik* recipes are to survive today, but I am not sure that the best answer is to make it more like a cake in modern terms. I have been rather more inspired by savoury versions of *pryanik* I have come across in regional recipes, notably from the Ukraine and the Baltics, where honey used to bind sweet mixtures is replaced by eggs and fat.

Sweet pryanik with honey and spices

350 g (12 oz) wholemeal flour
$\frac{1}{4}-\frac{1}{2}$ teaspoon each cinnamon and cardamom
4 tablespoons chopped almonds including 1 tablespoon
    bitter almonds
2 tablespoons candied peel
6 eggs
12 tablespoons liquid honey or to taste

Sift together the flour and spices, then add the nuts and candied peel. Beat the egg yolks and whites separately. Add the yolks and the honey to the flour, mix well, and fold in the whites. Spread thinly over a greased baking tray (about half a finger thick) and bake in a pre-heated medium oven for about 45 minutes, reducing the heat if the mixture starts to darken too much. It should emerge crisp and golden brown. Do use wholemeal flour for this recipe, otherwise you will lose both the colour and the texture desirable in a traditional *pryanik*. I like to dilute the honey with boiling water to cut down on what I find an excessive sweetness. Two thirds honey to one third water works quite satisfactorily. This biscuit-like preparation should be cut into squares while it is still hot in the tin, but left there to cool and harden. It is sometimes known as *kovrizhka*.

Sweet pryanik with rye breadcrumbs

Recipes like this one are a great comfort if you have failed with a batch of rye bread. They provide an excellent way to recycle the lost ingredients. Simply toast the bread slowly in the oven, then crush it either by hand or in a grinder. It may be used to make a sweet or a savoury biscuit. The simplest sweet version, which in fact produces something which is literally a candy rather than a biscuit, simply mixes these crumbs with thick fruit syrup or jam. Here is a more elaborate version, which may be made partly with biscuit crumbs if you have them. It reminds me of the sweet, sticky concoctions of breakfast cereal, butter and chocolate that used to circulate at school. I do expect it to be more popular with children than adults.

> 200 ml (⅓ pint) blackcurrant or raspberry syrup (ordinary jam
>   may be diluted with hot water to give a syrupy
>   consistency)
> 1 tablespoon honey
> ½ teaspoon cinnamon
> ¼ teaspoon each star anise and ginger
> pinch each of nutmeg and ground cloves
> 250 g (8 oz) milled crumbs
> ½ teaspoon baking powder
> 1 egg yolk

Mix the syrup and honey and warm in a pan with the spices. Add the milled crumbs and baking powder and mix well. Add the egg yolk and mix again. Spread about a finger thick on a greased baking tray and allow to dry out in a warm oven. Cut into squares while still warm. An alternative flavouring is mint oil (40 drops), in which case omit the honey and spices and add 200 g (7 oz) sugar.

Raised honey pryanik

> 500 g (1 lb) honey or 400 g (12 oz) brown sugar and a little extra milk
> 100 g (3½ oz) rye flour
> 2 egg yolks
> 200 ml (⅓ pint) milk
> 400 g (13 oz) white flour
> 1 teaspoon cinnamon
> ½ teaspoon ground cardamon
> ¼ teaspoon star anise
> 2 teaspoons lemon peel
> ½ teaspoon baking powder
> ½ teaspoon salt
> ¾ small (5 fl oz) carton sour cream or yoghurt

Warm the honey or dissolve the brown sugar in a little milk, and add to the rye flour. Beat well. Beat together the yolks and the milk and combine with the white flour and spices, lemon peel, baking powder and salt. Combine the two mixtures and add the sour cream or yoghurt. Spread the mixture about a finger thick on a greased tray, and bake in a warm oven for about 45 minutes. Cut into squares while still warm.

♦ This recipe may be adapted in two ways: into a sweet tea bread by adding 4 whole eggs instead of the 2 yolks, or into a savoury soft biscuit by omitting the sweetening and spices and adding caraway, cumin or coriander seeds to taste.

Savoury wheatmeal pryanik

> 3–4 tablespoons wheat berries
> 350 g (12 oz) wholemeal flour
> 1 teaspoon salt
> ½ teaspoon ground black pepper
> ½ teaspoon cardamom
> 40 g (1½ oz) butter or vegetable oil
> 6 eggs
> 1 tablespoon sugar
> 4 tablespoons milk

Cook the wheat berries in a little water for about 10 minutes until they are slightly soft. Add them to the flour with the salt, pepper and cardamom and rub in the butter or vegetable oil. Add the beaten egg yolks, the sugar and the milk and mix to a stiff dough. Beat the whites separately and add them to the dough. Spread thinly (half a finger thick) on a greased baking tray and bake in a medium oven for 45 minutes. Cut into squares while still warm. These biscuits are excellent with cheese. They may also be flavoured with caraway seed.

Baltic pumpernickel

> 100 g (3½ oz) butter
> 100 g (3½ oz) molasses sugar
> 1 teaspoon cinnamon
> 3 eggs
> pinch baking powder
> 500 g (1 lb) rye flour or finely milled rye crumbs
> 50 g (2 oz) finely chopped hazelnuts or wheat berries

Cream together the butter, sugar and cinnamon and add the eggs one at a time. Beat until very smooth and white. Add the baking powder mixed to a paste with a teaspoon of water, the flour and the nuts. Add a little milk or water if the dough is too dry to manage. Bake on a greased tray, rolled out to about half a finger's thickness and brushed with egg, for about 25 minutes in a medium oven. Cut into squares or rounds while the pumpernickel is still hot.

KORZHIKI

Korzhiki are more obviously biscuits than *pryaniki* and are usually translated as shortbread. But that is a misleading term, for they are softer than the biscuits we know and some recipes contain no butter at all, only eggs and cream to do the shortening. In the last century they were considered ideal to take on a journey.

Plain korzhiki

> 250 g (9 oz) flour
> pinch salt
> ½ teaspoon baking powder
> 1 small (5 fl oz) carton sour cream or yoghurt
> 1 egg
> 3 tablespoons caster sugar
> 2 tablespoons butter

Sift the flour, salt and baking powder into a mixing bowl, make a well in the middle, and pour in the sour cream or yoghurt, beaten egg, sugar and softened butter. Form into a dough which can be rolled out on a floured board about half a finger thick. Cut out with a biscuit cutter into rounds and bake on a greased baking sheet, brushing the *korzhiki* with beaten egg and pricking them with a fork first. They will take 10–15 minutes in a hot oven.

Plyetski
These are flat, fairly dry cakes made with yeast. This one is sandwiched together like a plum galette and is excellent if you like cake neither too sweet nor too dainty.

> 2 teaspoons dried yeast
> 160 ml (¼ pint) milk
> 500 g (1 lb) flour
> 100 g (3½ oz) sugar
> 2 egg yolks
> 60 g (2 oz) butter
> lemon or orange peel to taste
>
> FOR THE FILLING
> 2 medium apples, peeled and quartered
> 60 g (2 oz) currants
> 100 g (3½ oz) chopped figs (or dried prunes and apricots mixed)
> 100 g (3½ oz) hazelnuts
> 60 g (2 oz) sugar

Dissolve the yeast in the warmed milk and when it starts to foam add the flour, then the sugar and egg yolks creamed together, the softened butter and the peel. Mix well and leave in a warm place to rise. When it has doubled in size beat the dough well and leave to rise a second time. Meanwhile put the fruit, nuts and sugar in a pan with 4 tablespoons of water and cook gently until you have a soft mass. Roll out the dough in two equal-sized rectangles about a finger thick and place the first on a greased baking tray. Spread it with the fruit mixture, put the other rectangle on top and leave to rise. Brush lightly with egg and bake in a medium oven for 30 minutes, or until the cake has risen well and is light golden brown on top.

Poppy seed roll

Poppy seeds are one of the most popular ingredients in Russian baking. They are usually boiled, pounded and combined with honey to make a thick, sweet filling for plain cakes and sponges. Here the filling is wrapped up in a bun dough, raised with yeast.

3 teaspoons dried yeast
150 ml (¼ pint) milk
500 g (1 lb) flour
scant ½ teaspoon salt
80 g (3 oz) sugar
3 eggs
60 g (2 oz) butter
vanilla or lemon peel to taste

FOR THE FILLING
150 g (5 oz) poppy seed
60 g (2 oz) ground almonds
75 g (3 oz) honey
4 tablespoons caster sugar

Dissolve the yeast in the warmed milk and when it foams add the flour and salt, then the sugar and eggs creamed together and the softened butter. Flavour with a little vanilla or lemon peel to taste, and allow to rise twice. Prepare the poppy seed by pouring water over it in a pan, covering tightly and allowing to stand for 40 minutes. Drain through a fine sieve, pressing lightly to squeeze out the water, then pound the seeds in a mortar or with a wooden pestle in a basin. Put the seeds in a bowl and gradually add the almonds. Mix well and stir in the honey and sugar gradually until you have a mixture like a thick spread. Roll out the dough in a longish rectangle, about a finger thick, and spread with the poppy seed mixture. Roll up, transfer to a greased baking tray, and leave to rise for half an hour in a warm place. Brush lightly with egg and bake in a hot oven for 20–30 minutes.

Poppy seed tort

60 g (2½ oz) poppy seed
5 eggs
120 g (4 oz) sugar
125 ml (4 fl oz) single cream
3 bitter almonds + a few drops bitter almond essence
100 g (3½ oz) potato flour or arrowroot

Soak and pound the poppy seeds as in the previous recipe, then add all the egg yolks, the sugar, cream, pounded almonds, essence and flour, and beat until smooth. Fold in 3 of the stiffly beaten egg whites, pour into a buttered cake tin and bake in a slow to medium oven (350–375 °F) for 45–60 minutes. Don't test it with a skewer or it will collapse.

Khvorost'

A deep-fried doughnut plait, considered a Ukrainian speciality.

> 100 ml (about 6 tablespoons) milk
> 3 egg yolks
> 1 tablespoon single cream
> 1 tablespoon icing sugar
> ¼ teaspoon salt
> 2 tablespoons brandy, vodka or rum
> 300 g (11 oz) flour
> vegetable oil for frying
> cinnamon or vanilla sugar

Cream together the milk, egg yolks, cream and icing sugar, add the salt and brandy, and gradually sprinkle in the flour. Mix to a firm dough and roll out very thinly into a long rectangle. Cut into strips about 2 fingers wide and 10–12 cm (6 inches) long. Fold each in half lengthwise and weave together into a plait, joining the ends and brushing with beaten egg white. Several plaits may be joined together. Deep fry in oil for 2–3 minutes until golden brown, drain on greaseproof paper, and sprinkle with icing sugar mixed with cinnamon or vanilla sugar. The traditional fat used is pork lard, but I would suggest refined sunflower oil which has almost no taste of its own to leave behind and is very light.

A Russian cheesecake

This is one of my favourite Russian recipes. It is quick, simple, not too sweet and very versatile. Those first two virtues may be the reason why it is so often served in modern Russian hotels for breakfast, warm and with a generous spoonful of sour cream over the top. To my dismay most Western visitors turn it down as early morning food, which results in its being taken off the menu and fried eggs substituted. As far as I am concerned it may be eaten at almost any time of the day, warm or cold, and sits especially well on the tea table. But be warned: it is a very distant relative of the American cheesecake which seems to have set the British standard, and only a little closer to the German variety. The rich sweet mixtures of cream cheese and curd cheese that the Americans set over biscuit crumbs are often similar to Russian *paskha* set in the form of an open tart. This cheesecake, on the other hand, is basically baked curd cheese, only slightly sweetened and enriched. Its base is built into the mixture.

> 500 g (generous 1 lb) curd cheese
> 3 tablespoons butter
> 2 tablespoons semolina
> ½ teaspoon salt
> 2–3 tablespoons sugar
> 1 egg
> vanilla or lemon rind and 1 tablespoon lemon juice to taste
> 3 tablespoons raisins
> 3 tablespoons sour cream
> sour cream for serving

Beat the cheese or put it through a mincer to lighten and smooth it. Add 2 tablespoons of melted butter, the semolina, the salt, the sugar creamed with the egg and the vanilla or lemon. Mix well and add the raisins. Transfer to a well-buttered baking dish, smooth over the top and spread the sour cream over it. Dot with the remaining butter. Bake in a medium to hot oven for 25–30 minutes. Serve hot or cold with more sour cream, which should be fairly liquid and may be diluted with yoghurt, buttermilk or ordinary milk.

Sweet Things

The Russian sweet tooth is proverbial. Originally it meant honey with everything. In the sixteenth century, the richer classes discovered the sweetmeats of the East, which included dried and crystallized fruit, and in the seventeenth Peter the Great brought back knowledge of how to make chocolate from Holland. The aristocracy developed a taste for fine desserts in the eighteenth century, and found in France the rich delicate concoctions of eggs and cream and fruit in champagne which nothing Russian could match. The later nineteenth century, which witnessed the growth of good bourgeois home cooking tailored to a modest budget, introduced heartier, more sustaining puddings on the English model. Christmas plum pudding was enjoyed all the year round by the Nabokov family. Sugar, introduced in the eighteenth century and first refined in Russia in the early nineteenth, had replaced honey in all but specialized recipes by the 1860s.

The Russian native tradition in sweet things covered a wide variety of preparations: fruit pastilles and dragées, sweet fruit preserves, honey and fruit drinks, sweetened *kasha*, pies and pasta filled with sweet cheese, fruit, poppy seeds and honey, fresh berries, and sweet, fruit-flavoured cheeses. These were not meant primarily as the last course of a meal, but could be eaten at any time of the day. The favourite time for many of them was breakfast.

Fresh berries are worth singling out. Russians go berrying with all the same degree of 'quiet passion' as they pick mushrooms. Loganberries, cranberries, wild strawberries and raspberries are celebrated Russian 'gifts of the forest'. For Soloukhin, perhaps the foremost Russian nature writer this century, the wild strawberry evoked poetic memories of childhood:

We used to collect little bouquets of wild strawberries which indeed were no less fragrant than the freshest flowers. So that the berries would not fall off pieces of soft equally fragrant bread, we pushed each berry down into the soft part of the loaf and ate it with sips of milk. The best way of all to eat wild strawberries is like this: pour some cold milk into a bowl, add lots of fine sugar, stirring gently until it dissolves, and then sprinkle the berries into the milk.

VALENTIN SOLOUKHIN, *'Tret'ya okhota'*

The best Russian sweet dishes today are probably not those that follow a meal but those which are offered spontaneously at any time of day, like Soloukhin's strawberries. Neither the art of dessert nor the art of confectionery has flourished this century. In a modern Russian restaurant you are unlikely to be offered anything other than ice cream, though there may be excellent iced berries and sugar in season. As a hangover from the serving of grand bowls of fruit salad you will often find ready laid on a lunch or dinner table a glass of sweet fruit syrup containing a few pieces of tinned fruit. I never appreciated this habit, but I did very much enjoy the serving instead of a single chocolate truffle, which Russians chase down with sweet champagne.

Gurievskaya kasha

This fine pudding is said to have been created by the Russian Finance Minister Dmitry Guriev to commemorate his country's victory over Napoleon in 1812. Two years later it was already being shown off in Paris. The original was complicated. Milk or cream was gently simmered until it formed a skin. This round skin was removed whole, put on one side and the milk left to form another. In this way ten or twelve skins were collected. They were then used to separate layers of semolina cooked in milk or cream, nuts and preserves. Form-wise I have stuck to a simpler version in which the taste is just as good.

Gurievskaya kasha bears some resemblance to what I am told are bastardized versions of English and Scottish flummery, made with cream thickened with semolina or oatmeal, and like Scottish flummery it is often eaten warm. Without the nuts and fruits it recalls the taste of *crème brûlée*. Some modern cooks have suggested putting it in a soufflé dish, covering the top with caramel and baking it to bring out the similarity. I like *Gurievskaya kasha* made with cream, with fresh soft fruit (peaches, apricots, raspberries, strawberries, cherries, plums) in season and a minimum of sugar.

350–400 ml (⅔ pint) double cream
200 ml (⅓ pint) milk
OR
600 ml (1 pint) full cream milk

2 tablespoons brown sugar
vanilla essence to taste
2 tablespoons semolina
40 g (1½ oz) walnuts and almonds, chopped and mixed
about 2 tablespoons drained tinned fruit, fruit preserves or
  chopped fresh soft fruit

Combine the cream, milk, sugar and vanilla essence in a pan over a
low heat. Gradually sprinkle in the semolina, stirring all the time until
the mixture thickens. Add the nuts and spoon into individual serving
dishes, first a layer of semolina, then a layer of fruit, ending with fruit.
Serve warm. The mixture may also be arranged in this way in a large
dish for serving hot or cold. For a *brûlée* version omit the fruit, spoon
the semolina mixture into a baking dish and pour over a few tablespoons of caramel. Put in a medium oven for 10 minutes. If the
pudding is to be eaten cold, the semolina may be poured warm into a
buttered mould to set, unmoulded when cold and served with
caramel.

VARIATIONS
The *kasha* may also be flavoured with lemon peel or any of the oriental
spices: cinnamon, star anise, cloves, saffron. In winter, chopped
stewed dried fruit such as apricots and figs are a useful variation, and
nicer, unless you have home-bottled fruit or home-made all-fruit jam
at your disposal.

Baked grain pudding with curd cheese
Barley works best here, and makes a very nourishing, mild dish
popular with children. A French nineteenth-century version
suggested making it with cream to please adult diners, and sprinkling
the sugar on after the cooking so that it need only be mildly sweet.
I have found this variation excellent. Also try these mixtures of
grain, milk, cheese and eggs in savoury versions by omitting the
sugar.

250 g (9 oz) curd cheese
600 ml (1 pint) milk or milk and cream
½ teaspoon salt
5 eggs
6 tablespoons barley
2 tablespoons sugar (optional)
pinch of nutmeg (optional)

Blend together the cheese, milk and/or cream, salt and eggs until you have a smooth mixture. Place the washed barley in a baking dish, pour the cheese mixture over, stir, and set to cook in a slow oven until the grain is thoroughly cooked and the pudding browned lightly on top, about 1½ hours. Serve hot sprinkled with sugar and nutmeg and, if you dare, with more cream.

Orange breakfast cheese

>   450 g (1 lb) *tvorog* (curd cheese)
>   1–2 tablespoons thick sour cream
>   1 tablespoon softened butter
>   a little salt to taste, depending on the sourness of the cheese
>   2 teaspoons sugar
>   1–2 teaspoons dried powdered orange peel

Mix all the ingredients together well, tie up in muslin or put in a plastic box covered with muslin or a clean cloth, and press under a weight in an airy dry place such as a well ventilated larder for about 3 days before eating.

Strawberry, raspberry or cherry breakfast cheese

This is really a simplified version of Easter *paskha* (page 263). Fresh soft fruit is chopped small and sprinkled with a little sugar, and both fruit and juice are combined with *tvorog*, sour cream and sugar to taste. Russians make a cold, liquid pudding with child appeal by adding milk to this mixture.

Cottage cheese and sour cream

A delightful instant breakfast or pudding consists of cottage cheese with sour cream and home-made preserves, ideally *varenye* (page 308), or sugar.

Ryazhenka

This is a yoghurt made with baked, that is, evaporated, milk – bought in Russian dairies it is the colour of light caramel, creamy and only slightly sour. Make it with evaporated milk diluted with its own volume of water. Heat the blended milk and water to blood heat in a pan. Mix a little plain yoghurt with extra evaporated milk, and put a teaspoon in each pot to be filled. Pour over the warmed milk, stir and leave covered in a warm place for 24 hours. Serve chilled, with or without sugar.

Sweet vareniki
Follow the recipe for *vareniki* on pages 228–9, using a filling of cherries. Stone and chop the cherries, sprinkle with sugar, and leave for a few hours until they exude some of their juice. Drain them as dry as possible before using to fill the *vareniki*. Serve either with a sauce made from the cherry juice and sour cream, or just with sour cream, sweetened to taste. The sauce may be warmed in a pan and served separately in a jug, or it may be poured over the cooked *vareniki* in a baking dish, put in the oven for 10 minutes to brown lightly on top, and served from the dish. Curd cheese *vareniki* (page 229) may be served sweet by filling them with sugar and adding cream.

Sweet kasha
All the usual grains may be cooked with milk instead of water and served sweet, flavoured with spices, honey, lemon and dried fruit. Many of the results are familiar favourites like rice pudding and oatmeal porridge. For breakfast, as a change from oats, try millet porridge. The dry grains may be soaked in advance or cooked straight away. Cook first for about 10 minutes in water, skimming the surface to remove any scum, then drain and finish in milk or milk and water. The millet will take about 30 minutes in all to cook. Russian rice pudding is seasoned with cinnamon or star anise, sweetened with sugar and enriched with butter.

Barley pudding is a good variation. Bring 6 tablespoons of uncooked barley to the boil in plenty of water and cook for 5–10 minutes until it begins to swell, skimming the surface to remove any scum that appears. Drain, add 600 ml (a generous pint) of milk, and cook until the barley is soft, stirring often. Sweeten with sugar or honey. A particularly Russian way is to serve it with honey and poppy seeds. Soak 3 tablespoons of poppy seed in boiling water for 10 minutes, drain, repeat the process, and pour off the water as soon as little droplets of oil appear on the surface. Pound the drained seeds in a mixing bowl or non-metal mortar, adding a few drops of boiling water and 2 teaspoons of honey. Blend in with the barley. More honey or sugar may be added to taste.

Sweet syrniki
CURD CHEESE FRITTERS
See page 220.

Blinchiki

SWEET PANCAKES

I find pancakes too heavy for pudding unless I have had a very light meal, but the Russian stuffings are good if you can find an opportunity to try them out. Rasputin's Russian restaurant in London told me that their apple, pineapple and cinnamon *blinchiki* are one of the most popular items on the menu.

Prepare ordinary unleavened pancakes, cooking them on one side only, and lay them cooked side up on a plate. Fill with a mixture of cooked apple, dried fruit and cinnamon, well drained of juice, or with curd cheese, using 1 egg and a tablespoon of butter to every 500 g (1 lb) to bind it, and seasoning with sugar, nuts, vanilla, lemon peel, and soaked dried fruit to taste. Roll up each pancake separately, fry lightly in butter until the outside is brown, and serve hot, sprinkled with sugar. For the simplest *blinchiki* serve plain pancakes with plenty of sour cream or butter and warmed honey. The following is a basic pancake mixture:

> 3 eggs
> 500 ml (1 pint) milk
> ¼ teaspoon salt
> 250 g (8 oz) flour
> 2 tablespoons butter

Mix the egg yolks with a quarter of the milk. Add the salt, then gradually add the flour and the melted butter. Stir until smooth, add the rest of the milk stirring all the time, and finally the beaten egg whites.

Lithuanian sweet pancakes

This French variation is much lighter, though with nothing obviously Lithuanian about it.

> 50 g (2 oz) flour
> 200 ml (⅓ pint) milk
> pinch of salt
> 75 g (3 oz) sugar
> vanilla to taste
> 3 eggs
> 2 tablespoons butter
> 2 tablespoons apricot jam or puréed cooked dried apricots
> apricots or cream for serving (optional)

Blend the flour to a paste with a little cold milk. Bring the rest of the milk to the boil with the salt, sugar and vanilla, and gradually stir in the flour paste. Cook, stirring, for 2–3 minutes. Remove from the heat and add the egg yolks, the butter, and the sweetened puréed apricots or jam, and when these are well mixed, add the beaten egg whites. Cook in butter as for pancakes, turning once, and serve filled with more apricots. I do think using dried apricots makes all the difference here. Jam, unless you have made it yourself and controlled the ingredients, can be a nasty, over-sweet concoction with little taste. With dried fruit, on the other hand, you start from basics and can add sugar to taste. The result will be far less cloying. Petit suggests serving these *blinchiki* with a sauce of apricots and madeira, which I personally would find overwhelming. Thin cream, or, at the other end of the scale, a blob of clotted cream that will melt on the hot rolled pancake, is preferable.

Olad'i (sweet)

These fritters belong to the same family as *blinchiki* but are made with a yeast batter and cooked in plenty of oil. Their name comes from the Greek word for oil, *elaion*. They are cooked in a shallow pan with a good ½ cm (¼ inch) of olive or sunflower oil, either plain or with thin slices of apple or soaked raisins mixed into the batter when it is first poured into the pan. Plain *olad'i* may be served with honey or with a portion of curd cheese topped with sour cream. They should be very light and must be eaten straight away.

> 2 teaspoons dried yeast
> 400 ml (⅔ pint) milk
> 1 tablespoon sugar
> 2 tablespoons melted butter
> ½ teaspoon salt
> 2 eggs
> 500 g (1 lb) flour
> 3–4 apples, sliced, or 3 tablespoons soaked raisins (optional)
> olive or sunflower oil for cooking

Dissolve the yeast in the warm milk, add the sugar, butter, salt and eggs, and sprinkle in the flour. Mix to a smooth batter, cover, and leave in a warm place to rise. Beat well and allow to rise again before using. Add the apples or raisins if using. Heat a generous amount of oil in a small pan, and cook the *olad'i* by pouring into the pan a good tablespoon of mixture at a time. Turn once, drain on greaseproof paper, and serve. *Olad'i* are occasionally to be found on Russian breakfast menus, but when produced in quantity in hotel kitchens they are rarely successful in my experience.

Sweet drachena
See page 218 for the savoury version. Made to slightly different specifications and sweetened, this makes a light sponge pudding good to eat with cream.

>   3 eggs
>   4 tablespoons sugar
>   500 g (1 lb) flour
>   500 ml (1 pint) milk
>   50 g (2 oz) butter
>   pinch salt

Mix the egg yolks with the sugar, add the flour gradually, stirring, then the milk and butter to make a smooth mixture. Add the salt and the beaten egg whites. Turn into a buttered soufflé dish and bake in a medium oven for half an hour.

Apple pie
Sweet pies tend to be much the same whether they are called Russian, English or French, I find, but I do like the habit of baking the fruit, cream and pastry ingredients all in together, to which a Russian friend stakes unique claim. It is quick and rich-tasting, especially if the fruit has plenty of juice. Use good cooking apples, or a summer fruit like cherries, blackberries or plums.

>   6 eggs
>   100 g (3½ oz) sugar
>   1 small (5 fl oz) carton or more sour cream
>   1 kg (2¼ lb) apples
>   60 g (2½ oz) flour
>   cinnamon to taste
>   ½ tablespoon butter
>   fresh breadcrumbs

Beat the egg yolks with the sugar. Pour in the sour cream and add 3 grated apples, the flour, the rest of the apples chopped fairly small, the cinnamon and the 6 beaten egg whites. Pile this mixture into a baking dish greased with butter and sprinkled with breadcrumbs, and bake in a medium oven for 40 minutes.

Curd cheese pie

FOR THE PASTRY CASE
225 g (8 oz) butter or margarine
350 g (12 oz) flour
2 tablespoons sugar
1 egg
1 tablespoon sour cream (see filling ingredients below)
pinch salt
5 tablespoons water or a mixture of water and rum or vodka

FOR THE FILLING
100 g (3½ oz) butter
6 egg yolks
450 g (1 lb) curd cheese
1¼ small (5 fl oz) cartons sour cream minus the 1 tablespoon
  used for the pastry
pinch salt
100 g (3½ oz) caster sugar
vanilla to taste

Rub the fat into the flour, add the sugar, egg, sour cream, salt and the liquid and line a pie dish with the pastry. Cream the butter, add the egg yolks, cheese, sour cream, salt, sugar and vanilla, and mix well. Fill the pastry case with the cheese mixture and bake in a hot oven for no longer than 20 minutes. Serve hot or cold, sprinkled with sugar.

Air pie

This strange sounding concoction is none other than a fruit soufflé made entirely with egg whites, and is one of the few Russian puddings with a native heritage. Its original name was 'beaten pie', and it may be made with a purée of any fresh or dried fruit. Gooseberries, apples, strawberries, plums and blackcurrants are particularly recommended.

300 g (10 oz) uncooked fruit
4 tablespoons sugar or to taste
6 egg whites
caster sugar for serving

Prepare a fruit purée with as little extra water as possible, ideally by baking (apples) or steaming (soft fruit). Add sugar to taste. Beat the egg whites until very stiff, pour in the hot purée, and bake 10–15 minutes in a greased soufflé dish in a hot oven. Serve immediately otherwise the pie will sink. It may be sprinkled with caster sugar and eaten with cream or milk. It is not attractive once it has gone cold. Altogether an excellent way of using up egg whites, and a very light end to a meal.

Smetannik

CREAM AND JAM TART

> flaky pastry made with 250 g (8 oz) flour, 200–250 g (7–8 oz)
>   butter, 16 tablespoons water, pinch salt
> 450 g (1 lb) good jam, preferably strawberry, cherry or
>   raspberry, home-made, *or* cooked soft fruit with sugar
> 100 g (3½ oz) ground almonds
> milk
> 3 tablespoons sour cream
> 1 egg yolk
> 1 teaspoon cinnamon

Line a pie dish with the pastry rolled out thinly, leaving enough over to cover the finished pie, and spread the jam roughly over the surface. Put the almonds in a pan, gradually stir in warm milk, and cook, adding more milk as necessary, until the mixture is the consistency of a thick sauce. Remove from the heat, add the sour cream, egg yolk and cinnamon, mix well and pour over the jam. Cover with a pastry top, seal the edges and bake in a medium oven for 45–50 minutes.

Cherry (summer fruit) pudding

> 450 g (1 lb) cherries
> 5–6 tablespoons sugar or to taste
> 1 egg
> 1 small (5 fl oz) carton sour cream
> 1 teaspoon flour
> ½ teaspoon cinnamon

Stone the cherries and sprinkle with half the sugar. Beat the egg and sour cream together and add the remaining sugar, the flour, and the cinnamon. Pour this mixture over the cherries, mix well, put in a baking dish and cook in a medium to hot oven for about 30 minutes. Blackcurrants or blueberries are excellent substitutes for cherries.

Buckwheat pudding with sabayon sauce
The name gives away everything about this made-up nineteenth-century pudding, which resembles an English Christmas pudding. It is served with the best of French sauces and gets its bulk from a staple Russian food plant.

550 ml (1 pint) milk
1½ tablespoons butter
5 tablespoons caster sugar
180 g (7 oz) buckwheat (uncooked weight)
pinch salt
30 g (generous 1 oz) each raisins and currants
1 tablespoon mixed peel
grated peel of ½ a lemon
6 eggs

FOR THE SABAYON SAUCE
3 egg yolks
¾ glass sweet sherry or madeira ⎱ OR equal quantity light
4 tablespoons water ⎰ table wine

3 teaspoons sugar
squeeze lemon juice

Bring the milk to the boil with the butter and sugar and add the washed buckwheat. When it is cooked, remove from the heat and add the salt, dried fruit, mixed peel, lemon peel and egg yolks. Mix well and add the stiffly beaten egg whites. Put the mixture into a buttered pudding basin sprinkled with sugar and steam it for a couple of hours. To make the sabayon sauce, beat all the ingredients together and heat gently, stirring all the time, until the sauce thickens. Serve with the pudding. Alternative accompaniments are rum butter or cream.

Buckwheat pudding with rum and cream

90 g (3 oz) buckwheat (uncooked weight)
4 tablespoons sugar
600 ml (1 generous pint) single or sour cream or a mixture of
cream and milk (see recipe)
½ liqueur glass rum

This is a de-luxe grain pudding with adult appeal. The original calls for nothing but sour cream, which makes it very rich and expensive, but I have had good results from mixing cream and milk.

Mix together all the ingredients, turn into a buttered baking dish and bake in a medium oven for an hour.

Sharlotka

Charlotte russe, a cold sweet confected out of sponge fingers and cream, was invented in Paris in the early nineteenth century by Antoine Carême. He was probably tempted to call it Russian in honour of his time as chef to Tsar Alexander I. *Sharlotka* is a hot and distant relative popular in Russia since then.

> about 250 g (8 oz) stale (black) rye bread
> 150 g (5 oz) butter
> 2 cloves or vanilla to taste
> cinnamon (optional)
> lemon peel
> 12 tablespoons sugar or to taste
> 150 ml ($\frac{1}{4}$ pint) white wine
> 6 apples
> 10 g (generous 1 oz) raisins
> brown or white breadcrumbs

Grate or crumble the black bread, whichever is easier, and fry it in most of the butter, with the vanilla or cloves, the cinnamon, the lemon peel and a third of the sugar. Take off the heat and moisten with the wine. Peel the apples, chop them quite small, and mix with the raisins and the rest of the sugar. Butter a charlotte mould or any tall sided dish and line it with breadcrumbs. At the bottom spread a thin layer of the black bread and wine mixture, cover with a layer of the apple mixture, continuing alternately and ending with a layer of crumbs. Bake in a slow oven for an hour, and serve very hot, with thin chilled cream.

Fruit salad with champagne

This was a favourite at aristocratic tables in the nineteenth century and was usually given a German or French name. Urbain Dubois entitled this magnificent concoction *à la russe* in his *Cuisine de tous les pays*:

> $\frac{1}{4}$ large pineapple
> 4–5 fresh peaches
> 4–5 fresh apricots
> a bunch of cherries

2 handfuls of fresh red plums
1 litre (1¾ pints) fresh fruit juice or fruit purée
juice of 2 oranges
vanilla syrup (made by cooking 200 ml (⅓ pint) water with
    sugar and vanilla to a thin syrup)
1 bottle champagne
2 large wine glasses Bordeaux

Peel and chop the pineapple. Remove the stones from the other fruit and chop. Squeeze the juice from the peelings into a bowl, add the fresh fruit juice or fruit purée, the orange juice, and 1 glass vanilla syrup. Add the champagne and wine, mix, and chill well before serving.

♦ Corners can be cut, but not many. Tinned pineapple juice is acceptable out of the fresh fruit season. In the season you should be able to get very ripe soft red fruit to purée, ideally strawberries. Replace champagne with sparkling wine.

Kutyá and uzvar

Compotes of dried fruit are popular all over Russia and in the South. The Ukrainians prepare a particular *uzvar* for Christmas Eve which they eat with sweetened grain. It also marks feasts in honour of the dead. This grain dish alone, or sometimes the combination of fruit and grain, is known as *kutyá*. Soak dried fruit (figs, apples, pears, peaches, apricots, prunes, large raisins) overnight or longer in plenty of water. Cook the fruit in a little fresh water, adding honey or sugar to taste.

Eat with wheat grains cooked in milk like a rice pudding. Use 6 tablespoons of bulghur wheat to 350 ml (⅗ pint) milk and sweeten with sugar or honey to taste. Or make a rice pudding using milk of almonds. Steep 225 g (½ lb) crushed almonds in a muslin bag in a generous litre (2 pints) water until you have a well-flavoured milky liquid. Wring out the bag well into the bowl. Cook 12 tablespoons pudding rice in this liquid, sweetening according to taste. Serve hot or cold with the fruit compote. These dishes marked the last day of the meatless fast before Christmas.

Kisel (fruit purée) and fruit soups

Kisel for me falls into the same category as blancmange. It probably came to Russia at about the same time that genuine blancmange, made with light cream and milk of almonds, arrived. It was thickened with potato starch, a new ingredient in the late eighteenth century, and was ideally based on cranberries or loganberries, which made it slightly tart. Made with fresh berries and served with lashings of double cream, the *kisel* hot and the cream extra cold, it had and still has some pretensions to elegance if you like the liquid texture. But it has been temptingly easy to simplify into a bowl of thickened fruit flavouring, and even at its best I can't help thinking of it as children's food, perhaps part of a family meal which might not offend the adult palate but certainly would not challenge or delight it! This is a prejudice which bowlfuls of *kisel*, even wine *kisel*, have not dispelled. I encounter the same problem with the fruit soups some writers wistfully describe as a Russian speciality. Firstly, they are no more than thin *kisel*, and secondly, their true heritage is at least partly German. One Russian acquaintance with high gastronomic standards told me she thought *kisel* and fruit soups (sometimes called by their German name, *Kaltschalen*) had been introduced to Russia by German children's maids via the aristocratic nursery.

But plenty of good cooks have recommended *kisel*. If you like the idea, make it with fresh, tart fruit, slightly sweetened, and do not over-thicken it. Serve it hot or cold with plenty of whipped chilled cream. Cornflour and arrowroot are plausible substitutes for potato flour. Use ½–1 tablespoon of starch per cup of fruit purée, diluting it first with a little water or fruit juice, then adding it to the warm purée and heating the whole *kisel* gently, stirring all the time, to thicken it. Tartness may be increased to taste with a squeeze or two of lemon juice. *Kisel* to be served cold demands slightly more starch than a warm version, but don't exceed the upper limit or you will be faced with a most unattractive gelatinous mass.

Fresh cranberries and loganberries are not easy to come by in our markets, which is a pity for genuine *kisel*. My second choice would be sourish cherries, gooseberries, redcurrants or blackcurrants. Barberries, which used to grow wild in this country and were popular bottling fruit, would be excellent if only they too were available. They have a light red colour and a pleasantly acid flavour, and when cooked become slightly gelatinous, obviating the need for any starch to bind them. They are widely used both fresh and dried and powdered by the Armenians.

Gogol'-Mogol'

This strange-sounding dessert, which was immensely popular at the height of Russian–French Imperial cooking in the reign of Tsar Alexander III, is basically a French *sabayon* or an Italian *zabaglione*. It was enjoyed sufficiently in Russia to become naturalized. I include it here to show how far Russian sweet concoctions travelled from native *kashitsy* under elegant foreign influences. The following recipe was included in Soviet Russian cookery books right up to the late 1950s, even though it belonged to an age of good food and prosperity far out of reach.

6 egg yolks
3 tablespoons sugar (or to taste)
lemon peel to taste
orange-flavoured liqueur such as cointreau or rum
250 ml (½ pint) fortified wine (marsala, muscatel, malaga, madeira, port, sherry)

Beat together in a bowl the yolks, sugar, lemon peel and a dash of rum or orange liqueur to taste, add the wine and beat over hot water until thick and foamy. Serve with sponge fingers or ratafia biscuits.

ICE CREAM

'There, you see, I *did* ask,' whispered Natasha to her little brother and to Pierre, glancing at him again.

'Ice cream, only you will not be allowed any,' said Maria Dmitrievna.

Natasha saw there was nothing to be afraid of and so she braved even Maria Dmitrievna.

'Maria Dmitrievna! What sort of ice-cream? I don't like ice-cream.'

'Carrot-ices.'

'No, what kind, Maria Dmitrievna? What kind?' she almost shrieked. 'I want to know!'

Maria Dmitrievna and the countess burst out laughing, and all the guests joined in. They all laughed, not at Maria Dmitrievna's repartee but at the incredible audacity and smartness of this little girl who had the pluck and wit to tackle Maria Dmitrievna in this fashion.

Natasha only desisted when she was told there would be pineapple ice. Before the ices champagne was served. The orchestra struck up again and the count kissed his 'little countess' and the guests rose to drink her health, clinking glasses across the table with the count, the children and one another. Again the footmen bustled about, chairs scraped, and in the same order in which they had entered, but with faces a little more flushed, the company returned to the drawing-room and the host's study.

LEO TOLSTOY, *War and Peace*

Morozhenoe

Ice cream has been immensely popular in Russia since it was introduced in the eighteenth century as a delicacy for the aristocracy. By the end of the nineteenth century it was possible to buy as a piece of standard household equipment a *morozhenitsa*, consisting of a deep metal receptacle fitted inside a bucket filled with ice and salt. The receptacle contained the ice cream mixture and was fitted with a lid and a long stirring tool which dislodged mixture as it froze at the sides. But it probably remained something of a treat until in an immensely popular move in the 1920s Anastas Mikoyan set up the first Soviet Russian ice cream factory. That industry never looked back. Ice cream parlours are as popular in Russian cities as they are in the Mediterranean, and the product sold is of a purity and creaminess that constantly astounds Western visitors. There is no difference between a good Russian recipe for ice cream made at home and a good recipe from any other country. Here is a basic mixture:

> 1 egg yolk
> 60 g (2–3 oz) sugar
> 200 ml (⅓ pint) single, whipping or double cream as
>   preferred
> few drops vanilla essence or grated lemon peel

Cream together the egg yolk and sugar, add the cream and the flavouring, and heat gently, stirring all the time, until the mixture thickens. I prefer to do this in a bowl over a double boiler. It not only prevents the 'cooking' of the ice cream in every sense but saves losing any of this costly mixture round the sides of the pan. The bowl may be placed straight in the freezer, covered. Stir frequently to ensure a smooth, creamy result. Serve alone, with fruit syrup, fresh or bottled fruit, or chopped nuts.

Two variations are *plombir* and *zefir*. In the first, whipped cream is introduced to a basic mixture which is beaten when it is half frozen, and then the whole put on ice for several hours before serving. *Zefir* is usually a mixture of cream and fruit which is whipped just before serving.

Plombir

> 6–7 tablespoons single cream
> 2 egg yolks
> 50 g (2 oz) sugar
> a few drops of vanilla essence
> 200 ml (⅓ pint) whipping or double cream
> lemon peel or candied peel to taste (optional)

Mix together the single cream, the egg yolks and the sugar, add the vanilla, and stir over a double boiler until the mixture thickens. Cover the bowl and freeze. Meanwhile beat the remaining cream until it is thick. When the first mixture is half frozen beat it thoroughly, add the whipped cream and peel and leave this mixture to freeze again. *Plombir* is particularly good served with fresh orange segments.

Zefir

> 200 ml (⅓ pint) double cream
> 30–40 g (1–1½ oz) sugar
> few drops lemon essence, vanilla essence or grated lemon
>   rind to taste
> 150 g (5 oz) strawberries or other soft fruit; drained tinned
>   fruit may be used, or a good whole fruit jam, but the
>   quantity should be halved

Chill the cream and whip until thick. Add the sugar and flavourings and mix in the fruit. Freeze. Whip again just before serving. *Zefir* is often served on a meringue base, a convenient way of using up egg whites left over after making ice cream.

Eating Out

One of the world's finest restaurant cultures died with the Revolution and its aftermath. Of the veteran restaurateurs and gastronomes who watched it crumble, one opened a tiny cookery museum in Moscow in the late 1970s. The old menu cards and elaborate glass and silverware were a nostalgic tribute to the lost catering prowess of the city. 'Moscow has gained celebrity for its cutlets of all kinds, its divine cold sucking pig, and for its cold boiled beef, which is almost snow white,' wrote an English traveller at the turn of the century. Fish for the table used to swim in a pond in the floor of the Berlin restaurant, and German food was a speciality. All that glamour and variety has gone.

Noon was a busy time for restaurants in the pre-revolutionary city. They catered largely for businessmen, and the atmosphere around the *zakuski* table appears from contemporary descriptions to have resembled that of a respectable gentlemen's club. *Zakuski* were reputedly best at the Hermitage, the Bolshoi Moskovsky and the Slavyansky Bazar restaurants. An early twentieth-century guide called the Hermitage, where the famous Russian–French chef Olivier worked, one of the great historic restaurants of the world. A positive army of chefs and sous-chefs prepared French–Russian meals: sturgeon in champagne, saddle of lamb in the Scottish manner *à la Nesselrode* (an early nineteenth-century Russian diplomat who gave his name to several classic French dishes), salad and salted cucumbers, *bombe surprise*. For game they used a store room so large it was worth a special excursion to see, and for an additional charge guests could dine off Sèvres china.

The Hermitage rooms were light green, high-ceilinged, and decorated elaborately with stucco. As in several restaurants of the time, the walls and ceilings were overlaid with ornate mirrors which magnified the splendour and the atmosphere of the rooms endlessly. The *zakuski* table was housed under a musicians' gallery. The waiters wore long white tunics with a red cord at the waist in Tartar style. On Sundays and Holy Days they wore coloured silks. The Hermitage was sufficiently snobbish to deny all knowledge of Russian wines, but kept a well-stocked and very expensive French wine cellar. Wine imports were heavily taxed by the authorities.

The atmosphere at the Slavyansky Bazar was far more Russian. The waiters spoke only that language. The Old Russian Hall, painted in glaring reds and greens on white with a vaulted ceiling in wood, was a special attraction and the scene of noisy concerts. To serve its highly praised *zakuski* the Slavyansky Bazar used wooden platters edged in silver, and offered what must have been a wonderful spread of salmon, beef, sucking pig and crayfish, punctuated with bowls of sour cream. There was an excellent *solyanka* to follow, with *rastegai* (small salmon pies), and the house speciality, an orange salad.

The man with time to spare and the freedom to enjoy it took a light dinner around five in the afternoon, in summer preferably at one of the restaurants in Petrovsky Park. If he wanted a thoroughly Russian meal he would probably have gone to Testov's, in the city, where Grand Dukes and nobles went to eat native dishes and speak their native language as a change from the Frenchified daily round.

Supper would be around midnight, perhaps at the Yar or the Golden Anchor where there would be a music-hall cabaret. At the Yar, live sterlet would be brought to the table on a silver dish covered with a napkin, for the diner to make his choice. The atmosphere was close and informal, with dancing and singing and the gypsy bands that often seem best to express Russian spontaneity and celebration. The cabarets were excellent, and many were transported wholesale to Paris after the Revolution.

St Petersburg, though its restaurants were considerably more French, was no less of a gourmet's paradise than Moscow. One of the great attractions of the northern city was its setting on the water. Some of the finest restaurants were built in the Islands suburb, surrounded by lawns and gardens. In winter when the river and canals were frozen they were popular for sleigh parties. Ernest's, with its red décor and gypsy band, must have provided a wonderful welcome after the cold outside.

In modern Russia the best eating and drinking is undoubtedly done at home. But the habit of going to restaurants to find a festive atmosphere remains. Diners enjoy themselves with a verve I have rarely witnessed outside Russia. They come invariably in big parties to celebrate a birthday, a wedding or some other family occasion. Plates of dull food stand and get cold while vodka, champagne, chocolate and ice cream are brought in quantity. A loud band jollies and blasts couples on to the dance floor. Good eating and conversation are the last things on anyone's mind.

Beverages

TEA

To the Mongols who ruled the country for over 200 years until the mid fifteenth century the Russians owe two great features of their daily civilized life: tea and the samovar. Of all beverages, tea alone has the proverbial power to relieve *toska*, the sadness and melancholy which traditionally burden the Russian spirit. The samovar which dispenses it is a time-honoured symbol of Russian hospitality. It stands for the hearth, the warmth of a Russian welcome, the restorative powers of a glass of tea around the stove after hours in sub-zero temperatures. The word means 'self-boiler' and the samovar is just that, a portable water heater made traditionally of brass and fuelled with pine cones or charcoal. On top of it rests a teapot containing a powerful infusion. To pour a glass of tea, a little of this concentrate is diluted with boiling water from the urn. This way it is always fresh, never stewed.

Sadly, the modern samovar is a plug-in electrical device distinguished by its mass-produced shoddiness and the fact that no one wants to buy it. It is perhaps a fitting epitaph on the death of a culture. In the nineteenth century the samovar and the tea glass holder, found in daily use in the lowliest and the richest households, inspired some of the finest secular silverwork ever produced in Russia.

Statistically the Russians are among the world's top three tea-drinking nations (with Britain and Japan). The leaves are grown in the Caucasian Republic of Georgia, in southern Russia on the northern shores of the Black Sea, and large quantities are imported from India and Sri Lanka. China tea used to be the favourite among the aristocracy. Soviet Central Asia follows its own tradition of green (unfermented) tea, drunk in teahouses (*chaikaniya*) and often spiced with cinnamon.

The best Russian tea today is served on Russian overnight trains. At the end of every carriage, where the attendant has a small galley, there is a samovar constantly on the boil.

Russian tea is served fairly weak, steaming hot and without milk. The custom, pointing to oriental origins, has always been to serve something very sweet alongside it, rather than to sweeten the tea itself. It is not uncommon to see a Russian drink his tea through a sugar lump, or with a spoonful of jam. In trains it is invariably served with very sweet wafer biscuits. In the nineteenth century the aristocracy took their tea with cream and jam, or, as an alternative to jam, sweet syrups which went under the confusing names of *sidr* (also used for cider) and *sherbet*. The first was made with oranges and lemons, the second with almonds. It was a wonderful way of showing off home-made fruit preserves.

COFFEE

Peter the Great brought back the habit of coffee-drinking after visiting Holland at the beginning of the eighteenth century. It has never gained the popularity of tea in central Russia, although it is now available everywhere in hotels and restaurants. The standard of the brew is not high. Exceptions are the Baltic states, where coffee-drinking in the afternoon is a long-established tradition, and the South. The Armenians serve so-called Turkish coffee, thick and sweet in small cups with a glass of water alongside.

CHOCOLATE

Hot chocolate, an imported luxury in the last century, was a breakfast favourite with the children of the middle and upper classes. The adult aristocracy, according to an English traveller in the 1830s, also enjoyed it in the form of 'afternoon chocolate out-of-doors'. On such occasions a table would be laid in the open air and steaming mugs of cocoa served with blueberry tarts.

FERMENTED MILK

Fermented milk drinks are drunk throughout the Soviet Union. They go under a host of different names, but are essentially compounded of yoghurt and buttermilk. The Russians take *kefir*, a thick buttermilk available in varying degrees of milk fat content, as a nourishing drink, on journeys or for breakfast. *Kefir* was first brought to Russia in the nineteenth century as a health drink from the north Caucasus. Its preparation is apparently a secret. Cow's milk is cultured with *kefir* enzymes and yeast to produce a thick, refreshing, slightly sparkling drink with a grainy texture before it is stirred. To the ancient Caucasians it was known as 'the grains of Mohammed'.

In Armenia *kefir* is served as a non-alcoholic *apéritif* or first course of a meal. Further East, yoghurt or buttermilk are made into a long drink with soda water, seasoned with salt and served with ice. The drink is called *airan* and is excellent in the heat. There are also a variety of sour milks, and the legendary *kumys*, fermented mare's milk. *Kumys* is produced industrially in Russia, from skimmed cow's milk.

All these fermented and cultured milk products are highly popular all over the country and enjoy a reputation for promoting health, longevity, fertility and good digestion. (See also yoghurt, page 24.)

SOFT DRINKS

Many Russian hotels make up soft drinks by diluting fruit syrup with water, a curious practice deriving from the tea and syrup habit. In city streets and parks, soft drink machines dispense the same kind of sweetened water for a negligible sum. At home a quick hot drink is made by pouring boiling water over a spoonful of jam in a glass. A similar infusion used to be made with boiling water and dried powdered berries.

Russian mineral waters are excellent, and invariably to be found on hotel and restaurant tables. The chemical composition of each mineral water bottled is given in precise detail on the label. They come from hundreds of spas in Russia and the Caucasus and bring with them centuries of belief, shared with the Austro–Hungarian world and still current today, in the curative and restorative powers of the 'waters'. The first of these came into being in Karelia, where the soil is rich in iron. Peter the Great sent soldiers there to restore their strength after the war with Sweden at the beginning of the eighteenth century.

FERMENTED FRUIT DRINKS

The most ancient Russian drink, known since pre-Christian days, was made from the sap of the birch tree, collected in spring and left in large tubs to ferment naturally. This *beryozovitsa* was a sweetish drink which only gave way to *kvas* (see below) in the Middle Ages as the daily beverage. There is a modern mass-produced version with sugar and preservatives added which is not at all pleasant.

Other ancient drinks were made with honey, like our own mead.

Medok was made by fermenting honey water, hops and yeast together. *Sbiten'* was a hot spiced honey drink with no alcoholic content. Its popularity was overtaken by tea.

Sbiten'

> 5–6 tablespoons honey
> 2 litres (3 pints) water
> 100 g (3½ oz) sugar
> 2 teaspoons mint
> 2–3 teaspoons dried St John's Wort (optional)
> 2 cloves
> 5–6 peppercorns
> 1 teaspoon cinnamon
> ¼ teaspoon powdered ginger

Put the honey in a pan, bring to the boil, and add a cup of warm water. Stir and skim the surface. Bring the sugar to the boil in another cup of water. Simmer the herbs and spices in the remaining water for 20 minutes, leave to stand for another 10 minutes then strain. Mix all three liquids together. Heat through without boiling and serve in tea glasses.

Mildly fermented fruit drinks made with apples, pears and berries were also popular throughout Russia in the days before bottled soft drinks.

KVAS

... Our Russian *kvas* has all the makings of one of the healthiest and most nutritious drinks. It also has healing properties, particularly against consumption ...

ELENA MOLOKHOVETS

From the sixteenth century this unique Russian beer, sweet, mildly acid and mildly alcoholic, superseded all other drinks amongst the mass of the people and is still considered the national drink. It is made by fermenting wheat, rye, buckwheat and sometimes barley with water and sugar. It is sold on town streets in big stationary barrels with the letters KBAC on them, which attract a cluster of people at any time of the day. It is used also as a soup base. Russian supermarkets now stock a *kvas* concentrate, enabling people to make the beer quickly and cheaply at home. It is a drink that most Western palates find hard to like. The taste of yeast in the street variety and in that made from a concentrate is very strong, and the warm temperature at which it is correctly served does not appeal. But I had one experience of good *kvas* which was a revelation, at the Russkaya Izba restaurant outside Moscow. It was a pale blond colour and almost clear, like a good flat cider. It was sweet and pleasant to drink, served slightly chilled with a cold lunch. The Izba specialized in traditional recipes and would not give away its secrets, but here is one which I have tried successfully at home:

> 1 tablespoon dried yeast
> 150 g (5 oz) malt extract
> 400 g (12 oz) rye flour
> 100 g (3½ oz) buckwheat flour
> 100 g (3½ oz) wheat flour
> 2½ litres (4¼ pints) water
> ½ tablespoon dried mint

Dissolve the yeast in a little warm water with a tablespoon of flour. Pour a little hot water over the malt. Mix the 3 kinds of flour together, and add the malt water and half the specified quantity of water in the recipe, stirring to prevent any lumps forming. Leave for 5 hours then add the rest of the water, the yeast mixture and the mint. Leave for 12–24 hours in a warm place, then strain and bottle with loose-fitting corks. Serve chilled.

VODKA

There is no pretending that vodka is not the national scourge and that the legendary Russian lack of moderation in consuming it is not true. Distilled from grain and repeatedly purified to increase the alcoholic strength and refine the flavour, basic vodka has no flavouring added to it. It is extremely clear and smooth. The best vodka on sale in Russia today is *pshenichnaya* or wheat vodka, but there are many cheaper varieties. The widely exported *stolichnaya* is of very good quality. The difference between Russian vodka and that made in the West is enormous. The Russian product has a very distinctive taste which makes it delightful to drink neat, the only way a Russian would ever countenance it. It is always served ice cold and drunk in small glasses in one gulp. Order it in restaurants by weight, that is 100 g for two moderate diners eating *zakuski*. The myths that surround the power of vodka are legion. Russian vodka is strongly intoxicating and leaves as bad a hangover as you can imagine. Intoxication does not come gradually but suddenly hits the drinker when he thinks he has passed the test. It is this which has resulted, given the Russian habit at all levels of wanting to drink guests under the table as a sign of hospitality, in the keeling over of notable political figures in Russian company.

Russians will say that Westerners do not know how to drink vodka, and advise sniffing a piece of black bread between gulps, eating sour cucumbers and pickled mushrooms, making sure you do not drink on an empty stomach. But these are the refinements of vodka-drinking and not a safeguard against its effects. Ironically, vodka was first introduced in Russia in the fourteenth century as medicine. One might be tempted to see it as a cure for national melancholy, like tea, although the Russian dissident novelist Andrei Sinyavsky has fairly challenged that theory and suggested that its true fascination is as a source of the fantastic. Vodka is white magic.

Anything that Russians add to their vodka is added in the bottle by way of sugar and/or flavouring and colouring. Here the permutations are endless. Lemon vodka, which is slightly sweet and an appropriate colour, is a great favourite. The old medicinal remedies are remembered with pepper vodka, *pertsovka* – a chilli pepper is steeped in a bottle of vodka for hours or days, resulting in a fiery drink which brings tears to the eyes of the healthy and is a favourite folk remedy for colds and 'flu. Other additions include all kinds of sweet berries, caraway and aniseed, green herbs, tea, cherry stones, juniper and almonds. Saffron colours vodka yellow, mint makes it green, and cochineal is sometimes used to make it red, especially in the home brews recommended in the last century. Sweet vodkas, which to my taste are not worth the name compared with their unsweetened parents, come in every variety from raspberry to mint. They are sometimes used to make long drinks. I experienced an intriguing one in the Lithuanian capital of Vilnius, where it was served as a local speciality. The base was caraway vodka, with barley water and a little honey.

WINE

There is no native tradition of wine-drinking in Russia. Most of the country is too far north for a natural celebration of Bacchus. But importing wine from France was an established custom among the rich and powerful by the end of the Mongol period. Ivan the Terrible threw magnificent banquets at which the drinks included Romanée (Burgundy), *kvas*, malmsey, *medok* and fruit vodkas. The nineteenth-century palate was delighted by French wines and champagne. This culminated in a snobbishness which meant, as one English traveller at the beginning of the present century recorded, that no restaurant worth its reputation would admit even the existence of Russian equivalents. They did, however, exist in the south of the newly expanded empire. The first Caucasian restaurants to open in Moscow in the 1870s served Caucasian wines with the speciality of the house, *shashlyk*. The Imperial family, who imported wines from France and Hungary, set the finest tradition in Russian champagne with their Abrau Durso estate on the Black Sea.

The viticultural picture today is a curious one. The state encourages wine-drinking and produces 'mass wines' from pulp-processing factories all over the north of Russia, at least partly in a bid to lure people away from the more pernicious vodka. There is a good market both at home and potentially abroad, and all over the southern Soviet Union, in the republics where the climate is suitable, more and more land is coming under cultivation to produce wine. But by Western standards Russians do not know how to drink wine. They like fortified wines, sweetened with a lot of added sugar, and sweet champagne at any temperature. One still hears tell that sweet drinks are better in the Russian climate because they provide more warmth. And as if they were not sweet enough, the favourite accompaniment to wine and champagne is chocolate.

Traditions at home in the Caucasus, the Crimea and Moldavia are quite different. There the habit of wine-drinking is deep-rooted. Pride of place goes to Georgia, one of the oldest regions in the world to cultivate the vine. Many Georgian wines appeal to the classic *goût russe*, the sweetest tooth known to gastronomy. One of the most characteristic reds, *kinzmarauli*, was dictator Josef Stalin's favourite and still tops the list for Russian enthusiasts. But the area also produces very reasonable dry white table wines, *tsinandali* being among the best known, and some heavy, dry reds whose salient quality is their 'extractiveness'. This word indicates a dense, opaque wine that drinks well alone or is a good partner for robust dishes. *Mukuzani*, typical of the category, stains the imbiber's lips a deep purple. The great virtue of these wines, apart from their cheapness on the Russian market, is their naturalness. Hardly any sulphur dioxide is added as a preservative, and to my knowledge they contain no noxious potassium ferrocyanide to stop them going cloudy. They are low in alcoholic content and excellent for everyday drinking. Moldavia produces mainly white table wines on a par with the produce of Romania, Yugoslavia, Bulgaria and Hungary, while the Crimea is known for its 'champagne', exported as sparkling wine.

The future of Soviet wine does not augur well for quality.[1] Money and expertise are being poured into the traditionally Moslem republic of Azerbaijan to create a new wine industry there, but without any guiding native wisdom from the soil. At the moment the republic produces almost entirely 'mass' fortified and dessert wines which are no good for anyone's health or taste buds. These, incidentally, are often given the names of apparent European equivalents, such as *portvein, kheres* and *shato ikem*.

But, true to Soviet fashion, there are pockets of excellence within the sprawl of mediocrity. One such treasure house is the collective farm which took over the Abrau Durso estate and has continued to produce a few million bottles of excellent champagne a year by traditional hand methods. Only a quarter of those bottles reach the West. It is the finest champagne Russia produces, and is, I have on hearsay, indispensable at Kremlin banquets. The bottles were once labelled with the Imperial double eagle. The château itself lies in a most picturesque valley not far inland from the Black Sea port of Novorossisk.

---

[1] The October 1979 *Guide Gault-Millau*, a demanding survey of international wines, described Soviet wines as 'mediocre at best' with 'almost as much bouquet as ozone', but noted that by the year 2000 the Soviet Union, already the world's third largest producer, would probably be the first. Their survey was limited by poor supplies abroad for tasting.

Family and servants around the samovar (1889).

Preserving

Time, space, and an appreciation of the virtue of wasting nothing are essential here. 'Preserve to prize in March what you disdained in October' was sound wisdom when the seasons still affected our daily diet. Bottling, spicing, sousing, pickling, salting, and drying have remained popular in Russia because winter still deprives many people of vegetables and fruit. The age of convenience food has been slow to come, and the national economy cannot even now guarantee a constant supply of frozen and tinned goods. Memories of the famine of the 1920s and severe war-time deprivations are extraordinarily strong among ordinary people. Shortages of everyday foodstuffs are still common, and when harvests fail they cause havoc. This picture evokes in me both political cynicism and cultural nostalgia. Moscow's Central Market in winter houses scores of stalls selling pickled cabbage, pickled garlic, pickled cucumbers, pickled aubergines, pickled tomatoes, soused apples and dried mushrooms, but little else. The lack of freshness is monotonous. But the blackcurrants bottled at the end of last summer's holiday, or the soup whose aroma recalls the smell of the damp August forest in early morning, do wonders for jaded midwinter spirits.

DRYING

Apart from mushrooms (see page 212) you may find it useful to keep a stock of dried lemon and orange peel, which are especially good in cake-making and in sweet bread. Pare the rind from fresh fruit very thinly and allow it to dry in hot sun, in a very slow oven, or in a hot airing cupboard. Store the dry peel in airtight jars, in strips or ground to a powder in a grinder.

Cherries are also good to dry. Clean and dry cooking cherries which are unblemished and not too ripe, and without removing stalks or stones dry on trays in a very slow oven. Either tie in bunches and string up in a warm, dry room, or keep in glass jars. Sweet jars are excellent if you dry a lot of fruit. The dried cherries may be used for their sourish flavour in many Caucasian dishes, or sweetened and reconstituted in baking, puddings and savoury sauces.

Ground, dried barberries were once used to flavour bread but I do not make this as a serious suggestion today. Apples and pears on the other hand are well worth drying in early autumn when they cost almost nothing. They may be used in pies and other sweet dishes and also in breakfast cereals. Clean the pears and dry them whole on baking sheets in the oven. Apples should be peeled and either quartered or cut in thick rings before drying. In the south of Russia fruit is dried in the open air, but it is impossible to rely on nature alone in this country.

SWEET FRUIT PRESERVES

Russians distinguish between *varen'ye*, which should contain large chunks of fruit or whole berries and has plenty of syrup to spare, *dzhem* (from the English *jam*) which is firmer, often set with pectin and made of puréed fruit, and *povidlo*, fruit jelly or cheese. *Varen'ye* is generally superior in quality as far as what is on sale is concerned, and is close to home-made preserves. Its slightly less firm consistency makes it good to use in baking, on ice-cream and on curd cheese. Russian restaurants frequently serve the former as a dessert, while curd cheese with *varen'ye* quite often occurs on menus. Good *varen'ye* stands the ultimate test of being taken with tea. Tea Russian-style is weak and black, and the *varen'ye*, usually blackcurrant or redcurrant, is served in a small dish about 4 cm (2 inches) in diameter alongside the glass. It is eaten with a spoon. Middle Eastern preserves which keep the fruit whole and are often eaten alone as a sweet course or with coffee or diluted in a glass of water are probably *varen'ye*'s closest relatives. Older versions of *varen'ye* were made entirely of fruit and honey.

Blackcurrant or redcurrant *varen'ye* is made with equal quantities of fruit, sugar and water. For each 450 g (1 lb) of sugar and fruit use about 200 ml (⅓ pint) water. Wash the fruit whole, drain, remove any stalks, sprinkle with sugar and leave for a couple of hours while some of the juice is exuded. Then put the juice, water and remaining sugar in a pan. Cook quickly for 15 minutes without stirring, skim off any scum that forms, and continue simmering until the syrup is transparent and sets on a cold saucer. Add the berries, stirring as little as possible, and simmer in the syrup for a few minutes. Allow to cool slightly before bottling in small jars.

SPICED OR MARINATED FRUIT AND VEGETABLES

These excellent preserves in good vinegar, sometimes with sugar and often spiced, are used extensively in Russian cooking as accompaniments to poultry and game and in baked or braised vegetable mixtures, such as *solyanka* in a pan and sauerkraut. They are not pickles in the English sense of the term, and certainly shouldn't be thought of merely in that category. My favourites are marinated mushrooms and marinated cherries.

The mixture of vinegar and water is my own modification of old recipes calling only for vinegar, since I have found that these result in a very sharp preserve. Part of the fault lies in the usual strength of the wine vinegar we buy today, about 6 per cent proof, where the vinegars described in recipes from a century ago were around 3 or 4 per cent proof. With a strong wine vinegar you may find it advisable to use up to half water in the marinade. Cider vinegar, which is less acid, will probably make up three-quarters of a vinegar-water mixture. Do not under any circumstances use malt or spirit vinegar! One variation I came across almost by accident was the use of rough, flat cider that had turned vinegary before I had time to drink it. Apart from the taste, the tell-tale sign is the formation of a light veil in the liquid, which gradually grows into a thick, folded, sticky, semi-translucent skin called the *mère de vinaigre*. The liquid may be strained off and used as cider vinegar. How much you dilute it with water for preserving will depend on the strength of the cider, but the proportion should be no more than 1 part water to 3 parts vinegar.

Marinated mushrooms
See page 211.

Marinated grapes or plums

> 275 ml (½ pint) liquid, 2 parts water to 1 part good white wine vinegar
> ½ teaspoon salt
> 8 tablespoons sugar
> grated peel of ½ a small lemon
> 450 g (1 lb) firm grapes or plums

Bring all the ingredients to the boil except the fruit, simmer for 10 minutes, and allow to cool. Pack the cleaned, dried fruit into jars, pour the liquid over, cover with a thin film of oil and leave in a cool place to mature.

Marinated cherries or plums

> 450 g (1 lb) cherries or plums plus a few more very ripe
>   specimens to make juice
> white wine vinegar
> sugar
> spices to taste: cinnamon, cloves, peppercorns, bay leaf
> salt

Make up the marinade to about 275 ml (½ pint) by mixing half vinegar and half juice, made with the extra ripe fruit cooked in a little water until very soft then strained. Add the sugar (8 tablespoons per ½ pint), a pinch of one or two spices and a little salt. Simmer for 10 minutes and allow to cool. Pack the prepared fruit into jars and pour over the marinade. Cover and store.

Marinated melon

Choose a firm, slightly less than ripe melon (not water melon, which is a different family altogether). Remove the outside and the pips, and cut the flesh into segments the shape of potato chips but rather fatter. Put them in a large bowl with 1–2 cloves and cover with a white vinegar. Leave overnight. Next day bring to the boil and simmer until the melon is just tender. Strain off the fruit and pack into jars. Pour the liquid through muslin or a filter paper to clarify it. Add twice the quantity of water, and for every 275 ml (½ pint) of marinade pour in about 200 g sugar (7 oz). Bring to the boil and simmer until a thin syrup is formed. Allow to cool and pour over the melon. Cover and store.

Marinated pears

Choose firm, just underripe pears. Peel, slice lengthways and simmer in water with a little sugar until almost soft. Strain the pears and pour cold water over them in the sieve. Boil up 550 ml (1 pint) of vinegar and water with up to 450 g (1 lb) of sugar, 1 clove, a pinch of cinnamon, a bay leaf, a few peppercorns and ¼–½ teaspoon of salt. After 5 minutes lower the pears into the mixture, bring to the boil 2 or 3 times, pour into a bowl to cool and then bottle.

Marinated cauliflower

Use only the white part of the cauliflower. Divide it carefully into florets, bring to the boil in salted water and simmer for about 5 minutes. Drain and pack into jars. Cover with vinegar and water boiled up with 1–2 teaspoons of sugar per 275 ml (½ pint) liquid, a bay leaf, ¼ teaspoon of salt and a few peppercorns and allowed to cool. Cover and store.

SALTED VEGETABLES

The art of preserving vegetables in salt originated in Ancient China, and is another fundamental aspect of Russian cookery which was introduced by the invading Tartar hordes from the mid thirteenth century. It is said that sauerkraut was the staple food of the slaves who built the Great Wall of China. Only the name of this preserve, famed for its powers to impart longevity and good digestion, comes from the German–Austrian world with which we in Britain so readily associate it. The Russians distinguish between 'little-salted' preserves, made in hours or at the most a couple of days, and fully salted or fermented preserves that can take anything from 7 days to 2 months to mature. They can be made at home in stone crocks, in glass bowls or wide-necked jars or in plastic containers. Avoid metal or anything porous. I made my first batch of sauerkraut in a small washing-up bowl with great success.

Salted and fermented cabbage

SAUERKRAUT
It is not difficult to buy sauerkraut reasonably cheaply from delicatessens and good supermarkets, but made at home it is undoubtedly superior. It is less sour and far crisper. Russian housewives (for it is only they who do the shopping, believe me) taste sauerkraut from the various buckets on sale in the same way that the legendary French housewife goes round the market sniffing melons. They pick it up with their fingers, raw, dripping with brine, and toss it into their mouths. If it is too sour, or fermenting has gone too far, the response is a grimace and a shake of the head.
(1) Chop a Dutch cabbage finely, preferably in thin strips, or grate it if you have the patience and like your sauerkraut fine. Stir into the cabbage 1 scant tablespoon of coarse salt for every 500 g (1 lb) cabbage. Sprinkle a little rye flour over the bottom of whatever container you are using to preserve the cabbage (it must not be metal), fill it with the salt and cabbage mixture, and pour over a little warm water. One or two sliced carrots or eating apples may be added for aroma and flavour, or juniper berries or fresh cranberries. Cover and press down with a weight if you can arrange it, although I have found that the

cabbage ferments perfectly well not under pressure, merely covered and left in a warm place. It will take 7–10 days. At the start of the ferment, bubbles will appear on the surface. When they disappear, the cabbage is ready. During the ferment stir the cabbage several times downwards with a wooden spoon handle to release any gases that form and to promote the souring process.

(2) The process may be speeded up by blanching the cabbage in boiling water first, pouring over cold water to cool it, and then proceeding as above. The cabbage will take about 5 days to mature this way.

Salted cucumbers
If language is a reliable guide, the French first learned of these delicacies from the Russians and called them *agoursi* after the Russian word *ogurtsy*. It is as such at least that they find their way into *Larousse*. To prepare them you need small ridge cucumbers.

(1) *Quick semi-salted cucumbers*
Wash and dry the cucumbers, put in a wide-necked jar, whole, and cover with a brine solution of 2–3 tablespoons of coarse salt to 1 litre (2 pints) of water, brought to the boil and allowed to cool before using. Add to the jar a few dill seeds or sprigs of dill weed and a clove or more of garlic to taste. Cover and keep in a cool place. The cucumbers are ready after 2 days. The process may be speeded up yet further by nipping the ends off the cucumbers and pouring the brine solution over them while it is still hot. This way the cucumbers may be used after a few hours.

(2) *Fully salted cucumbers*
Line the bottom of a wooden barrel, stone crock or plastic bowl with carefully washed oak, cherry or blackcurrant leaves, sprinkle these with dill, slivers of garlic, and fresh tarragon if you have it. Put the cucumbers, preferably up-ended, into the container so that they are tightly packed together, if necessary in layers, interspersed with more leaves and herbs. Pour over a cooled brine solution of 1 litre (2 pints) of water to 2–3 tablespoons of salt, and cover the container. The brine solution should almost cover the cucumbers. The lid of the container should stop them floating above the brine but not put pressure on the cucumbers. A large plate placed inside the top of the container will do very well. Cover the vessel with a clean cloth to keep out dirt and keep in a cool place. The cucumbers are ready after 3–4 weeks.

(3) *Salted-pickled cucumbers*
Over washed cucumbers in a jar, flavoured with sprigs of dill weed
and garlic, pour a warm solution of 1 litre (2 pints) of water to 2
tablespoons of salt and 2 tablespoons of wine vinegar. Cover. Next
day, when some of the liquid has been absorbed, top up the jars with
cold solution, cover, and leave in a cold place to mature. These are the
longest-lasting of the three preserves given here.

HERRINGS

Salted herrings
Clean and gut the herrings, selecting plump fresh fish. I also prefer to
remove the heads at this stage. Soak them in vinegar or lemon juice
overnight, then drain well. Use a stone crock or a plastic or glass
container with straight sides, or, for large quantities, a barrel or plastic
bucket. For each pair of herrings you will need 2 teaspoons of coarse
salt, 1 teaspoon of vinegar, 2–3 crushed allspice berries, and a bay
leaf, broken into pieces. Line the bottom of the container with a layer
of these ingredients, lay the herrings belly up on top, sprinkle with
the salt, etc., and continue in layers for as many herrings as you want
to lay down. End with a layer of salt. Cover with foil, weight down
and keep in a cool place, preferably the refrigerator, until needed.
Soak to remove the salt before use.

Marinated fresh herrings
Gut, fillet and wash the herrings and arrange in a crock, bowl or
plastic box in layers, bellies upwards, covered with thinly sliced
eating apples, peeled and cored. Sprinkle the top of the batch with
pepper and pour over oil, ideally olive. If this seems extravagant (it is)
use a vegetable oil that you like the taste of, or refined sunflower oil
which has virtually no taste, or mix sunflower and olive oil in afford-
able proportions. Cover and keep in a cool place or freeze. The
traditional Russian way was to put the marinated herrings outside in
the snow.

Household mustard
Take equal parts by volume of black mustard seed and honey. Crush
the mustard seed in a mortar, and if you like it very fine sieve out the
husks. Put the honey in a pan and cook until it reddens. Add the
mustard and, a spoonful at a time, cider or wine vinegar which has
been brought to the boil and cooled. Mix to a smooth paste of the
desired liquidity, and bottle.

Russian Shops and Markets

My favourite shopping was done in Russian markets. In Moscow's Central Market the aroma of fresh dill was overwhelming. At the height of the summer season vegetables of every shape and colour and an abundance of greenery glistened, newly washed, on marble slabs. In one corner the sauerkraut and salted cucumber sellers would shovel their wares by the kilogram out of enamel buckets into plastic bags. There would be Russian, Georgian, Armenian and Azerbaijani stalls all competing with one another in price and quality. Southern farmers would fly in fresh produce – tomatoes, aubergines, okra, melons, peppers, peaches, plums and wonderful fresh herbs like basil and tarragon – every day. Every stall was a hive of small-scale and extremely lucrative private enterprise, and if ever there was a long queue somewhere you knew that one farmer had excelled himself and had some fruit or vegetable that everyone wanted to buy, at a price that no one else could offer. Nuts and dried fruit of all kinds lay in open boxes, ready to be shovelled into more of the plastic bags you should have remembered to bring with you. Berries mingled with freshly cut flowers, pot plants and a stall selling loofahs for the bath.

In another hall, less inviting for all but the heartiest carnivores, was stall after stall of fresh meat. Before a holiday there would be rabbits and occasionally hares. In a third hall, gleaming white and well-scrubbed, Russian women sold *tvorog* from huge mounds, and patted out bricks of fresh butter. One or two would be selling honey, and trying to tempt passers-by to try any of ten or more varieties brought in from the country still on the comb. In late summer the mushroom sellers would arrive and set up stalls outside, displaying a score of different kinds of mushrooms. In winter a few would return with long strings of dried mushrooms, priced out of most people's reach and always a cause of passing indignation. Add to this Georgian women selling excellent cane baskets, a tiny bread shop with twenty different loaves, the smell of boiled sausages and soup from the stand-up buffet, and a constant bustle of people with green leaves sprouting from their shopping bags, tasting, prodding, patiently queueing or sometimes turning away with disdain, and you have an atmosphere to rival that of any market in the world.

Russian shops are less attractive. Most have been made into supermarkets of a kind and all are state-owned. The produce is cheaper, poorer quality and far less abundant than that in the markets. There are almost always queues, which can mean standing for two hours or more to buy lemons or oranges or whatever prize has appeared unexpectedly on the counter. State supplies are plagued by constant and unpredictable shortages of everything except cabbage.

Shops in the last century were far more varied and richly stocked. They contributed to Russian culture rather than detracted from it. One of the most famous was Milyutin's on St Petersburg's Nevsky Prospekt, where, according to the French chef Petit, in Russia in the 1850s, one could buy excellent groceries of all kinds: cheese, conserves, lobsters, oysters, pâté de foie gras, bear, hams, truffles, wines and liqueurs. A Russian friend of mine has fond childhood memories of Milyutin's biscuits, and it was Milyutin's too that boasted strawberries and raspberries in April at a great price. It stocked pomegranates from the Caucasus and from Portugal, plums from the Crimea, pears from France. Further along the street, at the English shop, the Nabokov family bought the imported English food that had such great snob value amongst the aristocracy, everything from fruit cake to golden syrup for young Vladimir's breakfast. Nevsky Prospekt was crossed by one of the city's many canals, and at the main bridge customers could descend to where an enormous variety of fresh, frozen and salted fish, *vyaziga* and caviare were offered. St Petersburg's own river, the Neva, yielded the finest fresh salmon in summer. Fresh salmon trout were brought to the fish barges from nearby lakes, and a small, very delicate trout was carted in from the nearby Imperial estate of Gatchina. Many good things were to be had too from Lake Ladoga in Karelia to the north, including burbot, freshwater bream, smelts, *sig*, live sturgeon and the highly prized sterlet. Russia's icy climate has meant that deep-freezing is no new aid to the provision of food in variety out of season, and there was a standing tradition of bringing to Moscow and St Petersburg frozen salmon of many kinds from Siberia, Archangel in the far North, Astrakhan and the Urals in the East. Baltic sprats (*kil'ki*) were brought down from the port of Revel, now Tallinn, capital of Estonia, and minnows, popular during Lent, from the river Velikaya in Pskov. Caviare arrived in barrels, salted and pressed, from Astrakhan and the Urals.

Meat also seems to have been of excellent quality, although much of the best of it was brought up from the Caucasus. Gourmets looked out for elk and chamois from the South in winter. In pre-revolutionary days one went to one shop, the *bulochnaya*, for white bread, and another, the *pekarnya*, for black. Flours and grains were bought from *labaznie lavki* or cornchandlers', a word and a shop that have disappeared from modern Russian life. It is tempting to characterize the nineteenth-century world of Russian food by its abundance and variety, provided by the rich land, waters and forests and swollen with imported fruits, preserves and delicacies. The twentieth by contrast is barren, and has been plagued by shortages and even famine. The wonderful old wooden signboards that used to hang outside bakers', cornchandlers', grocery and fruit shops, depicting Ceres and the fruit of the land, overflowing sacks of grain and rows of well-ordered kitchen storepots, are indeed relics of a bygone age.

Select Bibliography and Further Reading

Sergei Timofeyevich Aksakov, *Collected Works* (in Russian), 6 vols., St Petersburg, 1886. Aksakov (1791–1859), writer, nobleman and one-time official censor, plagued with intermittent ill-health, spent much of his life in the Russian countryside, eventually retiring there in his late forties. It was in this latter part of his life that he wrote the fine nature studies and the autobiographical *Family Chronicle* and *Childhood Years* for which he is best known.

Marie Antonin Carême, *L'Art de la cuisine française au dix-neuvième siècle, Traité élémentaire et pratique*. Continued by A. Plumerey, 5 vols., Paris, 1833–44.

N. N. Davis (ed.), *The Gourmet's Guide to Europe*, London, Grant Richards, 1903.

Dr John Doran, *Table Traits with Something on Them*, 2nd edition, London, 1854.

Urbain Dubois, *Cuisine de tous les pays*, Paris, 1872.

Nikolai Gogol, *Dead Souls*, London, Penguin, 1961.

Robin Howe, *Balkan Cooking*, London, J. M. Dent, 1965.

Kniga o vkusnoi i zdorovoi pishche [A Book of Tasty and Healthy Food], 7th edition, Moscow, 1977.

Kulinarnyi sbornik [Collected Recipes], Moscow, 1915. A collection of recipes from contemporary magazines.

M. A. Markevich, *The Epicure in Imperial Russia*, San Francisco, 1941.

Elena Molokhovets, *Podarok molodym khozyaikam* [Gift to Young Housewives], St Petersburg, 1861–80, and many subsequent editions.

Prosper Montagné, *New Larousse Gastronomique*, English edition, Hamlyn, London, 1977.

Vladimir Nabokov, *Speak, Memory*, London, Weidenfeld & Nicolson, 1967.

N. P. Osipov, *Starinnaya russkaya khozyaika* [The Traditional Russian Housewife], Moscow, 1794.

Helen and George Papashvily, *The Cooking of Russia*, Time-Life International, 1971.

A. Petit, *La Gastronomie en Russie*, Paris, 1860.

V. V. Pokhlebkin, *Natsional'nye kukhni nashikh narodov* [The National Cuisines of Our Peoples], Moscow, 1978.

I. Radetsky, *Almanakh gastronomov* [The Gastronomes' Almanac], 2nd edition, St Petersburg, 1877. The first Russian cookery book by a professional Russian chef.

Russian Journal of Lady Londonderry, 1836–37, ed. W. A. L. Seaman and J. R. Sewell, London, John Murray, 1973.

Russkii domashnii deshevyi povarskii stol [Economical Everyday Russian Cooking], Moscow, 1879. A collection of dishes compiled by French and Russian chefs working in well-known restaurants in Moscow.

Sofka Skipwith (née Princess Sophy Dolgorouky), *Sofka, the Autobiography of a Princess*, London, Hart-Davis, 1968.

Sofka Skipwith, *Eat Russian*, London, David & Charles, 1973.

Valentin Soloukhin, 'Tret'ya okhota', in *Selected Works*, vol. II (in Russian), with other studies on nature, Moscow, 1974. A delightful essay on the Russian passion for picking mushrooms and berries.

Anna Thomas, *The Vegetarian Epicure*, Penguin, 1974.

Zhizn' i priklyucheniya Andreya Bolotova, opisannye samim im dlya svoikh potomkov, 3 vols., Moscow/Leningrad, 1931; reprinted by Oriental Research Partners, Cambridge, 1973.

Index

How to use this index: Russian foods and dishes are listed individually. Recipes are listed again in English according to the main ingredients or type of dish.